HOPE
in
COUNSELLING
and
PSYCHOTHERAPY

SAGE has been part of the global academic community since 1965, supporting high quality research and learning that transforms society and our understanding of individuals, groups and cultures. SAGE is the independent, innovative, natural home for authors, editors and societies who share our commitment and passion for the social sciences.

Find out more at: **www.sagepublications.com**

HOPE
in
COUNSELLING
and
PSYCHOTHERAPY

DENIS O'HARA

Los Angeles | London | New Delhi
Singapore | Washington DC

Los Angeles | London | New Delhi
Singapore | Washington DC

SAGE Publications Ltd
1 Oliver's Yard
55 City Road
London EC1Y 1SP

SAGE Publications Inc.
2455 Teller Road
Thousand Oaks, California 91320

SAGE Publications India Pvt Ltd
B 1/I 1 Mohan Cooperative Industrial Area
Mathura Road
New Delhi 110 044

SAGE Publications Asia-Pacific Pte Ltd
3 Church Street
#10-04 Samsung Hub
Singapore 049483

Editor: Kate Wharton
Production editor: Rachel Burrows
Copyeditor: Helen Skelton
Proofreader: Sharika Sharma
Indexer: Martin Hargreaves
Marketing manager: Tamara Navaratnam
Cover design: Jennifer Crisp
Typeset by: C&M Digitals (P) Ltd, Chennai, India
Printed in India at Replika Press Pvt Ltd

Library of Congress Control Number: 2012949196

British Library Cataloguing in Publication data

A catalogue record for this book is available from
the British Library

ISBN 978-1-4462-0169-5
ISBN 978-1-4462-0170-1 (pbk)

To Fiona for her love and understanding and for being a fantastic mum.
To Evan and Keeley for their love and patience.

Contents

About the author

Denis O'Hara is Associate Professor of Counselling and Psychotherapy at the Australian College of Applied Psychology and previously programme leader in the MSc in Counselling at the University of Abertay, Dundee, UK. Dr O'Hara is also an honorary fellow of the Australian Catholic University, Brisbane and a chartered psychologist and associate fellow of the British Psychological Society. He has been a university lecturer for over twenty years and has maintained a private counselling and psychotherapy practice for most of his career. He has written extensively on hope and conducted research investigating the application of hope to a range of areas, such as bereavement by suicide, therapist hope, and hope in children and adolescents. Dr O'Hara is a keen psychotherapy educator, researcher, and supervisor, and enjoys providing professional development training. He believes that it is important to maintain a reflective stance towards one's work and to integrate theory and research into professional practice.

Preface

People throughout the ages have sought help and wise counsel from a variety of sources for problems in living. While we can be sure that the questions and queries presented to those who listened varied greatly, one issue did not vary – the search for hope. This is because hope is an indispensable component of life. Without hope we cease healthy functioning. Hope is like the air we breathe and the food we eat, it is essential for life. These might seem like large claims for a concept or quality of which we are often only vaguely aware in our daily lives. While this may be so, many of the researchers referred to in this book have found that hope is commonly understood by people to be one of the most important human qualities to maintain. It seems that hope supports and guides much of our life focus and activity, but does so often without being noticed for the part it plays. Hope is everywhere yet hardly visible. It features in our everyday language in both mundane and profound phrases such as, 'I *hope* dinner is on the table when I get home' to 'I *hope* my chemotherapy works this time'. It's commonly found as a movie theme: in *The Shawshank Redemption* the quietly profound nature of hope is well captured in the words written by prisoner Andy Dufresne (Tim Robbins) to his fellow prisoner Red (Morgan Freeman). 'Hope is a good thing, maybe the best of things, and no good thing ever dies.' This powerful quality we call hope seems to sit in some indeterminate zone between the unconscious and the conscious. It is ever-present yet elusive.

In the modern era, the importance of hope has not diminished. With the emergence of the helping disciplines of psychology, psychotherapy, social work, nursing, and others, hope has gained increased notoriety as being an important aspect of human health and recovery. Building on the existing literature in theology and philosophy, nursing and psychology researchers have substantially added to our understanding of the place of hope in human functioning. While hope is often found in the background of daily life, it comes to the foreground at times of stress, illness, and struggle. Those working with patients and psychotherapy clients know that the discovery, development, and main-tenance of hope are an important aspect of their work. The mercurial nature of hope however has meant that it has taken a surprisingly long time for it to become a key focus of enquiry in the helping professions. We have known that hope is important but have not clearly known how to foster and work with it.

My desire to write a book on hope has grown slowly over about a fifteen-year period. The impetus for this has been threefold. In the first instance my interest arose from personal struggles. These struggles came from a mixture of physical ill health in my early adult-hood and existential questioning about the meaning of life, partly as a result. My intro-duction to the profound necessity of hope came in my late twenties when I found myself incapacitated by chronic fatigue. My struggle with this became, in many ways, a defining life event. I was initially so debilitated by it that within the first three months of the illness I could rarely venture outside the house. I very slowly improved over eighteen months and was not fully functional again until three years later. The experience of severe chronic fatigue left me, as it has many others, wondering if normal life could again be possible. By its nature, chronic fatigue is an experience which raises questions about existence and therefore about hope and despair.

The second stimulus for writing a book on hope came from my work as a psychologist and psychotherapist. It doesn't take long working as a therapist to realise that the need for hope is an essential feature of clients' concerns and inquiries. Whether directly stated or not clients bring to therapy not just pragmatic problems of living but existential ones. Their core issues tend to be about meaning-making, about making sense of life itself. My own observation as a therapist is that clients need hope to stay engaged in the process of healing and recovery, and people in general need hope for daily living.

The third reason for putting pen to paper on the topic of hope is my interest in findings in the research literature. As an avid reader of all things psychological, it became clear to me that while hope was once not commonly found in psychology texts, it has, over the past thirty years, become a highly researched field of interest. While this is the case, there remains a relative dearth of literature on how to work with hope in therapy. It seems that it is time for a text which both explores hope in general and which also examines how to apply hope in therapeutic contexts.

Structure of the book

As suggested above, hope is a mercurial topic and so to grasp its nature and function a comprehensive examination is required. Before one seeks to work with hope in therapy it is first advisable to have a thorough understanding of it. Thankfully, there is a rich variety of literature that provides an intricate tapestry of ideas about the topic. These ideas, though, need to be processed and organised in a way that supports the practitioner in his or her work. As well as being equipped to work with hope in the practice of therapy, helping professionals need to contribute ongoing research into how best to help people find, develop, and foster hope in their individual growth and recovery. With these concerns in mind, this book has three aims:

1 To introduce the reader to hope and to provide a solid theoretical grounding for the topic based on a breath of literature from several disciplines
2 To explore how to work with hope and operationalise it within therapeutic contexts
3 To encourage and provide ideas and resources for future research on hope.

Reflecting these aims the book has been divided into three sections. The first section focuses on understanding the nature and function of hope. It draws on literature from theology, philosophy, and on research studies from nursing and psychology. In addition, an examination of how different theories of counselling and psychotherapy operationalise hope is provided. The final chapter in this section examines how despair and anxiety can be expressions of a loss of hope. The second section explores how hope can be worked with in therapy. The first chapter in this section examines therapist hope and what place it has in the therapeutic enterprise. The next chapter looks at practical strategies for fostering client hope. The final chapter in this section takes a deeper look at hope and its relevance for those who struggle with severe and enduring psychological problems. The last section of the book promotes the need for further research on hope and places an emphasis on practitioner research. The importance of conducting research that seeks to combine theory and practice is asserted. To encourage future research a range of research instruments are listed with some included in an appendix.

The use of 'we'

Please note that throughout this book when referring to the author(s), the personal pronoun 'we' is used. This is because I wish to acknowledge my wife, Fiona's, contribution to the development of the ideas communicated within these pages. Fiona has made a seminal contribution to the ideas herein and to the quality of the text, and so it only seems right to me that I refer to our combined efforts and desire to see hope better understood and worked with in therapy via the use of the collective pronoun 'we'. As Fiona wouldn't let me include her name on the front cover, I have included it here.

Finally, it is our hope that this book causes you to pause and to consider this most curious of qualities we call hope, especially how it applies to you personally and professionally.

Acknowledgements

Both Fiona and I are enormously thankful for the support of a number of people at the University of Abertay, Dundee, UK. We first want to thank Emeritus Professor John McLeod for his encouragement throughout the project. Other staff at the university have also been a great support especially, Julia McLeod, Mhairi Thurston, Joe Armstrong, and Robin Ion. As well as support in the UK, we have benefited from moral and practical support from colleagues at the Australian Catholic University. I particularly would like to thank Professor Gail Crossley and Associate Professor Anne Tolan for their support and encouragement over the years.

It would be difficult to write a book on this topic without the support of the publisher. We would particularly like to thank Commissioning Editor Alice Oven for first believing in the idea and Assistant Editor Kate Wharton for her help throughout the project. I would also like to thank Senior Managing Production Editor, Rachel Burrows, for managing the detailed editing of the manuscript. There are many others at SAGE involved in the cover design and production whose names we don't know but whom we would like to thank as well. We would also like to thank a number of unknown reviewers who provided very helpful feedback on the original proposal and on subsequent drafts of the book.

As part of developing this text Fiona and I conducted a number of research studies on hope. These studies would not be possible without the willing participation of many people and so we want to express our appreciation for their time and effort in contributing further knowledge in this area by completing questionnaires and participating in interviews. We also want to thank our students for listening to reports on our research findings. We hope they were interesting.

Finally, I (Denis) would like to thank my family, Fiona, Evan, and Keeley for allowing me the time away from them to write the following pages. I can't express my gratitude enough.

SECTION 1

UNDERSTANDING THE NATURE OF HOPE

1

Introducing hope

If we asked an average group of people to brainstorm a list of factors that contributed positively to mental health and well-being, it is likely that they would identify several in common. The list might include: the provision of basic needs like food, clothing, shelter, etc.; care and emotional support from significant others; financial provision through gainful employment; pleasure through leisure pursuits; and a positive mental outlook. People who look to their future with a good measure of positive expectancy are likely to think well of themselves and of their opportunities in life. Such people probably have a number of life goals, generally look forward to their working day, and experience some form of enjoyment in their relationships and life pursuits. Of course, no one is exempt from experiencing challenging life events. Even the most positive individuals will at times experience more difficult emotions like sadness, worry, or despair. Mentally healthy people though seem to have an orientation to life that allows them to be grounded and optimistic even in the most challenging of circumstances.

This view is reflected in the World Health Organization's (WHO) definition of health as:

> a state of well-being in which every individual realizes his or her own potential, can cope with the normal stresses of life, can work productively and fruitfully, and is able to make a contribution to her or his community. (WHO, 2001)

It is important to note that mental health and well-being is understood to be much more than the absence of disease. In fact mental health may exist in the presence of physical illness. A comprehensive understanding of health, especially mental health, focuses on what factors support health and well-being, rather than on factors that cause disease. This view, known as the salutogenic approach to health, claims that health is much more open-ended than in a disease model of health and is dependent on the skills necessary to organise resources in society, the social context, and the inner resources of the self. 'This framework suggests that what we perceive as being good for ourselves (subjective well-being) also predicts our outcome on objective health parameters. In other words, if we create salutogenic processes where people perceive they are able to live the life they want to live they not only will feel better but also lead better lives' (WHO, 2005: 51).

It appears that having a positive life orientation is one of the ingredients of a healthy life. If this is so, then we need to understand more precisely what such a personal worldview is, how it functions, and how it can be fostered. In the following chapters, this positive life orientation will be referred to in various ways using such terms as optimistic, sanguine, hopeful, and resilient, to name a few. While these and other related terms will be examined, the primary focus of this book will be on the nature and function of hope. The capacity to hope, it will be argued, is essential for health and well-being. Those without hope are certain to struggle with themselves and their life circumstances. Our examination will highlight the fact that hope is a more complex notion than might generally be thought. It is a word used in everyday speech to refer to relatively mundane thoughts such as 'I hope it's not going to rain today' and also to more profound ideas like 'There's no hope for me'. Hope is a word that captures a range of nuanced meanings and therefore requires a thorough scrutiny.

Before we venture too far into the research literature it might serve us well to start with a few definitions of hope. The following definitions are drawn from commentators from different disciplines and provide a breadth of perspective on the nature of hope.

HOPE IS:

'a movement or stretching forth of the appetite towards an arduous good.' (Aquinas, 2006a)

'a process of anticipation that involves the interaction of thinking, acting, feeling, and relating, and is directed towards a future fulfilment that is personally meaningful.' (Stephenson, 1991: 1459)

'a multidimensional life force characterized by a confident yet uncertain expectation of achieving a future good which, to the hoping person, is realistically possible and personally significant.' (Dufault & Martocchio, 1985: 380)

'the sum of perceived capabilities to produce routes to desired goals, along with the perceived motivation to use those routes.' (Snyder, 2000: 8)

A number of key characteristics of hope are represented in these definitions. They suggest that hope involves:

- Appetites/desires
- Anticipation
- Confident expectation
- Life force
- An arduous process
- Realistic possibilities

- Issues of personal significance
- Perceived personal capability
- Goals, pathways/routes, motivation/agency
- An interaction between thinking, acting, feeling, and relating.

As we explore the topic of hope each of these characteristics will be examined in more detail. To develop the definitional aspects of hope a little further we now turn to the dictionary for further clarification.

Hope as a noun

Hope is defined in the Oxford dictionary as both a noun and a verb. As a noun, hope is: *a feeling of expectation and desire for a particular thing to happen.* Eliott and Olver (2002) noted that when hope was described as a noun it was represented as an entity, and therefore in a sense as existing independently of the individual. In this respect, hope was 'out there' and could either be gained or lost. One of the interesting features of hope as a noun is that it is viewed as having an *a priori* existence. If hope already exists the implication is that it cannot be created but rather only be gathered in lesser or larger amounts. Hence, hope can grow and increase or equally it can diminish and vanish. Another feature of hope as a noun is that it must have an object. There is a hope for or of something happening. This object may be something concrete or something less tangible such as a state of being. In either form, hope has an object of desire.

Hope viewed as a noun tends to orientate the hoper to a modernist view of reality where aspects of reality either exist in principle, as in Platonic forms, or as physical and measurable entities. When hope is conceived of as already existing in the real world in some form or other it carries the notion that it can be *gained*, *given*, or *discovered*. This has both positive and negative aspects. The view that hope might exist in some fashion and that it needs to be procured somehow means that there is a potential positive expectation of either gaining the object of hope or of gaining more of the quality of something desired, for example, affection. On the negative side, the object of hope may be withheld or be unavailable.

Hope: given or taken

Another feature of hope as a noun is that it is often conceived of as being outside of one's control. This is best illustrated by research on the participation of patients in medical treatment. Eliott and Olver (2002), for example, reported that patients undergoing medical treatment often link hope with cure. Hope then becomes associated with the presence or absence of an objective, empirical fact. When a medical report is good, for example when there are no further cancer cells found after an operation, hope is delivered. Hope in this context is seen as being in the hands of the doctor. If the doctor delivers a positive word, hope is possible; alternatively, a negative report is more likely to lead to a loss of hope. There is a sense here of hope as being able to be either *given* or *taken*. When hope exists as an entity outside of the person there is a danger that it is represented as an absolute, with its possibility or impossibility already predestined.

A negative feature of hope seen as being outside of one's control is that it can lead to inaction. If hope is 'out there' then there is nothing I can do about it. All I can do is wait for my fate to be delivered. In psychological terms we might speak of someone with this orientation as lacking self-efficacy (Bandura, 1982). Such persons do not believe that they can effect any change in their circumstances, whether physical or emotional, because it is out of their control. In the medical context this view renders the doctors as having all the power. Only they can make any difference to the individual's state of being.

Hope understood as something pre-existing has a positive dimension as well. Many people relate to hope as an aspect of spirituality. In monotheistic religions, for example, God is the giver of hope. "'I know the plans I have for you", declares the Lord "… to give you a hope and a future'" (Jeremiah 29:11, New International Version). God in this scheme is a benevolent, powerful being able to offer and provide hope. Sometimes this offer of hope is seen as the potential attainment of some temporal desire, like health, a relationship, a job, or some physical object. Equally God's offer of hope may be to gain some eternal state such as heaven or eternal peace. The interesting thing here is that hope is understood as being possible because a power greater than the individual is able to provide it.

Hope discovered

Another response to viewing hope as existing objectively is to actively seek hope. While similar to a view of hope as being received, its focus is potentially more active. This more self-efficacious view sees the person as being on a journey of discovery. If hope is lacking and it exists in principle, then it should be able to be found. Many people enter counselling and psychotherapy with such an assumption. It is as if they have recently lost something they previously possessed and now need to find again. Such people come to therapy to enlist the therapist's aid in helping them find their elusive hope. Like hope *given,* hope *discovered* implies that hope itself has a quantitative characteristic – hope can grow or diminish. Such a view also has a positive and self-empowering aspect, for if hope can grow in quantity then human effort can make a difference. The more I seek that which I am after and the more I rid myself of blockages to its attainment, the more likely it is that I will attain my goal.

Hope as a noun implies that hope has some form of independent existence and in some way is outside the person. It does not, however, have to remain outside for whether hope is *given* and *received* or actively *sought* and *discovered*, hope can be gained and become the individual's psychosocial and spiritual possession. The different aspects of hope as a noun are summarised in point form below.

Hope as noun

- Hope is a pre-existing objective entity
  - It can increase and decrease
- Passive engagement
  - It can be given or provided
  - It can be received
- Active engagement
  - It can be pursued and discovered
  - It can be possessed

Hope as a verb

Hope as a verb is the act of desiring, of having confidence, of believing or trusting in someone or something (Webster's Dictionary, 2006). An interesting aspect of hope as a verb is that it introduces a subject. There is someone doing the hoping. Hope as a noun highlights more of the *objective* nature of hope, while hope as a verb highlights its *subjective* features. In hope as a verb the actional dimension is personalised, providing more power to the individual to choose the object of hope. In their study on hope and cancer patients, Eliott and Olver (2002) found that patients who referred to hope in its verbal form were less dependent on the doctors' pronouncements for the maintenance of their hope. While a good report from the doctors was welcomed, it did not necessarily determine the person's ability to hope as this capacity was already subjectively held. *To hope* was already an engagement in an active process. To hope meant that there was a belief that something positive and desirable was possible.

Hope used as a verb tends to focus on possibilities; here the future is more open-ended. In contrast, hope used as a noun is more likely to refer to definitive outcomes, a prescribed response. Hope as an action requires some behavioural response from the individual. Hope has to be evidenced in some way and usually involves a level of risk or trust in another or in some possibility. The action, for example, might simply be a choice to contact a friend and arrange a social chat even when one feels unwell and unsociable. It may be the act of risking the possibility of being vulnerable in a close relationship or of ceasing further medical treatment in preference for a short-term improvement in the quality of life. Such expressions of hope involve more than conceptual acknowledgements of desired outcomes, rather, they require some self-empowered action by the hopeful person.

Hope as a verb also involves a sense of motivation, an energy directed to an action. As we will see later in the section on positive psychology and hope, hope involves the capacity for agency, that is, belief in one's own capacity to effect change in one's world. When used as a verb, hope implies action. An illustration is helpful here. If Bill were to say, 'I hope that

I get the job I applied for soon', then he is using the word 'hope' as an action; Bill is engaging in the act of hoping. But what is this action? One important aspect of hope is that it is intentional. It is directed at the attainment of some desired object or state of being. The etymological meaning of 'intention' provides us with a helpful base from which to understand hope as an action. Intention is made of two Latin words '*in*' and '*inteo*' where '*in*' has the same meaning in Latin as it does in English and '*inteo*' means 'to hold'. Hence, hope as intention means *to hold* in mind the object of one's desire. This holding requires some effort and usually some emotional response because what we hope for is by definition something that is currently not present. This delay challenges us to continue to believe in the possibility of attaining that for which we seek and therefore not to be despondent, anxious or overly frustrated. The different aspects of hope as a verb are summarised in point form below.

Hope as verb

- Hope is a subjective reality
- Hope is open-ended
- Active engagement

  - It is motivational/emotional
  - It is intentional
  - It is created

A reciprocal relationship

In summary, hope can be a noun, conceptualised as objectively existing, and also owned and internalised by the individual, and as a verb, an action state. These various facets of hope have a reciprocal relationship.

The reciprocal nature of these aspects of hope is highlighted by the hoping process undertaken by the hospital patient. When the doctor delivers a good report, hope as an external entity is offered. This hope however, has to be accepted and owned; it has to become the patient's hope. The patient who owns the hope of a cure or of a recovery must also continue to maintain hope. There has to be a process of holding the hope in place. At times the doctor's report may not be as positive as at other times. It is then that the patient must place more reliance on their own hope as both a belief and as an action. At times it is only the patient's internally held hope that remains alive. Each form of hope supports the other and carries the weight of expectancy.

Another example of the reciprocal nature of the different aspects of hope can be found in the counselling room. Many times counselling clients come to counselling because they have lost hope. This loss of hope may be around self-belief, a relationship, health or social functioning. Often the client expects that the therapist will be able to offer hope. Sometimes this offer is a new way of thinking, and in being explained

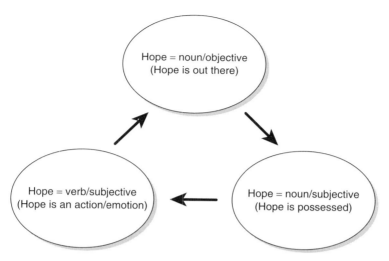

Figure 1   Reciprocal relationship between the three versions of hope
Source: adapted from Eliott & Olver, 2002.

alters the client's perception of self and life, thus returning hope (noun/objective). In a sense, the therapist is seen as possessing the secrets of hope. Sometimes the client sees the therapist as a person skilled in aiding others seek for hope. In this case the therapist is not understood as possessing hope as an entity as such but as someone who knows how and where to look for it. Sometimes the discovery is that hope already exists in the client and has, as it were, been lost or misplaced. The therapist's role then is to aid the client's self-discovery of hope (noun/subjective). The therapist's role might also be to aid the client to actively hope (verb/action/emotion), to encourage feelings and behaviours that maintain hope.

Spheres and dimensions of hope

It should already be obvious that hope is a multifaceted concept and because of this it can be used to express a range of meanings. Sometimes the word hope can even be used to convey seemingly contradictory ideas. Recognising the many nuances of hope, nursing researchers Dufault and Martocchio (1985) have developed a meaning framework that helps to identify different facets of hope while maintaining its overall coherence. They argue that there are two main spheres of hope containing six common dimensions. The two spheres are *generalised* and *particularised* hope and, in their view, these spheres are related but distinct in nature.

Spheres

Generalised hope

Dufault and Martocchio (1985: 380) define generalised hope as 'a sense of some future beneficial but indeterminate developments' and explain that it is broad in scope and not linked to any concrete object or quality of being. This form of hope might be understood as a state of mind or life orientation. The researchers provide an example from their research interviews with terminally ill patients to illustrate the nature of generalised hope. One patient stated, 'I don't hope for anything in particular, I just hope', while another commented, 'Hope keeps me going. It is an outlook that makes everything worthwhile' (1985: 380).

These statements highlight some of the features of hope previously discussed. First, both comments demonstrate that hope can be a state or attitude of mind without the need for a specific desired goal or object. Second, the two comments illustrate the use of hope as both a noun and a verb. This is all the more striking when we consider that the comments were made by people who knew they had terminal illnesses. The first comment, 'I don't hope for anything in particular ...' at first glance is confusing. Hope here is an action but an action without any seeming object or direction. However, when hope as an action is, in part, understood as a *holding in mind* then the action appears clearer. This still begs the question, 'Holding what in mind?' We believe the answer is best understood as a holding of a positive life attitude in mind. In the context of life challenges and struggles, it becomes more obvious that holding a positive life attitude or orientation becomes quite an action in its own right.

A qualification is worth noting here. It might be said that a positive life orientation is simply optimism. It is true that optimism is such a life orientation, and in many ways has much in common with hope. However, optimism and generalised hope differ in an important way. The optimist believes that 'good, as opposed to bad, things will generally occur in one's life' (Scheier & Carver, 1993: 26). The person with generalised hope also holds this view. The difference is that optimism is a predominantly cognitive state; the optimist expects that life *will* work out well and as expected. The hopeful person is more realistic and recognises that life may not work out as planned but still determines to hold a positive expectancy. In delineating the hopeful person from the optimist, Van Hooft (2011: 53) states, 'Her hopefulness is constituted by a willingness to act in pursuit of her goals, to accept the risk, to make the required efforts and to accept the outcomes even if they are disappointing. It is a practical stance rather than a cognitive belief'.

Generalised hope provides a broad perspective for life, and its pragmatic stance provides an inbuilt flexibility and openness to life's vagaries.

Particularised hope

Particularised hope, as the name suggests, is focused on the attainment of a specific outcome. The objects of hope may be concrete in nature or abstract. Particularised hope is characterised by the expectation that:

- What exists at present can be improved
- What a person does not have at this time can be attained or received
- The desired circumstances surrounding an event will occur
- What is valued in the present can be part of the hoping person's future
- Unfavourable possibilities will not occur. (Dufault & Martocchio, 1985: 380–1)

In being focused on specific objects of desire *particularised hope* helps to clarify and affirm life priorities. This type of hope helps us persevere when obstacles and life challenges are encountered. Ultimately, it is what we hope for that provides us with a reference point for meaning in life; it illuminates what is important.

Generalised and particularised hope work in cooperation. Sometimes the success of *particularised hope* adds support to a waning *generalised hope*. At other times generalised hope bolsters specific hopes when the objects of desire are not gained or received. Generalised hope may also provide a propitious climate wherein particular hopes can be formulated and risked. At times of great struggle, only generalised hope may be available. Dufault and Martocchio (1985: 381) provide another example in their account of a woman in the last phase of her long illness and who stated, 'At this stage, you just hope; there is nothing left to do but hope. Hope is quite enough'. We see here someone who knew that the time for the pursuit of goals was at an end. Her hope was not for the attainment of something particular. Her hope was in possessing an attitude of being. Ultimately, both forms of hope are required to embrace the challenges of life.

Dimensions of hope

Dufault and Martocchio (1985) identify six dimensions of hope: affective, cognitive, behavioural, affiliative, temporal, and contextual. They suggest that each of these dimensions has components that structure the nature and experience of hope. Collectively these dimensions form the processes of hope.

Affective dimension

Given that hope is multidimensional, its various dimensions can be in operation independently or collectively. The affective dimension is concerned with the sensations and emotions of the hoping process. Components of the affective dimension include:

- An attraction to the desirable outcome
- A sense of personal significance of the outcome for the hoping person's well-being
- Feelings of confidence about the outcome
- Feelings related to some uncertainty about the outcome
- A broad spectrum of feelings that may accompany hope. (Dufault & Martocchio, 1985: 382)

Hope has a strong emotion-based aspect. While many commentators on hope situate it within a cognitive framework, others describe hope as an emotion (Averill, Catlin, &

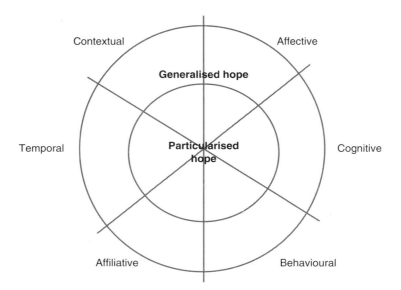

Figure 2   Spheres and dimensions of hope

Source: Dufault & Martocchio, 1985.

Chon, 1990; Averrill, 1994; Scioli, Nyugen, & Scioli, 2011). Averill et al. (1990) argued that hope is an emotion by comparing it with the characteristics of basic emotions. They found that hope conforms to the parameters of an emotional model of behaviour. Hope is difficult to control and more like a passion than an action. Hope can be irrational in that if people are strongly attached to the object of their hope, they may convince themselves that the chances of gaining that object is higher than is actually possible. Finally, these researchers found that like other emotions, hope motivates behaviour.

The first component of hope as an affect is its attraction to a desirable object or outcome and this can be expressed using terms like longing, yearning, aching. The second affective component is personally significant. This is well illustrated in the statement by a patient recovering from an operation for cancer who said, 'I hope to return to work, at least part time. It means everything to me … I *ache* to get back'. We see here both the attraction to the desirable object, in this case a return to health and work, and also the depth of personal meaning that this has for the person.

To capture a sense of confidence about outcomes the hopeful person uses such expressions as 'feeling positive', 'assured', 'happy', and/or 'seeing the light at the end of the tunnel'. However, hope also has a dualistic aspect; on the one hand there is a sense of confidence, but on other a lack of certainty. Some affective responses to uncertainty are nervousness, doubtfulness, tenseness, vulnerability, and worry. Uncertainty is especially associated with waiting and delay – a fundamental characteristic of the hoping process. Hope is not hope if the object of desire appears immediately one desires it. This would be better described as magic, not hope. Hope exists in the *in between* world of waiting. The relative balance between certainty and uncertainty is mediated by other dimensions of hope, such as the cognitive, contextual, and affiliative dimensions.

The feelings of certainty and uncertainty can also exist concurrently. These feelings may at times be confusing as they initially can appear to be at odds. The tendency to think in either/or terms only adds to this confusion. It is more helpful to think of hope as having a constellation of affective expressions, many co-existing or alternating in rapid succession.

Cognitive dimension

The cognitive dimension of hope focuses on a wide range of thinking and imagining processes. The components of the cognitive dimension include:

- Identification of objects of hope, such as desired good, goal, state of being, or outcome
- Examination and assessment of reality in relation to hope
- Discrimination of actual and potential internal and external hope-promoting factors from hope-inhibiting factors
- Perception of the desired future outcome as realistically probable or possible though not certain
- Imaginative use of past and present facts that permits belief that the boundaries of favourable possibility are wider than they might seem, and the boundaries of unfavourable possibility are narrower than they seem. (Dufault & Martocchio, 1985: 384)

Hope from a cognitive perspective is reality-based. There is an expectation that that which is hoped for will eventually appear. To maintain a reality-based expectation, the hoping person continually assesses and reviews the grounds for hope. Many factors affect the maintenance of hope. Some of these are contextual, others are based on the resources of the individual, and still others are grounded in supportive relationships.

Logic and reason allow the hopeful person to bolster their resources when external circumstances provide little encouragement for the fulfilment of that for which the individual hopes. At the same time, hope may be abandoned if new information calls into question the legitimacy of the hoped-for outcome. Those who are able to maintain their hopes in difficult circumstances are able to muster a battery of cognitive strategies to realign and reposition themselves to gain their hopes where possible, or to reframe their meaning-making when hope has to be abandoned.

Behavioural dimension

As mentioned earlier, the behavioural aspect of hope is focused on action. Action can be an activity that brings about a desired outcome or it can be activity that is unfocused and ineffective. Hopeful persons like optimists are more inclined to take action to achieve their ends because they believe in the possibility of a positive outcome. Positive belief encourages positive action. However, some actions do not have a direct bearing on the outcome as such. Some actions are more subtle and focus on the maintenance of belief, attitude, and perseverance. Action can be understood to occur in a number of different areas: psychological, physical, social, and spiritual.

Psychological action

Action in the psychological area is cognitive in nature and involves planning strategies, organising ideas, reframing, and reality testing. An important aspect of psychological action is the mental preparedness to wait and it has two sides. The first is a form of waiting which involves observing the contextual climate and assessing when it is time to take other actions. The second is a form of waiting which is required when one has no control over external circumstances. This type of waiting might be described as an active passivity. One sometimes waits because that is all one can do.

Physical action

Action in the physical area involves taking practical steps to achieve one's goals. Such action might include dieting and exercising or seeking medical help to maintain physical health. Physical action might also involve travelling and risking new cultural experiences if the desire is for a life full of travel and multicultural encounters.

Social action

Behaviours in the social area are those that promote social engagement and relational connection. The old saying, 'If you want a friend, be a friend' captures some sense of the direction of the action in this area. Making choices about when and with whom to engage socially are all aspects of social actions that engender and help to maintain hope.

Spiritual action

The spiritual aspect, like the social aspects of behaviour, overlap with the affiliative area. They all involve some level of relationship albeit focused in different directions. Relating in the spiritual area focuses on some awareness of a higher power whether that is understood as God, spirit, nature, or force. Actions in the spiritual area might include praying, meditating, participating in religious practices, reading religious or spiritual literature, participating in a spiritual retreat, and contributing to charities.

Actions that help to encourage hope are not always focused on specific outcomes. Some actions are more about creating an environment or life atmosphere. Such actions may even be as mundane as keeping a routine, engaging in leisure pursuits, keeping a social calendar. These actions correspond well to generalised hope and collectively support a positive, hopeful life orientation.

Affiliative dimension

'The affiliative dimension focuses upon the hoping person's sense of relatedness or involvement beyond self as it bears upon hope' (Dufault & Martocchio, 1985: 386). This dimension involves relationships across a wide spectrum of connections including any sense of attachment to family, others, nature, and the spiritual realm. It is about intimacy, mutuality, and otherness. Otherness can include family and friends but equally it may include animals and nature or aspects of society at large like the underprivileged or those suffering from famine in other countries. The desire to be surrounded by the beauty of the natural world to enjoy pets is another aspect of relationship. Similarly, the desire for spiritual experience or communion with the transcendent is another expression of the affiliative dimension of hope.

Hope in relationships often involves a desire for a particular response from another. The hope may be that another appreciates or has empathy for what one is presently going through. It may be the hope invested in a doctor's response by a person suffering from a difficult illness, in particular, that the doctor will see them as a person and not just as a patient. Responses from others can directly influence one's hope. Sometimes others bolster hope by identifying with one's point of view or agreeing with one's perspective on life, and simply supplying emotional support.

Temporal dimension

The temporal dimension is concerned with the hoping person's experience of time as it relates to the process of hoping. Hope is most specifically focused on the future but it is also influenced by the past and the present. The issue of time is a significant feature of the hoping process especially as it relates to waiting and delay, as mentioned earlier, but it is also significant in terms of time specificity or non-specificity.

Particularised hopes are usually focused on gaining the objects of desire within a given time period. The time period may be short, medium or long-term depending on the nature of the object of hope and of its relative importance. Someone hoping to gain a new job might be focused on the short-term time frame, while an aspiring actor, desirous of an Academy Award, may view this as a longer-term process. Still other hopes may be stretched beyond the fabric of time to eternity. We are all capable of holding several hopes at one time, each with different time expectations. All hopes have a time delay though, and this delay must be managed if hope is to be sustained. The maintenance of hope within the context of delay presents its own challenges and requires perseverance. The various dimensions of hope must all be mustered to manage the delay between the establishment of hope and its fulfilment or abandonment.

Non-time-specific hopes can serve as a protective device against disappointment. Generalised hope, for example, orientates the individual to a particularly robust life attitude. It expects the best but is at the same time grounded in reality and able to accept the limitations of the human condition while still remaining positive. Non-time-specific hopes do not require a focus on time and therefore the constant surveillance of the opportunities to fulfil hopeful expectations. Having some non-time-specific hopes encourages a broader hopeful outlook and the pursuit of particular time-specific hopes as well.

As well as the future, the temporal dimension of hope also involves engagement with the past. Time past exerts an influence on hope for several reasons. The first is that it creates a storehouse of positive memories that help to frame hope. If the individual has had many experiences of hopes fulfilled then the memory of these provides encouragement and belief in the possibility of other hopes being fulfilled. The past becomes a reference point for belief and a reservoir of personal experiences of the possibility of hope.

A second feature of time past stored as memory is that it may also serve to support hope by providing memories of *unfulfilled* hopes. Dashed hopes do not necessarily have to be interpreted negatively. They may serve as lessons in reality grounding. Experiences of unfulfilled hope may also provide experience and knowledge about how best to manage in difficult circumstances. The psychological, affiliative, and behavioural resources used in the past also become a reservoir of knowledge of how to manage difficulties.

Finally, the present is also an important aspect of time that can influence hope. The ever present 'now' is often quite confronting. Questions like 'Do I like the present moment?', or 'What do I want to change about the present?', or 'What is missing from the present?' are provocative and provide a grounding for the future to emerge.

Contextual dimension

Hope is envisioned and activated within a given context. The contextual dimension of hope focuses on those life circumstances that surround, influence, and challenge an individual's hope. Hope is occasioned by a perception of need or desire. Desire for something can emerge at any time and can reflect normal developmental processes in the physical, cognitive, psychosocial, and spiritual domains. For example, it is normative for someone in their twenties to begin thinking about finding a life partner. A person in their thirties is often focused on career development and building financial security. Similarly, it is quite typical of a person in their mid-forties to begin a life review and to re-engage with questions about the nature and meaning of existence.

Maslow's hierarchy of needs is one way of framing the many contextual features of hope. As is well known, Maslow (1987) argued that human needs are hierarchical in nature. That is, it is much harder to focus on a higher need when lower needs are not met. For example, the person struggling to find enough food to eat is less likely to be hoping for a new house. However, when our basic physiological needs are met, the emergence of other perceived needs is more likely. These needs as set out in Maslow's hierarchy are physiological, safety, security/belonging, esteem, and self-actualisation. There is a strong argument that Maslow actually included an additional need to his hierarchy in his later writings, that of self-transcendence. (Further comment on this need will be made in later chapters.)

When an individual comes to an awareness of a need, a strong drive for its satisfaction is invoked. At the earlier stages of life these needs are often focused on physical, security, and esteem needs. Children and teenagers, for example, are often focused on hopes about obtaining physical objects that signify belonging or esteem. The ownership of the latest sports shoes, skateboard, or mobile phone often holds an underlying meaning for the teenager that says, 'I fit in' or 'I am now "cool"!' The later stages of the needs hierarchy capture quite a different focus, which eventually looks past the immediate needs of the self and expands to the needs of others, the wider society, and the transcendent. Whatever context stimulates and activates a need, whether that is a need to belong or to transcend the self, the basic processes involved are part of the activity of hope.

What hope is not

One of the challenges of defining hope is that there are many similar terms that appear, at first glance, to be synonymous with it. We have already mentioned the common identification of hope with optimism, but what of other terms like desire, wish, want, and self-efficacy? A number of studies have been conducted to examine the relationship between these different constructs (Magaletta & Oliver, 1999; Bryant & Cvengros, 2004; Bruininks & Malle, 2005). Many times these studies have compared the different variables, like self-efficacy, optimism, and hope, with an outcome variable like well-being. While it is not our aim to report the designs and results of a long list of such studies, it is perhaps helpful to summarise some common findings.

The majority of comparison studies report the finding that the various constructs/ terms listed above are discrete notions in themselves, although often complementary. For example, optimism, as already noted, has some similar characteristics with hope in terms of it implying a positive expectancy about life and life events. It is, however, different from hope in that it does not always focus on specific outcomes, but on generalised expectations.

Another example of the discrete but complementary nature of some of these constructs is found in a comparison of hope and self-efficacy. Self-efficacy is concerned with how people judge their capabilities and how these judgements influence their motivation and behaviour. As Bandura (1982: 122) defined it, 'Perceived self-efficacy is concerned with judgements of how well one can execute courses of action required to deal with prospective situations'. The person who has a positive belief in their capacity to effect a positive change in a particular situation is more likely to be motivated to stay focused on the topic of interest and also to take action to effect a change. Central to Bandura's understanding of self-efficacy is the view that the cognitive assessment of one's capacity to effect change is specific to the situation and not a generalised trait. Snyder et al. (2000), however, argue that a cognitive perspective of hope, while similar to self-efficacy, is focused both on situational and cross-situational goals and self-motivational thoughts. That is, the nature of hope is both *dispositional* or trait-based, and *state* or situationally based.

One study in particular sought to explore the conceptual and psychological differences between hope and the related mental states of desire, wish, want, joy, and optimism by examining folk definitions and real-life examples of these various states (Bruininks & Malle, 2005). In the first part of the study fifty-two undergraduate students were asked to describe these six mental states listed above. The researchers then used a coding system based on a set of feature descriptors and rated the number of times the participants mentioned these features (see Table 1).

The number of participants who mentioned a particular feature was computed for each of the six mental states of interest. A base rate was established by calculating the average number of participants who mentioned that feature. From this it was possible to make comparisons across each mental state and also the overall base rate. Table 2 itemises the frequencies of the features described for each mental state.

Table 1 Coding features associated with related mental states

1 *Cognition:* Related words such as: *belief*, *know*, *conscious of*, *think*, *imagine*, *consider*, and *remember*. These were cognitions one would experience concurrent with a particular state.
2 *Emotion:* Phrases including the words *feel* or *feeling of* were coded for this feature, as well as words such as *sentiment*, *mood*, *passion*, *longing*, and *yearning*.
3 *Temporal:* This feature was divided into the categories of *in the future* and *in the past*.
4 *Personal control:* This feature was divided into *high* and *low personal control*.
5 *Likelihood:* This feature was divided into *likely* and *unlikely*.
6 *Function:* Phrases that expressed the function of the state were coded for this feature (e.g., 'hope keeps a person focused on his/her goals').
7 *Object of the emotion:* Phrases such as *hopeful for* or *joyous about* were coded for this feature.
8 *Cause:* This feature consisted of circumstances that caused the emotion.
9 *Expectancy:* Words or phrases related to the expectancy of an outcome.
10 *Action:* Any action caused by experiencing a particular state was coded for this feature. This feature was divided into *take action* and *can't take action*.
11 *Consequences:* Phrases that implied consequences of experiencing.
12 *Physiology:* Any physiological symptoms mentioned in relation to experiencing the state were coded for this feature (e.g., *racing heart*, *can't sleep*, *short of breath*).

Source: Bruininks & Malle, 2005.

Wanting

Only five participants described wanting as being cognitive, whereas a strong majority described it as being an emotion. Surprisingly, wanting was not typically linked to the future. Unsurprisingly, wanting also corresponded to an object (representational object) that was desired. In many ways wanting was similar to desire and, as the researchers noted, may be considered a colloquial expression for desire.

Desire

The majority of respondents described desire as an intense emotion and, unlike other mental states, it was linked to a physiological response. Interestingly, only twelve per cent described desire as a cognition and no one described it in terms of expecting a positive outcome. Desire was most often described in relation to a desired object.

Wishing

Twenty-six per cent of participants (more than for any other mental state) described wishing as occurring when a person experiences little personal control over gaining a positive outcome. Thirty-three per cent of the participants (far more than for other states) described wishing in terms of *not* expecting the wished for object or event. It was strongly linked with an object and moderately associated with the future.

Table 2 Frequencies of features to describe each mental state

				Mental state			
Feature	**Hope**	**Optimism**	**Want**	**Desire**	**Wish**	**Joy**	**Base rate (%)**
Cognition	21	41(+)	5(−)	6(−)	20	0(−)	30
Emotion	29	9(−)	32	47(+)	34	50(+)	65
Future	40(+)	20	7(−)	15	23	2(−)	35
Past	0	0	0	0	0	12(+)	4
High control	0	1	0	2	2	3	3
Low control	5	0	1	2	13(+)	1	7
Likely	9	14(+)	1	3	2	1	10
Unlikely	3	1	0(−)	2	22(+)	0(−)	9
Function	16(+)	1	1	7	1	4	10
Representational object	42	40	45	46	47(+)	21(−)	78
Caused by	6	0(−)	3	3	2	16(+)	10
Expect positive outcome	30(+)	18(+)	1(−)	0(−)	1(−)	0(−)	16
Don't expect pos. outcome	1	0	1	0	17(+)	1	6
Take action	6	9	2	5	10	0(−)	10
Can't take action	2	0	0	0	3	1	2
Consequences	0	0	2	6(+)	3	0	4
Physiological	1	0	0	5(+)	0	4	3

Note. (+) number is above the row base rate; (−) number is below the base rate (both *ps*<.01). *N*=52 for each state.

Source: Bruininks & Malle, 2005.

Joy

Joy was described by nearly all participants as a very positive emotion and no one described it as being a cognition. Joy was not linked to a future outcome but rather to a state that is experienced when a future outcome has been realised. Joy was less linked to the attainment of a physical object.

Optimism

Optimism received the highest rating as being a cognition and was strongly linked to the future and a representational object. Interestingly, while the link with the future was strong it was significantly weaker than hope's link with the future. One of the most distinguishing differences between optimism and hope was in the expectancy of a positive outcome. Thirty-five per cent of participants associated optimism with a positive outcome compared with a fifty-eight per cent link between hope and a positive outcome.

Hope

Seventy-seven per cent of participants described hope as being associated with the future. Unlike the other mental states, hope was described by thirty per cent of participants as serving a function. Often this function was related to the maintenance of goals or to controlling negative feelings. Hope was consistently described as an emotion and also as being linked to the expectation of a positive outcome.

Positioning mental states

In a third study conducted by Bruininks and Malle (2005) participants had to identify the six mental states from short narratives which described one of each discrete state but where any identifying words were removed and replaced with the word 'represent'. Hence, if the narrative read, 'I hope that the future will turn out okay', the word 'hope' was replaced by 'represent'. The participants had then to identify

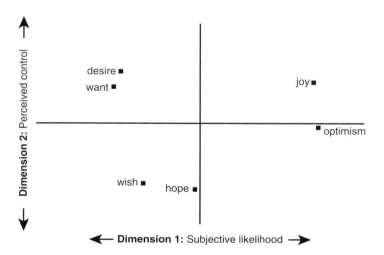

Figure 3 Scatter plot showing locations of the mental states in two-dimensional Euclidean distance model space

Source: Bruininks & Malle, 2005.

each narrative with the mental state it was conveying. The data were subjected to a multidimensional scaling analysis (SPSS ALSCAL), which recovers for each participant response the spatial location that best fits the data. One of the dimensional relationships that provides an insight into the differences between the mental states is between the dimensions of *subjective likelihood* and *perceived control*. Where the six mental states are situated in relation to each other based on these dimensions is represented in Figure 3.

When hope is viewed from the perspective of the dimensional comparison between perceived control and subjective likelihood we gain a particular insight. Hope, it seems, can exist even when an individual does not necessarily hold a high expectation that the object of hope will be gained. Equally hope can exist even when an individual perceives that he or she has little control of the circumstances surrounding the hoped-for outcome. This finding fits well with the notion of *generalised hope*.

Summary

As has been outlined in this chapter, hope has many discrete features but also many aspects that complement other mental states. One of the reasons that hope and other such mental states are often confused is because of their similarity. Hope, however, has some very distinct qualities and characteristics. Unlike optimism for example, hope has both a generalised and a particularised sphere of focus. *Generalised hope* allows for a positive but indefinite future which is grounded in reality. That is, its positive attitude does not deny the possibility that life may not work as originally hoped, hence, it maintains a positive outlook come what may. On the other hand, *particularised hope* does focus on specific future outcomes, expects to attain these, and has a strong action focus. It is possible at times for both forms of hope to co-exist and at other times for one to wax and the other to wane.

Hope can be understood to have both an external objective existence (i.e., to be out there somewhere) and an internal, subjective existence (i.e., to be owned by the individual). Hope is also an action that is acted upon in a range of dimensions including cognitive, behavioural, and affiliative, which are influenced by an individual's view of time and context. More than any other mental state, hope is strongly linked to the future as an orientation, is a balance between cognition and emotion, and expects a positive future outcome.

We have seen that hope is a multidimensional construct that can present contradictory features. At times hope represents a strong goal orientation and at other times it represents a positive expectation about life even when there is no possibility of the hoped-for outcomes. Most commentators say that hope is essential for life and wellbeing. While this may be so, there are many different views about the function and importance of hope. In the next chapter we will explore how hope has been understood from the perspective of different disciplines of thought.

QUESTIONS FOR REFLECTION AND DISCUSSION

1 Think of a time in your life when your circumstances either tempted you to lose hope or actually caused you to lose hope.

    a What were your dominant thoughts at the time?

    b What was your view of yourself?

    c What began a movement back to a hopeful outlook?

2 In counselling and psychotherapy, can hope be given to the client by the therapist? If so, how?

3 If hope can ebb and flow, wax and wane, what steps or strategies can a person take to increase the likelihood of enlarging their hope?

4 In your view, is hope largely a trait-based quality (i.e., an aspect of personality) or a state-based (context-specific) quality? Why?

5 Think of a person who you know that you would describe as full of hope. What qualities characterise that person?

2

Theoretical perspectives on hope

Introduction

Study of the nature and function of hope is not new to the academic disciplines. Hope was discussed by the ancient Greeks, by Christian theologians like Aquinas, and later philosophers like Kant and Kierkegaard. In more recent times, existential philosophers like Sartre and Marcel among others have continued the examination of hope. In theology, there are important modern works by Moltmann, Pieper, and Kelly. Hope has also been explored in other spiritual traditions, notably within Sufism and Buddhism. Different spiritual traditions have influenced thought and practice within counselling and psychotherapy and while it would be instructive to look at a wide range of these traditions, we have only addressed those that illustrate significantly different views of hope. In this chapter we present an outline of how hope has been understood from within the framework of different spiritual, philosophical, and academic traditions. Our aim here is to provide a breadth of perspective that may serve as a theoretical backdrop to later explorations of how hope may be fostered within counselling and psychotherapy.

Hope as a virtue

Within Western thought and some Eastern thought, hope has long been considered one of the central virtues. The ancient Greeks regarded a virtue as a personal trait or quality that enabled one to live a moral and ethical life. It was both a quality of being and a practice of the will. The virtues were considered the foundations of both personal and collective well-being. Many religious and philosophical traditions identify with several virtues in common, but a list of all virtues would be quite extensive. The ancient Greeks emphasised four cardinal virtues: *temperance, prudence, courage*, and *justice*. Aristotle understood a virtue to be a balance point between a deficiency and an excess of a trait. Hence, the virtue of generosity, for example, is regarded as a balance between miserliness and extravagance, and courage is the mean between recklessness and cowardice. From this perspective Aristotle developed the idea of the 'golden mean', that is, the desirable middle between two extremes.

The Christian tradition acknowledged the cardinal virtues of the Greeks and added to these the three theological virtues of *faith, hope* and *love*. Thomas Aquinas, one of the great philosopher/theologians of the medieval period, argued that hope presupposes desire, meaning that we only hope for that which we desire. He distinguished hope from desires and wishes by maintaining that hope must fulfil four conditions:

1   Hope must be for something good as opposed to something bad, such as fear
2   Hope's object must be in the future
3   Hope's object must be something arduous and not easily attained
4   This difficult object or state must be something possible to attain.

Aquinas, in the tradition of the ancient Greeks, also took the view that one should be dedicated but measured in the pursuit of one's hope. This was in fact an application of the 'golden mean'. The pursuit of hope requires motivation because the object of hope is not easily attained, but equally this pursuit should not be a headlong rush towards one's goal for fear of over-running the mark.

Aquinas spoke of hope as being both a *passion* and a *virtue*. When framing hope as a passion, he was highlighting its emotional dimension. When framing hope as a virtue he was emphasising its theological dimension and regarded it as a habit of mind. Like the Greeks, Aquinas understood a virtue to be a disposition or commitment of the mind. As a religious believer, Aquinas saw hope as an essential virtue because it aids the individual in attaining both temporal and eternal happiness.

The Sufis, a contemplative or mystical sect of Islam, also see hope as an important virtue, which sustains the devotee on his or her quest for spiritual union. Rumi (n.d.), a well-known thirteenth century Sufi master, asserted that 'we must always have hope'. To illustrate the importance of hope he explained:

> Now, when we hope expectantly for a reward, we will surely work with greater effort. Expectation becomes our wings, and the stronger our wings the farther the flight. If, on the other hand we lose hope, we become lazy and of no value to anyone.

Hope as a theological virtue involves a choice to think in a certain way. It is a habit of mind that embraces possibilities. To hope presumes that one will press on and work hard to achieve the object of desire. To hope, however, does not necessarily presume that one will achieve one's desires. Rather, hope is activated because one believes that to expect the good and to discipline the mind will in itself produce positive change in the self. As Aquinas explained it, 'The perfection of hope lies not in achieving what it hopes for but in embracing its standard' (Aquinas, 2006a, 17: 2).

It is clear from the forgoing outline that hope has had a long tradition within religious and spiritual traditions. In the following section we will explore further how hope is understood within two of these traditions, Christianity and Buddhism. We have selected these two traditions for several reasons. The first is because both have been highly influential in the development of counselling and psychotherapy. The second is because they represent in some respects quite disparate approaches to spirituality, one a monotheistic religion and the other a non-theistic religion. While we would like to include discussion of other religions/spiritualities and their views of hope, we have limited our examination to the two that have more directly influenced counselling and psychotherapy in the West.

Spirituality and hope

Christian perspectives on hope

Hope has long been a central theme within the Christian spiritual tradition. As mentioned earlier it is one of the three theological virtues. The explicit identification of hope was seen very early in Christian writings. References to hope are dotted throughout the Old and New Testaments. An example can be seen in the New Testament book of 1 Thessalonians 5:8: 'But since we belong to the day, let us be sober, putting on *faith* and *love* as a breastplate, and the *hope* of salvation as a helmet' (my italics). Hope is also often mentioned in the Old Testament in relation to the expectation that desires would be fulfilled. The loss of hope is considered a serious state of affairs. Proverbs 13:12 states: 'Hope deferred makes the heart sick, but a longing fulfilled is a tree of life.'

Immediately in these writings we are introduced to some of the characteristics of hope. First, hope has something to do with endurance; second, hope has protective qualities most likely for the mind as it acts like a helmet to protect thought; and third, the loss of hope can leave one emotionally troubled.

Hope as promise

One of the most significant Christian commentators on hope is the theologian Jürgen Moltmann. Moltmann claims that the authentic Christian perspective on life is one that is orientated towards the future. He argues that God is 'a God with "future as his essential nature"' (1993: 16). Genuine Christianity for Moltmann is not focused on doctrinal theses but rather on an expectant, ever-emerging view of the future based on the ongoing power and activity of Jesus Christ. Christianity in his view is a hope-based religion where hope is founded on God's promises. The identification of 'promises' as a seminal theme within a Christian worldview is based on two dimensions of promise. The first is the individual promises dotted throughout the scriptures, and the second is the representative nature of promise evidenced in the actions of Christ. For the Christian, Christ's resurrection from the dead established two fundamental principles: one, that death, the symbol of all pain and suffering, could be conquered, and two, that He in remaining alive evidences the possibility of a never-ending future for the individual and for humanity.

In the Christian mind, this resurrection or Christ event is one that radically alters the previous universal reality, which was limited by the *past* and *present*. Without the possibility of an ongoing *future*, humanity was understood to be ensnared by the cyclical repetition of the past and by a known present. As Moltmann (1993: 20) expresses it, 'hope … kindled spans the horizons which then open over a closed existence'.

In Moltmann's view, the way we relate to history is important as it orientates us to a particular vision of life. For example, a history without promise is a *history of commemoration*. Cultural events often act as anchor points for worldviews, but these can function in either positive or negative ways. When negative historical memory is regularly revisited, it solidifies cultural identity. A momentous national defeat in battle, for example, can become the touchstone of a society's personality – we the victims, the underdogs. Moltmann gives an example from ancient societies. He states, 'In Greek and Roman mythologies, the past is re-presented as an everlasting foundation' (1993: 109). His point is that such cultural histories are not defined by promise but by past events. Moltmann argues that when promise is introduced into history, history takes on a new character because it is no longer a cyclical process of commemorations of past events but is a site for celebrating promises fulfilled. A good example of this is the Feast of Passover within the Jewish calendar. For the Jew and Christian alike, this is a celebration of the fulfilment of God's promise to the Jewish people that they would be freed from enslavement in Egypt. For the believer, the Passover now becomes a cultural event that says, 'God will fulfil His promises and create a better future'. History is now no longer a cyclical remembering of the past, but rather a signpost to a new promised future.

One of the objections to a worldview that is orientated to an unfolding future is that it obscures an awareness of the present. One of the best expressions of this complaint is from Pascal (1958: 49) who said:

> We do not rest satisfied with the present. We anticipate the future as too slow in coming, as if in order to hasten its course; or we recall the past, to stop its too rapid flight. So imprudent are we that we wander in times which are not ours, and do not think of the only one which belongs to us …

For Moltmann, however, the individual living in the eternal present is the person who has stepped out of history. As he explains (1993: 29):

> The present is not a concept of time. The eternal conceived as the present is arrested temporal succession. The moment characterizes the present as a thing that has no past or no future. The moment is an atom of eternity.

In this view, the person who is only ever 'present' is contemporaneous with himself or herself. 'And to be … utterly and completely contemporaneous with oneself today, is to gain eternity. [Such a person] turns his back on the eternal so to speak, precisely in order to have it by him in the one day that is today' (1993: 29). Moltmann suggests that the person who is supposedly ever living in the present moment is one who presupposes an immediacy with God. Such a person has no need for God's help or the Christ event, as history and the future are rendered meaningless.

A living in the present that *does* reflect a Christian perspective is an experience of surprise – a flash of the future, an apprehension in a moment of what is to come. Living in the present is also understood as experiencing a foretaste of spiritual union with God within the present moment – a realisation of the divine. However, theologians assert that such transcendent experiences are not meant to blind one to the present realities of the human condition (Kelly, 2006). Rather, it is argued that hope allows one to embrace the present while at the same time straining for a promised future. Kelly maintains that hope itself does not simply placate the Christian believer through revelry about the future but disturbs his or her experience of the present by highlighting the incongruity of the present with the future. Hope draws the individual and society towards the 'not yet': 'Hope anticipates a future fulfilment that is yet to be given' (Kelly, 2006: 6).

Hope as promise also creates a tension between the 'now' and 'not yet'. When promise is offered and therefore brought into consciousness, the individual is drawn towards the possibility of a future not yet present. Hope creates a period of tension between the offer or awareness of promise and its fulfilment. This is the space where the work of hope is done, where the patience of hope is tested and where hope matures. It is this liminal 'inbetween' world which causes the individual to become more self-aware, to question assumptions about oneself and about the character of God. Questions such as 'Who am I to have such hopes?', 'What happens to my view of life if my hopes are dashed?', 'Is God just playing with me?', 'Is God even there?' are an important feature of the liminal experience.

Patience is a key aspect of hope in this inbetween world. The Christian existentialist, Kierkegaard, is instructive here. For Kierkegaard (1844) the patience of hope is about enabling the individual to 'gain one's soul'. By this he means that the soul or self is not simply possessed by the individual but must be continually gained. The soul for Kierkegaard is best understood as a *relationship* between the temporal and eternal worlds, between the finite and infinite. In his view, the soul is more than an entity on a temporal journey capable of reflecting on itself, rather, it is a relational being in relationship both with itself and with otherness. For him the soul could only properly know itself in relation to that which, or rather, he who created it. The soul is continually being 'gained' because it is continually becoming. The liminal space between the offer of hope and its fulfilment draws the self into a deeper relationship with itself, with others, and with God, thus facilitating a greater gaining of the self. Patience therefore, is much more than a 'holding out' for that which one awaits. It is an active process of becoming.

The final aspect of a Christian view of hope is that of a social virtue. The individual cannot manage the tasks of hope alone for he or she needs a helping community. Hope 'enables the individual to join or rejoin the human race with confidence and freedom' (Kelly, 2006: 11, 12). We need to be surrounded by a milieu of hope where others can provide emotional and practical support, and where stories of hope fulfilled can be recounted. One enduring metaphor of Christianity is that of yeast, which ferments and transforms the whole loaf of society. It accomplishes this transformation by demonstrations of hopes fulfilled. Those who carry a Christian vision of hope carry the candle of hope for the whole society. In their view, a depressed society needs to be surprised by a communal spirit of hope. According to Kelly, genuine Christian hope is not afraid to get dirty in the muck of human struggle and misery. It purports to have the power to sustain the individual and the community through adversity.

According to philosopher/theologian Pieper (1986), the two enemies of Christian hope are *presumption* and *despair*. Presumption arises when one is impatient for the arrival of the promised future. It seeks to find its own answers and to draw early closure on the problems of life. Despair is the anticipation of the non-fulfilment of God's promises. Both these states relinquish patience and trust in the character of God and cause the devotee to cease to believe that God will fulfil that which he promises. The despair referred to here should not be confused with the ordinary despair of frustration and disappointment. This type of despair comes over every person at times, tempting us to give up hope, and is part of the normal ebb and flow of the human condition. Rather, the aforementioned despair is a determined state of being which tries to relieve the individual from disappointments. It says, 'God is not there' and 'Do not risk any further'. It says with Camus (1955: 170), 'to think clearly and not hope any more'. The difficulty with this sentiment is that hope cannot be so easily disposed of for it even resides in despair, for despair emerges when no possibility for that which is hoped for is imagined. Despair, in this sense, is still a state defined in relationship with hope. Unfortunately, all that is left when hope is not active is the *status quo*.

In summary, a Christian hope has several key elements.

1   Hope is based on the promises of God:

    ○   specific scriptural promises
    ○   a symbolic promise of the possibility of a never-ending future.

2   Hope provides for a linear not cyclical view of history.
3   Hope draws the believer towards the future.
4   Hope creates a tension between the 'now' and 'not yet'.
5   Hope is a social virtue.
6   Presumption and despair are enemies of hope.

Buddhist perspectives on hope

Buddhism, like Christianity, is one of the great world religions and has had wide influence particularly in the East but also increasingly in the West. All world religions converge at various points especially around their agreement on what constitutes the virtuous life. For example, the values of living at peace with others, of cultivating temperance and moderation in conduct, and of offering acts of charity are examples of common spiritual values. One of the differences between religious traditions is in how each instructs the individual to achieve or gain these values and act them out. Like the Christian tradition, Buddhism has had and continues to have significant influence on the practice of counselling and psychotherapy. To demonstrate this link it is important to first provide a brief outline of Buddhist thought. While the following will not do justice to a comprehensive appreciation of Buddhism, it will at least provide a backdrop for understanding how the tradition views the concept of hope.

The Buddha lived over two and half thousand years ago and, in reaching a state of enlightenment, set about teaching the spiritual path. He first proposed what has become known as the Four Noble Truths:

1 Life leads to suffering (dukka)
2 Suffering is caused by craving or wanting
3 Suffering ends when craving or wanting ends and this leads to enlightenment (Bodhi)
4 Reaching this liberated state is achieved by following 'the path'.

The Noble Eightfold Path is the fourth of the Four Noble Truths and instructs the follower how to achieve enlightenment. It is organised into three groups, which progressively outline 'right' belief and action.

A. Prajna is the wisdom that purifies the mind, allowing it to attain spiritual insight into the true nature of all things. It includes:

   i drsti: viewing reality as it is, not just as it appears to be
   ii samkalpa: intention of renunciation, freedom and harmlessness.

B. Sila is the ethics or morality, or abstention from unwholesome deeds. It includes:

   iii vāc: speaking in a truthful and non-hurtful way
   iv karman: acting in a non-harmful way
   v   ājīvana: a non-harmful livelihood.

C. Samādhi is the mental discipline required to develop mastery over one's own mind. This is done through the practice of various contemplative and meditative practices, and includes:

   vi vyāyāma: making an effort to improve
   vii smrti: awareness to see things for what they are with clear consciousness, being aware of the present reality within oneself, without any craving or aversion
   viii samādhi: correct meditation or concentration. (Source: Wikipedia)

One of the fundamental tenets of Buddhism is that suffering is caused by attachment to our wants and cravings, and if we are to be rid of suffering, which is the path of enlightenment, then we must disavow our wants and cravings. Within Buddhism there is often some distinction made between craving and desire. A craving is best understood as a desire that has developed too much energy within the individual and consequently exerts control. Desire might be better thought of as a generally positive life force. However, the two terms are often used interchangeably as the gap between craving and desire is quite small. For the Buddhist, desire that leads to attachment is understood to be a delusion. By this is meant that we are often confused or enticed to desire or want something because we think that it will provide us with happiness and contentment. We say to ourselves, 'If I only had that job, I'd be happy', 'If only I could be married, all would be well', 'If only I owned my own house, I would be content'. Happiness in this scheme is largely related to gaining something that is external to the self. Instead of a focus on self-transformation there is a focus on maintaining the self through gratification. In the Buddhist mind this is all viewed as self-delusion. What is required for a return to the path of enlightenment is for our delusions or illusions to be unmasked. We need to see that achieving these relationships or objects of desire will not produce happiness in and of themselves. Happiness comes from a total transformation of the self, even a loss of the self, and therefore a loss of desire.

Christianity and Buddhism have a lot in common on several of these points, especially that our desires are often forms of unhelpful attachment of which we are better rid. Most spiritual traditions in fact, see desire as problematic to some degree. A defining feature of Buddhism however is its belief in the centrality of personal moral choice as a means of disavowing wants and desires. It is regarded as no easy thing to rid the self of such wants and desires, so much so that it may take many lifetimes to achieve. The Buddhist concepts of reincarnation and karma are based on the view that personal progression towards enlightenment is fundamentally a moral issue. The better our choices in life, the more evolved we will be in the next life and so on until our choices are realised in a transcendence from this mortal cycle of existence. To enable us to make better moral choices we need to rid ourselves of our desires, and this is brought about by the progressive unmasking of our illusions of attachment. It is in this context that the Buddhist view of hope must be understood. If life is suffering brought about by our attachments and we can rid ourselves of these by ceasing to want or desire them, then hope has no real place or useful purpose. As one Buddhist scholar states, 'there is no hope in Buddhism' (Gombrich, 2011: 1). Gombrich goes on to assert, 'Since the only sure way to eliminate suffering is to eliminate wanting, how can hope be commendable?' (2011: 12).

Central to the Buddhist view is the notion that all major happenings in life relate to our moral choices. The individual in this respect is responsible for the direction his or her life takes, whether that be for good or ill. While this is sometimes viewed as a deterministic position, it would be more accurate to consider it a position that emphasises free will. The Buddhist does not assert that all everyday happenings are imbued with karmic energy, only significant ones. This position is central to understanding the limited place that hope plays within a Buddhist worldview. As Gombrich explains, 'Since the Buddha has taught that all major events in one's life depend on one's own moral decisions, hope can play a minimal role at best' (2011: 11). This perspective, however, does not obviate any reference to hope. There are still the common-sense references that the Western mind would certainly perceive as conveying some reference to hope. For example, a well-wishing comment to a friend about to undergo an operation such as 'I hope it all goes well' would not be out of place. Such a kindly thought though, would have at its base the assumption that the outcome of the operation will, most likely, be influenced by karma. On a day-to-day basis the Buddhist is hopeful in the general sense of expecting a positive future. This hope is founded on the expectation that his or her good moral choices will have a positive effect on the wheel of life.

How the future is conceptualised is a fundamental dimension of hope. As outlined in Chapter 1, hope has a temporal or time-based aspect. When spirituality is introduced into the discussion, time takes on at least two features: chronological time and time beyond the temporal, that is, eternity or nirvana. While eternity and nirvana are not necessarily synonymous in meaning, they do both capture a sense of the future beyond time. The Christian perspective on hope and time acknowledges that hope is intricately involved in both the human experience of the future as chronological time and as eternity.

The Buddhist view of the future is quite different from the Christian perspective outlined earlier. For the Christian the future is something that unfolds in response to God's plans for humanity and existence. The individual as well as the whole of humanity participate in the outworking of this hope-filled future. The Christian's responsibility is to believe and to take action which is consistent with this view of God's benevolent plan. A central aspect of this future existence is an ever-increasing union or relationship with God. Buddhism, conversely, does not relate the future to the involvement of an omnipresent, omniscient, omnipotent God, but rather the engagement of the individual in moral choices. It is these moral choices that have the power to facilitate the emergence of one's future through the process of karma.

The third grouping in the Eightfold Path is Samādhi, or the mental discipline required to gain mastery over one's own mind. Central to this discipline is the development of an awareness of oneself in the present moment. To facilitate awareness, the devotee practises meditation and different forms of concentration. These practices, which are designed to provide the individual with mastery over the mind through the disciplined dissolution of cravings and expectations, form the vehicle for the journey to enlightenment. The aim of so freeing the mind is the achievement of a greater awareness of oneself and of one's connectedness with all existence. It is these practices of Buddhism in particular that have found their way into the field of counselling and psychotherapy. Meditation and other activities designed to focus one's awareness on the present moment are often referred to as mindfulness techniques and have become common practices in therapy.

In summary, there are two seminal features of Buddhism that determine how hope is understood within this tradition. The first is the centrality of moral choice as the active human dimension of karma. The second is how time is prioritised in terms of a focus on the present moment. As significant aspects of the future are viewed as an outworking of moral choices there is less need to look to a future outside of the consequences of these choices. Hope in this respect is largely determined by oneself. In a related fashion, if the future is not viewed as an ever-expanding and surprising future based on God's unfolding plan, then the present moment becomes of greater importance. As hope is predominantly future-oriented it takes on less overall importance within the Buddhist tradition.

Existential perspectives on hope

Existentialism is both a philosophical system and also an approach to counselling and psychotherapy. The focus in the following discussion is on the philosophical dimension and especially how hope is understood within its different divisions. Existentialism did not arise from a single source, as many divergent voices helped shape it as a philosophical system. From its earliest beginnings in the works of Kierkegaard and Nietzsche there appeared within existentialism two divergent streams of thought – Christian and humanist. Kierkegaard is regarded as one of the first to articulate an existential philosophy, in particular a Christian approach, which proposed that the starting point for understanding life was not the traditional grand philosophies based on universal principles but on what he termed 'the single individual'. Kierkegaard argues that living one's life by trying to conform to what ethics dictate as being universal norms for appropriate human behaviour results in a meaningless life. This is because in conforming to an objective norm one loses one's individuality – actions governed by norms are the same as everyone else's. Living life on the basis of agreed philosophical ethics simply make one part of the crowd. Kierkegaard asserts that life only has meaning when we act according to our own subjective understanding. He argued that 'subjectivity is the truth' and that it should be the starting point for any philosophical enterprise rather than grand notions of universal principles. The difficulty raised by appealing to subjectivity as the measure of meaning and authenticity in life instead of objective moral ethics, is that belief and behaviour must be governed by some standard. Kierkegaard acknowledged that life is paradoxical in that moral ethics may be good in and of themselves, but may not lead to personal meaning and the authentic life unless they are personally appropriated. Kierkegaard addresses the problem of identifying a standard by arguing that the only answer is the *passion* of faith. By this he means that it is not reason that gets us through life but action, and action is derived from our deep desires and passions. It is our passions that bind us to life and cause us to want to live meaningful lives. For Kierkegaard, human passions are intimately linked to the source of life, God. Hence, to be true to oneself and to live an authentic life one has to be connected to one's passions, which are by nature ultimately God-given and oriented.

In arguing for truth as subjectivity, Kierkegaard highlights the essential paradox of existential living. He acknowledges two seemingly contradictory positions: one, that there are moral and ethical principles worthy of note that commanded a response from the individual, and, two, that these ethical principles can be countermanded at any time by the necessity of passion. The individual thus lives in an absurd world of contradiction. In a similar vein, the individual of faith gives everything to follow a belief in God whose existence cannot be proven. Living then is a passionate faith in a reality that transcends the world and provides a higher and personal meaning. To exist is always to be confronted by the question of meaning. For Kierkegaard and for existentialists in general, meaning comes first from action, not from thinking. We discover ourselves by first acting out our passions, not by thinking through the dilemmas of existence.

Anxiety is an important theme within existentialism and has been skilfully highlighted by Kierkegaard. In his view, anxiety demonstrates the tension between the temporal and eternal worlds. Kierkegaard uses the biblical story of Adam and Eve to argue that sin is an important part of the process of humanity becoming aware of the spiritual or eternal. This is the case because the sinner 'lives only in the moment as abstracted from the eternal' (Kierkegaard, 1844: 93). The sinner separates himself from the eternal (the decree not to eat of the fruit of the tree) and plunges into the temporal. As van Deurzen (2010: 11) explains, 'Instead of staying merged with the eternal or the ethical, Adam, in this, manifested his spirit and posited the moment, the temporal, making the opposition between the temporal and the eternal a possibility'. The result is that Adam (humanity) moved beyond 'un-self-conscious immediacy' – life before sin – and gained 'self-conscious reflection'. To put it another way, Adam realised that inherent in God's edict not to eat of the fruit of the tree was the implication that he was free to choose. Hence Adam came upon the realisation that he had freedom, but this freedom ultimately led to sin. Sin, however, had a twofold outcome, the first was the breakthrough into an awareness of the temporal, and the second was the anxiety that resulted from the newly created tension between the temporal and eternal. To be fully human is to grapple with our finite and infinite states made possible by our freedom to do so. The by-product of our freedom is anxiety, or as Kierkegaard (1844: 61) expresses it, 'anxiety is the dizziness of freedom'.

The writings of Nietzsche represent the beginnings of the humanist form of existentialism. Like Kierkegaard, Nietzsche struggles with the existing philosophical explanations for existence, especially any position that privileges an objectivist view of reality. He argues that universal moral or ethical principles are established by those who are in power. As far as Nietzsche is concerned, both the church and science are complicit in asserting that there are pre-existing universal principles from which causal relations are derived. Moral and ethical principles are the result of this thinking and have brought humanity to a state of docility and sickness. Nietzsche seeks to throw off this mentality and replace it with a form of nihilistic freedom. He proclaims that 'God is dead!' and therefore there are no longer any pre-existing universal laws governing human existence and choice. One problem with this position is that it imagines a universe without constraints, a place without any intrinsic meaning. However, such a universe provides both a problem and a benefit. The problem is that the weak individual is likely to fall victim to despair in the face of such meaninglessness. In this situation nihilism wreaks confusion and havoc. The benefit is that the strong individual is freed by nihilism to take responsibility for meaning. 'Nietzsche imagined such a person as the "overman" (Übermensch), the one who teaches "the meaning of the earth" and has no need of otherworldly supports for the values he embodies' (*Stanford Encyclopedia of Philosophy*, 2010a: 6).

Like Kierkegaard, Nietzsche reorientates the priority for meaning-making in the individual. Under his scheme, it is not universal moral, ethical, or causal principles that determine the nature of existence, but the individual. However, meaning and values cannot simply be founded on arbitrary decisions and impulsive behaviour. In relocating meaning as a subjective process Nietzsche had also to establish the grounds or standard by which such meaning could be measured as a success or failure. He found a useful analogy for the nature of such a standard in works of art. For the quality of a work of art to be judged it first has to be regarded as having a style. Interestingly this 'style' is not something that can be reduced to a general law or form. The style of a work of art is best understood as being within the art itself. The art is therefore judged on a style that is inherent to the artwork. In a similar fashion, the quality and success of subjective, moral and ethical determinations are to be judged on their aesthetic appeal.

Nietzsche's relocation of meaning in the individual, like Kierkegaard, led him to realise the precarious nature of existence. Nihilism can destroy or empower; it can leave humanity in despair or raise humanity to superhuman status (overman or *Übermensch*). Freedom to decide meaning means that individuals are left hanging between these two states of being:

> Man is a rope, fastened between animal and Superman – a rope over an abyss. A dangerous going-across, a dangerous wayfaring, a dangerous looking-back, a dangerous shuddering and staying still. What is great in man is that he is a bridge and not a goal; what can be loved in man is that he is a going-across and a down-going. (Nietzsche, 1896: 43–4)

Important existential concepts that developed in the twentieth century are those of 'facticity' and 'transcendence'. Facticity refers to the various objective qualities an individual possesses. For example, gender, colour, socio-economic status, abilities, and so on all constitute a third-person view of the facts about an individual's state of being. However, unlike the facticity of a non-human object, such as a stone or a chicken, the individual has the power to imbue these facts with a quality of existence that is greater than the third-person facts. Being is determined by the 'stance' one takes towards the facts because human beings are 'self-interpreting animals'. It is this capacity to be more than the facts that existentialists refer to as 'transcendence'.

Sartre, the French existentialist, captured the concepts of facticity and transcendence by the slogan 'existence precedes essence'. By this he means that it is not possible to define human existence on the basis of the facts alone. The nature of existence depends on the actions of existence. In classical philosophies existence was thought to be determined by the pre-existing essence of the object. Existence was therefore the playing out of the essence or nature of the entity. A rock acted according to its essence or 'rockness' and the chicken according to its 'chickenness'. In existentialism, meaning is decided not by essence but through and in existing itself.

While a great deal more could be said about the key themes in existentialism, our primary focus is on how existentialism considers hope. Given that despair, absurdity, anxiety, and freedom are core existential issues, it is not surprising that the question of hope arises. This is especially so when one considers that hope is the opposite of despair. Existentialism branches into two streams of opinion about hope: the humanist existentialists discard hope as unnecessary, while the Christian existentialists regard hope as an essential virtue to hold alongside the other existential themes.

Hope and existentialism: a rejection and an embrace

Rejection

Beginning with the humanist stream and in particular the writings of Sartre, we see a strong assertion that hope is a useless relic of bygone universalist philosophies. If the meaning of existence is determined solely by the individual, then the individual must take responsibility for the outcomes of his or her choices. Despair and hope are conceptualised on this basis. If I despair, I only have myself to blame for my poor choices. If interpreting my circumstances is dependent on me, then it is also up to me to decide what action to take to rectify them. In this system of thought there is no place for hope as there is no power outside the self on which the individual can base any meaning for existence. As Sartre (1946) expressed it, 'there is no God and no prevenient design, which can adapt the world and all its possibilities to my will'. Sartre went on to make an even clearer statement about hope. He said, 'When Descartes said, "Conquer yourself rather than the world," what he meant was, at bottom, the same – that we should act without hope' (1946).

In his famous lecture entitled, 'Existentialism is a Humanism', Sartre expressed strongly the view that people 'paint their own portrait' and that there is nothing but that portrait. On this basis he asserts that reality alone is reliable, and that is the reality that we ourselves determine. Given this, he suggests that hope serves only a negative function. He said 'that dreams, expectations and hopes serve to define a man only as deceptive dreams, abortive hopes, expectations unfulfilled; that is to say, they define him negatively, not positively' (1946: 10).

Camus agrees with Sartre that entertaining the possibility of hope is a waste of time. He holds this position primarily because he believes that there is no life after death. This position led Camus to question the nature of existence. His conclusion was that life is an absurdity. Life is absurd because it presents us with unsolvable contradictions. On the one hand we value our lives and yet on the other hand, we know that we will die, and in Camus' view, this renders our life endeavours as meaningless. Camus' answer to the absurdity of existence is to live life to the full, revelling in the pleasures of the senses. He sees hope as a delusion because it distracts the individual from living in the present with thoughts of an eternal future. The person busy with preparation for eternity is not living in the here-and-now. Hope minimises the value of life and weakens our capacity to deal with the vicissitudes of existence. For Camus (1955), it is only in being stripped of all hope that the individual is able to fully engage with life.

An embrace

Another perspective on hope, however, can be found within existentialist thought. Writers like Kierkegaard, Marcel, and Levinas all acknowledge the importance of hope, albeit in different ways. For Kierkegaard, hope is best understood as the practice of patience. In his approach to understanding the human condition, he focuses on the soul's encounter with the present moment. The soul is in a process of always becoming or, in his words, 'gaining itself' (1844). His view of the soul is not that of an entity with some pre-existing essence, but a self that only exists in and through its relationship with itself and otherness. The soul/self is by nature fundamentally relational. The problem of the soul, however, is that it has a tendency to fail to be authentically itself – to stay relationally engaged. The task of the soul is to continually press into being. Hence, the soul must constantly reorientate itself through relationships to 'gain itself'. Patience and therefore hope is required in this process of continually becoming oneself.

For Kierkegaard hope also has another aspect, an orientation of expectancy. This expectancy is understood in terms of a Christian telos of eternity. The soul or self is defined by its engagement in a dialectical relationship between temporality and eternity. This means that to be human is to be cognisant of both our mortality and our immortality. The self requires both a temporal hope and an eternal hope – a hope in our present condition and a hope for an ongoing benevolent existence beyond the grave. To continue in a process of becoming more authentically ourselves, both personal effort and also a recognition that the task is beyond us are necessary. Ultimately hope is dependence on God. There is in this position a contradiction between the importance of the struggle and the effort of maintaining hope, and an awareness that even our efforts are guided and enabled by God who is the source of life and the ultimate telos of all relationships.

Marcel (1995), a twentieth-century French existentialist, held views close to Kierkegaard's on the importance of hope. He also emphasised the central notion that the self is best understood as an entity in relationship with otherness. In view of this he developed the concept of *disponibilité* and *indisponibilité*, sometimes translated as *availability* and *unavailability*. Marcel assumes that the self will develop best when in relationship with others who are fully available and present to the relationship. The problem of *disponibilité* is that it requires an investment in the other, a belief in and expectation of the quality of the other. Essentially, *disponibilité* is *to hope* in the good intentions of the other towards us. In reality others will fall short of our expectations. Given this fact, Marcel suggests that encounters with others' limitations draw attention to our own inadequate expectations and our own limitations. The benefit is that relationships enable a greater self-awareness. However, the difficulty with this situation is that it is not always easy to maintain positive expectations of the other, in other words, to continue to hope. What is required is an act of *fidelity*, a commitment to maintain relationships. Marcel argues that it is in the act of commitment or fidelity that hope is required.

The only way in which an unbounded commitment on the part of the subject is conceivable is if it draws strength from something more than itself, from an appeal to something greater, something transcendent – and this appeal is hope (*Stanford Encyclopedia of Philosophy*, 2010b).

For Marcel, hope provides the ground for fidelity and the strength not to despair. He argues that hope is more than a general optimism about a positive future outcome. This he bases on a view of optimism that he refers to as arising from the *realm of fear and desire*. Fear and desire are anticipatory states in which we expect a specific desire or outcomes to eventuate or not. Optimism resides within this realm as it imagines a specific result or object. Alternatively, Marcel argues that hope resides in the *realm of hope and despair* where hope is better understood as an attitude of positive expectancy without a specific notion of how the future will reveal itself. This form of hope is akin to *generalised hope* as outlined in Chapter 1. Hope of this kind is simply defined as a positive expectancy of a future good without a specific object of hope in mind. Contingent with this view of the future is also a realistic acknowledgment of current contingencies, of a grounded reality. Marcel's hope is similar in form to Kierkegaard's patience of hope – an active expectancy. Like Kierkegaard, Marcel believes in a spiritual or transcendent reality beyond the human condition and relies on this in his formulation of hope. He states, 'Hope consists in asserting that there is at the heart of being, beyond all data, beyond all inventories and all calculations, a mysterious principle which is in connivance with me' (Marcel, 1995: 28).

The final existential view of hope we will comment on is that of Levinas (2001). While Levinas says little of hope specifically, he does comment on the idea of the future, which is directly related. Levinas understands the notion of 'the future' to be organised in three primary ways (Egéa-Kuehne, 2008). The first two of these he argues are based in utopian visions of the future. The future depicted by Aristotle as '*germ-like*' or as incremental growth, is the first of these. The future in this organisation is a linear expansion of life as it begins in or from the present moment. This growth metaphor assumes that the present is a lesser state than that which the future will be. In this conception, we can expect that things will gradually improve over time. The second version of the future is that of the *heroic journey*. It is based on the power of people to pursue and achieve their goals. This approach prioritises human ability, effort, and perseverance. It is winning despite obstacles.

The third version of the future is based on Levinas' central thesis – the importance of 'welcoming the other'. For Levinas, existence is first and foremost about a dialogical encounter with otherness. While this is a key theme in existentialism in general, Levinas develops it and highlights the central importance of prioritising the other over the self. On this basis, the future is not founded on some utopian vision of what life should look like, for to do so would require building towards an outcome that either, through incremental social change or through the power of self-effort, could deny the being of the other. Rather, the future is based on the present encounter with the other. In this respect, the future is unknown and generally unexpected. Levinas holds the view that people consistently exceed our expectations of them and surprise us. In other words, the future is much better thought of if it is not understood to be an extrapolation of the present or an outworking of our controlled interventions, but rather a fresh surprise of personal encounters. Such a view provides for a bright vision of hope as something that emerges between people, as something unexpected. Hope then is intricately linked to otherness and encounter. Hope therefore always has a social dimension.

Summary

Hope as a concept has a long history evidenced by its inclusion in literature from ancient times to the present. Hope has been understood variously as both a virtue and a curse. These contradictory views have surrounded the notion of hope throughout human history. We see these distinctions expressed in religious and secular settings. In Christianity for example, hope is a central virtue, while in Buddhism it holds much lesser importance. In a somewhat similar manner, hope is prized by some existentialist writers and denigrated by others. One thing is sure, hope is a confronting idea which requires careful consideration.

QUESTIONS FOR REFLECTION AND DISCUSSION

1   What were the ideas that most struck you from the chapter? Why?
2   The two main examples of spiritual approaches to hope provided in the chapter represented quite different views. In Christian spirituality hope is understood as a fundamental human quality or life virtue; in Buddhism hope is best seen as an outcome of moral choices but not central to healthy human functioning. What is your own perspective on hope and spirituality?
3   In a similar manner, existentialism incorporates two quite different perspectives on hope. In one form, hope is akin to patience and endurance and also of engaging with otherness; in the other form of existentialism, hope is seen as a set of empty dreams. In your view, what are the strengths and weaknesses of these two positions?

EXERCISE

Traditional spiritualities and academic disciplines have formed the philosophical backdrop to how hope is understood within a culture and therefore within counselling and psychotherapy. Make a list of cultural and spiritual ideas (assumptions) that have influenced the practice of counselling and psychotherapy in the West.

3

The emergence of hope in the literature of the helping professions

If it is true that the average person would include a positive mental outlook in a list of necessary features of mental health and well-being, or at least similar notions such as optimism, sanguinity, or hopefulness, it is a little surprising that it has taken the helping professions until relatively recently to explore the nature and function of hope. Of course counsellors, psychotherapists, psychiatrists, social workers, and nurses have often intuited the importance of hope in people's recovery from physical and mental illness, but little attention has traditionally been paid to it in their respective training programmes. As an example, in 1963 psychologist Paul Pruyser lamented, 'Most psychological textbooks do not carry the words hope or hoping in their index or chapter headings' (p. 86). Menninger in 1959 was one of first to emphasise the importance of psychiatrists inspiring hope in their patients, stating 'as scientists, we are now duty bound to speak up about the validity of hope in human development' (1959: 491). A little later in 1973, the noted psychiatrist Jerome Frank highlighted the importance of hope in psychological recovery. He observed that people sought out help through psychotherapy because they were demoralised in their own problem-solving efforts. Frank stated, 'Feelings frequently accompanying demoralization are anxiety to the point of panic, depression to the point of hopelessness, and feelings of powerlessness accompanied by suspiciousness and chronic anger' (1995: 90). Vaillot was one of the first to comment on hope in the nursing literature and, seeing it as a central dimension of nursing commented, '"to inspire hope would be the nurse's specific task" … they needed to ask "how can nurses inspire hope in their patients?"' (1970: 272).

Research on the topic of hope has grown substantially since these early investigations. The two disciplines that have developed the most extensive research in the area are nursing and psychology/psychotherapy. Before we explore the application of hope-based strategies in counselling and psychotherapy in later chapters it will be helpful to identify the current understanding of hope from the perspectives of these two disciplines. There is much common ground in the respective research but important differences as well. The review will begin with findings from the nursing literature, and then from psychology.

Hope in nursing research

Nursing researchers have done much to add to our knowledge about hope and its application in the helping professions. Nursing as a discipline has a breadth of applications ranging from general adult nursing to a wide set of specialist areas such as psychiatric/ mental health nursing, oncology nursing, and palliative care nursing, to name a few. Important studies on hope have come from each of these fields and much of this can be readily applied to the practice of counselling and psychotherapy.

The centrality of hope in nursing practice is probably best highlighted by a statement made by Vaillot (1970: 272) in the early stages of the nursing profession's inquiry into hope.

> There are some major yet seldom talked about issues here, most especially, to fail to inspire hope was *ipso facto* to fail in a duty of care, and it thus by implication – would be contributing to the client's demise.

Another early exploration of hope in nursing was conducted by Miller (1983) who drew on the relevant literature at the time to try to provide a definition of hope and to understand how it might be inspired in people with chronic illness. Miller's work was theoretical rather than empirical, but it added to the growing understanding of hope. She identified eight key elements of hope:

- Valued
- Private (personalised)
- Powerful
- An intrinsic component of life
- Providing dynamism for the spirit
- An expectation
- An inner readiness
- Central to human existence ('Everything human beings do in life is central to life')

Yet another early understanding of hope came from Dufault and Martocchio's (1985) study of cancer patients. As outlined in Chapter 1, they distinguished between two forms or spheres of hope, *generalised* and *particularised* hope, and identified six dimensions: *affective, cognitive, behavioural, affiliative, temporal,* and *contextual*. Soon after this study Owen (1989) explored the understandings of hope held by specialist nurses. Owen's conceptual model identified hope as having six features as itemised in Table 3.

One final list of conceptual components of hope identified in the nursing literature is worthy of note and this comes from the findings of Morse and Doberneck (1995). They analysed interviews with four groups of patients – patients with spinal cord injuries; patients undergoing heart transplant; breast cancer survivors; and breast feeding mothers – using conceptual analysis. Their analysis (see Table 4) identified what they regard as seven universal components of hope.

In summary, early nursing research sought to provide evidence for a clear definition of hope, especially as it applies to nursing. As research endeavours from other disciplines have also found, hope is not an easy concept to define. Having said this,

Table 3 Themes in Owen's conceptual model of hope

Themes of hope

Goal setting: Hopeful patients engaged in setting (and revising) attainable goals. It may be worth noting that the goals of these patients noticeably changed as death approached (e.g. smaller, more attainable, and more realistic).

Positive personal attributes: Hopeful patients were described as having several hopeful personality characteristics (e.g. courage, optimism, and a positive attitude).

Future redefinition: Hopeful patients were described as those who saw or perceived the future, and this future was not quantified in time.

Meaning in life: Hopeful patients were those who equated hope with a meaningful life.

Peace: Hopeful patients were described as being at peace or comfortable with their situation.

Energy: Hopeful patients were described as being those who possessed and gave out energy. Additionally, Owen reported that the hopeful patient needed energy to remain hopeful – hope required energy and gave energy.

Source: Owen, 1989: 77.

Table 4 Morse and Doberneck's universal components of hope

Components of hope

A realistic initial assessment of the predicament or threat.
The envisioning of alternatives and the setting of goals.
A bracing for negative outcomes.
A realistic assessment of personal resources and of external conditions and resources.
The socialisation of mutually supportive relationships.
The continuous evaluation for signs that reinforce the selected goals.
A determination to endure.

Source: Morse & Doberneck, 1995: 281.

there are a number of common findings from the studies identified above. In short, hope is:

- An intrinsic component of life
- Power and energy
- Future-oriented
- Goal-oriented
- Endurance
- An internal and external process of assessment of resources
- A social virtue
- A search for meaning.

Metaphors of hope from nursing research

Before moving on to explore some applications of hope in nursing, another review of hope is of interest. A very helpful summary of the research findings comes from a metasynthesis study conducted by Hammer, Morgensen, and Hall (2009). A metasynthesis aims to examine the findings of representative qualitative studies on a topic and synthesise them. The data for this metasynthesis were drawn from fifteen studies from seven different countries. The findings were analysed and grouped into a number of different conceptual categories that were further organised into metaphors of hope.

Living in hope – a being dimension

This dimension of hope reflects the inner experience of hope that is deeply embedded within the individual. It is a profound knowing that 'all will be well'. This aspect of hope is one that expects things will work out no matter what happens in life.

Hoping for something – a doing dimension

This aspect of hope captures an external 'doing' dimension. It is a pragmatic goal-setting orientation that continually responds to changing life circumstances. This external form of hope nurtures the inner form and might be considered a subjective probability of good outcomes for oneself or others.

Hope as light on the horizon – a becoming dimension

Hope as a light on the horizon incorporates several features of hope related to living fully in the present while imagining a positive but different future. It can be seen in a range of different expectations such as expecting positive medical results, being cured from a disease, or receiving a hopeful message from a physician. 'The light on the horizon helps to remove hopelessness and see the significance of life ... and it resembles stepping through an archway into the unknown where it is scary, but where passions lead and things come together' (Hammer et al., 2009: 553). This type of hope is encouraged through sensory attention to and appreciation of nature. Hearing the sounds of birds or seeing the beauty of flowers engenders a hopeful expectancy.

Hope as a human-to-human relationship – a relational dimension

Relational hope is about being known as a person. From this perspective hope is having a loving relationship with someone who accepts us for who we are – for example, knowing that our family is there for us and is supporting us encourages hope. Caregivers like doctors, nurses, and support staff showing interest and concern also engenders hope. 'Meaningful interpersonal relationships, faith, affirmation, and support confirm a sense of worth, feeling needed and "good enough," and help a person experience hope' (Hammer et al., 2009: 554).

Hope vs hopelessness and despair: two sides of the same coin – a dialectic dimension

In this dimension hope and despair are viewed as existing in a dialectical relationship. Hope and despair are understood to be necessary counterparts in human existence.

There exists a dynamic movement between a state of hopefulness and a state of despair, but with an expectation that it is always possible to return to hope.

Hope as weathering a storm – a situational and dynamic dimension

This aspect of hope is about confronting life circumstances with a will to engage and overcome difficulties. It is an energetic driving force and fighting spirit to endure and succeed. This aspect of hope operates with an awareness of the contingencies of life, of the changing seasons of one's progression through life. It looks for a positive future even when conditions are serious and not favourable.

Inspiring hope

Apart from extensive literature on defining hope within nursing there is also growing research on identifying hope-inspiring strategies within the field. Nurses understand that an essential aspect of their role is the task of inspiring hope in their patients. Hope-inspiring strategies have application in many and varied nursing settings and many of these strategies and approaches have direct application to counselling and psychotherapy.

In a study conducted to explore the nature of hope and the strategies that foster hope in caregivers of terminally patients, Herth (1993) identified six categories of hope-fostering strategies and three hope-hindering categories. The categories of hope-fostering strategies are (a) sustaining relationships, (b) cognitive reframing, (c) time refocusing, (d) attainable expectations, (e) spiritual beliefs, and (f) uplifting energy.

Hope-fostering strategies

Sustaining relationships

This category is characterised by 'presence of ongoing supportive relationships that serve as an anchor and support' (Herth, 1993: 542). These relationships are experienced as being warm, caring, encouraging, and lasting.

Cognitive reframing

Cognitive reframing is understood to be the conscious process of reworking threatening perceptions into more positive views of a situation. Some of the strategies that the caregivers used were envisioning hopeful images, calming, positive self-talk, and the use of humour. Fundamentally, cognitive reframing requires gaining a sense of perspective.

Time refocusing

Time refocusing involves the changing of one's view of span or focus of time. Such refocusing could include a shift in focus from future expectations to a more daily focus.

Another reported form of refocusing was attending to the importance of upcoming events and their special meaning for the individual.

Attainable expectations

This category describes the need to have attainable goals but also the capacity to reset those goals as situations change. This is understood to be an important ability, especially in situations that are constantly changing. As different patients within the study began to deteriorate in health, caregivers aided them in adjusting their goals and expectations. Goals became smaller as patients' health declined. These adjustments, however, enabled patients and caregivers to maintain a sense of hope.

Spiritual beliefs

Herth reported that 'The belief in a "power greater than self" or "natural order to the universe" was described by 92% of the caregivers as empowering hope' (1993: 543). Many of the patients engaged in various spiritual practices such as reading the Bible, listening to inspirational music, prayer, and meditation. The participants in the study expressed that these practices provided comfort and meaning that was beyond human explanation in their experiences.

Uplifting energy

Caregivers described their role as exhausting and expressed a need to replenish their own energies. Support was often provided by nurses, who helped the caregivers prioritise their responsibilities and schedules. Refreshing activities like listening to music and engaging in hobbies also revitalised the caregivers.

Hope-hindering categories

Three hindrances to hope were identified in the study. A hindrance to hope was defined as a factor that inhibits the possibility of attaining or maintaining hope. The identified hindrances were organised into three categories: (a) isolation, (b) concurrent losses, and (c) poorly controlled management of symptoms.

Isolation

'Isolation involved the physical, emotional or spiritual sense of separation from a significant other and/or higher power' (Herth, 1993: 543). Often this isolation was experienced as a loved one or a carer not having enough time to listen. The spiritual isolation involved a process of questioning of one's beliefs and values.

Concurrent losses

When caregivers experienced a number of losses within a short space of time, such as the death of a friend or loved one, loss of a job, or loss of income, this precipitated a sense of being overwhelmed, overloaded, and hopeless. The proximity of these multiple losses led to a break or incompleteness in the grieving processes as there was not enough time to process each separate loss.

Poorly controlled symptom management

Caregivers experienced their loved ones' intense and sometimes uncontrolled physical pain as a challenge to hope. They felt helpless when pain or symptom management was not adequate. The images of these times were noted as being difficult to deal with.

In summarising caregivers' views of hope within the study, Herth (1993: 544) quoted from one of the participants who stated that:

> Hope is like a rose with many petals, each petal different and each petal unfolding in its own time. Initially, the rose is just a bud, but eventually each petal will open and a new beauty, never before envisioned, will be seen.

Based on the collective views of caregiver, Herth summarised hope as 'a dynamic inner power that enables transcendence of the present situation and fosters a positive new awareness of being' (1993: 544).

The implicit projection of hope and hopefulness

Another study which shed light on the process of encouraging hope in patients was that conducted by Cutcliffe (2004, 2006a, b) who sought to explicate *if* and *how* bereavement counsellors inspire hope in their clients. Cutcliffe is a mental health nursing researcher and, in this study, interviewed bereavement counsellors about their practice. As Cutcliffe's work sits predominantly within the nursing literature, the findings of this study are reported here. However, his findings will be further examined in Chapter 7 where a closer look at inspiring hope through the counselling process will be taken.

Cutcliffe's grounded theory study revealed a core conception/variable – *the implicit projection of hope and hopefulness.* Within this conception were identified three sub-core variables: *forging the connection and the relationship; facilitating a cathartic release;* and *experiencing a good (healthy) ending.*

The implicit projection of hope and hopefulness was understood by the counsellor participants as an essential but implicit aspect of their work. They saw themselves as bringing hope to the counselling process. Each of the participants asserted that the process of inspiring hope was largely an implicit one. Speaking directly of hope was sometimes seen as being counterproductive within the context of bereavement counselling.

Phase One	Phase Two	Phase Three
Forging the connection and relationship	Facilitating a cathartic release	Experiencing a healthy (good) ending

←——————— The implicit projection of ———————→
hope and hopefulness

Figure 4   The integrated theory of hope inspiration in bereavement counselling

Source: Cutcliffe, 2004: 176.

Inspiring hope was understood by the counsellors as a process that developed through the counselling sessions and can be identified within the sub-core variables as seen in Figure 4.

According to this model, the projection of hope through counselling begins with forging a therapeutic relationship that then allows for cathartic release in the patient. The establishment of hope is concluded, at least as it is situated within counselling, via the management of a good ending. Cutcliffe's focus on the implicit projection of hope as being central to the process of instilling hope is evident in the segment from his work represented in Box 3.1.

BOX 3.1   THE CORE VARIABLE: THE IMPLICIT PROJECTION OF HOPE AND HOPEFULNESS

This core variable is the central aspect of this theory, in that all the other categories and subcore variables are linked to it and could be subsumed within it. This core variable explains how the bereavement counselors resolved the key problem of hope inspiration. The data collected from the counselors convey that a sense of hope and hopefulness permeated throughout the process of the bereavement counseling. The counselor's hope and hopefulness are not limited to any particular phase of the therapy. It is there at the start, it remains there during the therapy, and it is still there as the therapy draws towards an end. There is a continual implicit sense of hope for the counselor and this is introduced, implicitly into each encounter. As a result, at the end of the therapy, the clients possess some of this hope for themselves. The counselors were thus 'responsible' for bringing hope into the therapy and this was projected into both the counseling atmosphere and the client. (Cutcliffe, 2004: 177)

Hope in psychology research

Research on hope from within the discipline of psychology has made significant strides forward over the past twenty years. As already mentioned, a number of key early writers pointed the way in drawing attention to the significance of hope in human health and well-being (Frankl, 1959; Menninger, 1959; Erikson, 1964; Fromm, 1968; Stotland, 1969; Frank, 1973). From these beginnings an increasing number of studies have been conducted to further our understanding of the nature and function of hope within human psychological processes.

Writers on hope have tended to emphasise either its cognitive or affective aspects. In psychology, the most significant corpus of research has emerged from the work of C. Rick Snyder. Rick Snyder and colleagues developed a cognitive approach to understanding hope and produced and published a number of associated psychometric tests. These have been used in a wide range of research endeavours and therefore have influenced the field significantly. Snyder proposed that hope is fundamentally based on goal pursuit and on how individuals motivate themselves to attain their goals. He defines hope as 'the sum of perceived capabilities to produce routes to desired goals, along with the perceived motivation to use those routes' (2000: 8), and identifies three key components of hope: *goals*, *pathways* (planning to meet goals) and *agency* (goal-directed energy). Each one of these components of hope has to be active for hope to be fully present.

Goals

There are two types of goals within Snyder's hope theory. The first type is referred to as positive or approach goals. These may take three forms: (a) a first-time goal; (b) a goal that pertains to the sustaining of a present goal; (c) a goal which represents the desire to further an existing positive goal wherein one already has made progress. The second type of goals involves forestalling a negative goal outcome. A negative goal has two forms: (a) to stop something before it happens; (b) to deter or slow down the occurrence of something happening. These two types of goals and their sub-components can be seen in Table 5.

Other commentators of hope have argued that hope is only present when there is threat or deficit in an individual's life circumstances. Snyder refers to this form of hope as *repair* hope. While agreeing that this is an important form of hope, Snyder also argues that there are at least two other types of goals. The first of these can be seen in the

Table 5   The two major types of goals in hope theory

Type 1 – Positive goal outcome
A. Reaching for the first time
B. Sustaining present goal outcome
C. Increasing that which already has been initiated
Type 2 – Negative goal outcome
A. Deterring so that it never appears
B. Deterring so that its appearance is delayed

Source: Synder, 2002: 250.

very ordinary, almost mundane aspects of life – our daily agendas. He refers to these as *maintenance goals*. The second makes reference to goals that build on what is already satisfactory in life – goals that reach high above our everyday expectations. These he calls *enhancement goals*.

Snyder initially thought that hope was only present in the context of reasonably challenging but achievable goals. In other words, goals that appeared impossible to reach or simply too easy to attain were not regarded as hope-based. He later altered his view and argues that high-hope people often seek out unachievable goals and also that mundane goals form part of an intermediate range of goals which encourage focus and maintenance (Snyder, 2002).

Pathways

While goals set the target direction for our thoughts and actions they do not establish how we are to get there. Pathways are about the routes we take to reach our goals. As human beings we have a capacity to imagine the future and relate it to our present. Jockeys, for example, know in advance of a race the maximum weight they are allowed to be in order to enter. Knowing this, they are able to decide on and take action to manage their food intake and exercise regime to make sure they are within their target weight by the day of the race. In other words we are able to plan routes from the present to the future. These routes may not always be linear in nature, they sometimes take a circular path, but the clarity of goals sets up the possibility of planning pathways to reach them. The distinction between goals and pathways, however, is important. As Snyder expresses, 'Goals remain but unanswered calls without the requisite means to reach them' (2002: 251). He suggests that one of the tasks of the human brain is constantly to anticipate the possible route sequences from the present to the future.

Evidence suggests that high-hope people are good at identifying route possibilities and of having confidence in their decisions (Snyder et al., 1998; Woodbury, 1999). A high-hope person identifies a clear pathway and has the concomitant confidence to pursue it. In addition to a strong capacity to identify a primary route to a destination, high-hope people are also able to select secondary routes if the primary route is blocked or unsuccessful. They are flexible thinkers and are particularly good at imagining alternative pathways. Low-hope people, on the other hand, are less confident about deciding upon a primary route and are also poor at creating alternative pathways to their chosen goals. They are much less flexible in their ability to alter their plans and can become more easily stuck or frozen *en route*.

As high-hope individuals get closer to their desired goals they are constantly refining their pathways in order to arrive at their destinations as efficiently as possible. Snyder is of the view that 'high-hope people more so than low-hope people … more quickly tailor their routes effectively so as to reach their goals' (2002: 251).

Agency thought

Agency thought is the perceived capacity to achieve one's goals using selected pathways. This is the motivational dimension of Snyder's hope theory. People who are high in agency thinking continually reaffirm their own capacity to use routes to achieve their goals. Snyder found that such people often use phrases like 'I can do this,' and 'I am not going to be stopped' (Snyder et al., 1998). Agency thinking is an important feature of goal-directed thought, but is especially significant at times when the individual meets challenges or blockages to their goals. At such times high-agency people are very efficient at seeking out the best alternative routes to their goals (Snyder, 1994).

The synergy of pathways and agency thinking

Hopeful thinking requires a healthy interplay between pathways and agency thinking during the process of goal pursuit. If one of these factors is not present then hope is diminished or stalled. The interaction between pathways and agency thinking is an iterative process wherein thoughts move between pathway options and agency self-talk. In this process, one form of thinking supports the other, ultimately providing an additive effect to an individual's capacity to reach a designated goal. There is strong research evidence to support the iterative processes involved in pathways and agency thinking (Snyder et al., 1991; Snyder, 1995). Full high-hope people (i.e., those with high pathways and high agency) have fast and fluid movements between pathways and agency whereas full low-hope people (low pathways and low agency) have slow and halting iterations between pathways and agency.

Other combinations of high and low pathway and agency thinking also impede hope. Those high on pathways but low on agency have a capacity for strategic thinking but not the motivation to carry through on identified options. Those high on agency but low on pathways are stymied in their drive towards goal attainment because of lack of route direction. These mixed hope patterns slow down iterative thinking and thereby limit goal attainment.

Hope and emotion in Snyder's theory of hope

Snyder appreciates the importance of the emotional side of hope but subordinates it to the cognitive. His view is consistent with a broadly cognitive approach to human behaviour that understands emotions as products of particular cognitive schemas. Simply put, positive thoughts lead to positive emotions and negative thoughts lead to negative emotions. As Snyder's theory is based on a view of goal pursuit, he argues that a person's perception of the success or failure of a particular goal pursuit influences subsequent emotions. According to this view, naturally high-hope people would tend to have enduring positive emotions and low-hope people negative emotions, especially when focused on goal pursuit. These dispositional tendencies are theorised as relatively stable even in the context of goal blockage. Hence, the high-hope person who encounters a blockage to his or her goal attainment is more likely to maintain a positive emotional state or at least recover quickly from any emotional setback. Conversely, the low-hope person is less likely to do so.

Snyder also argues that emotions are an important feature of hope because they play a vital role in the memory storage of positive and negative thoughts. He states, 'as a mechanism for storage, memories are catalogued according to emotions – as well as to the contents (in abbreviated form) of the particular action sequences' (2002: 253). When primed by positive emotions, an individual will more likely remember positive goal pursuit activities. Conversely, when primed by negative emotions, more negative goal pursuit activities are likely to be remembered.

On the basis of this theoretical proposal, it may well be possible to aid clients in therapy by helping them to locate the sources of their negative emotions and to develop a deeper contextual understanding of them. Following the establishment of a wider awareness of these feelings, an exploration of positive future responses might be possible. The benefit here is that a shift in focus from negative to positive emotions, with supporting pathway elicitation, may serve to activate a more positive cognitive set that will further enhance present and future goal pursuit.

Snyder's hope model

This cognitive theory of hope is based on the view that a hopeful disposition and the concomitant skills are largely learned in childhood and through significant life experiences. As

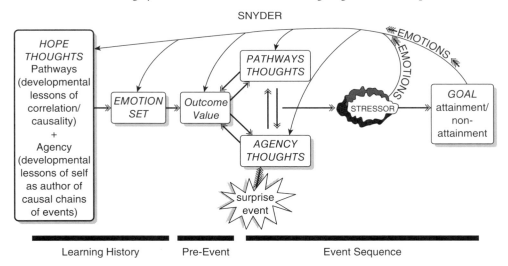

Figure 5   Schematic of feed-forward and feed-back functions involving agentic and pathways goal-directed thoughts in Snyder's hope theory

Source: Snyder, 2002: 253.

such, those who have not had the good fortune to form a positive hope-filled life orientation can do so if taught the necessary cognitive skills.

Figure 5 demonstrates the iterative processes involved in hope-filled goal pursuit. Initially a goal is assessed by the individual for its potential meaning and value. If the goal is highly valued, the emotional feedback will motivate the pathways and agency dimensions, beginning the iterative strategy process. The early feedback from the perceived benefits of the specific goal pursuit and the energy created from the pathways and agency thinking create an *emotional set* and help to create an affective tone. The feedback loops from previous goal pursuits (whether positive or negative) also provide both cognitive and affective information about the possibilities and benefits of continuing after the current goal. Positive feedback may reaffirm the *outcome value* of the pursuit, leading to further pathways and agency thinking. Agency thinking and alternative pathways are constantly being adjusted as the individual approaches their desired goal. Sometimes major blockages or *stressors* challenge goal attainment, resulting in further adjustments to pathways and agency processes. If stressors are overcome and the goal is reached, feedback is provided for future goal pursuits.

Positive psychology

In a book about hope, it would be remiss not to discuss the place and influence of positive psychology. While hope has its own bank of research and literature, it also can be contextualised as being an aspect of positive psychology. To clarify its place within this broader field, it will be helpful to provide a brief overview.

Positive psychology has built on the foundation stones of humanistic psychology in its aim to study highly functional and even exceptional human thought and behaviour. Carl Rogers' focus on the human tendency for actualisation is highlighted and extended by positive psychologists. It may be helpful here to be reminded in Rogers' own words of the human being's incredible capacity for growth and development. He states (1980: 115):

> Individuals have within themselves vast resources for self-understanding and for altering their self-concepts, basic attitudes, and self-directed behavior; these resources can be tapped if a definable climate of facilitative psychological attitudes can be provided.

In synergy with Rogers, writers such as Martin Seligman and Mihaly Csikszentmihalyi argue that psychology as a discipline originally intended to study the full spectrum of human behaviour from the dysfunctional to the highly functional, but that it was diverted from its broader aim after the Second World War to focus mostly on pathology. Proponents of positive psychology seek to return psychology to its other aim of studying high-functioning human behaviour and what enables it. While the knowledge gained from fifty-plus years of research on dysfunctional behaviour has been highly beneficial, much more is to be gained from exploring positive aspects of the human condition. As Seligman and Csikszentmihalyi explain, 'our message is to remind our field that psychology is not just the study of pathology, weakness, and damage; it is also the study of strength and virtue. Treatment is not just fixing what is broken; it is nurturing what is best' (2000: 7).

One of the obvious outcomes of a shift in emphasis from pathology to functionality has been a focus on prevention. The obvious logic is that if we understand how best to prevent physical and psychological ill health then individuals and society will benefit. In the exploration of features of preventative health, positive psychologists have identified a range of very interesting human strength-based qualities. As Seligman and Csikszentmihalyi (2000: 7) highlight:

> Prevention researchers have discovered that there are human strengths that act as buffers against mental illness: courage, future mindedness, optimism, interpersonal skill, faith, work ethic, hope, honesty, perseverance, and the capacity for flow and insight, to name a few.

As noted by these authors, hope is regarded as a strength-based feature of human health. In this respect, this book fits comfortably within the wider context of positive psychology. Along with positive psychology we acknowledge the importance of understanding pathological processes, but we also value the importance of understanding highly functional processes. In the quest for a greater understanding of preventative, strength-based human qualities, psychologists have identified a number of related but discrete constructs. Some examples of these include, hope, optimism, self-efficacy, self-esteem, and resilience. While each of these is worthy of study in its own right, there are also overlaps in meaning and function. Some of these have already been commented on in earlier chapters but it is worth distinguishing between them here.

Self-efficacy

Badura's self-efficacy theory is a goal-directed model similar to Snyder's hope theory. The level of an individual's self-efficacy is based on his or her self-assessment of the possibility of goal attainment. As a first step, the goal-seeker assesses the various contingencies associated with the goal. This is not unlike pathways thinking. If the goal, in principle, seems possible to attain the individual then assesses his or her own capability of reaching it. As Bandura (1982: 123) explains it:

> Self-efficacy judgments, whether accurate or faulty, influence choice of activities and environmental settings. People avoid activities that they believe exceed their coping capabilities, but they undertake and perform assuredly those that they judge themselves capable of managing.

According to Bandura, self-efficacy judgements determine how much effort people will expend and how long they will persist in pursuing their goals. Presented with obstacles or difficult experiences when pursuing their goals, those who are low in self-efficacy focus on self-doubts and tend to ease their efforts or give up on goal pursuit. Conversely, those who are high in self-efficacy confront challenges by increasing their efforts at goal attainment.

It appears that those individuals who judge themselves to be inefficacious in coping with the challenges of a task tend to dwell on personal deficiencies and imagine greater difficulties with the task than is warranted. This also has the effect of drawing attention away from the goal itself, leaving them less effective in reaching their target. Those who judge themselves as highly efficacious are more able to stay focused on the task at hand and therefore not only reach their goal, but to do so more efficiently.

The primary emphasis in Bandura's theory is on the self-appraisal (or agency thoughts), whereas hope theory is built on the dual function of pathways and agency thoughts. The other difference between self-efficacy and hope theory is that self-efficacy is posited to function in respect to a situation-specific goal. Snyder's theory is broader in scope and functions cross-sectionally as well.

Optimism

Optimism, as referred to in Chapter 1, has many similarities with hope but some important differences. Like hope, it provides for a positive view of the future resulting in motivation to pursue life interests and goals. Less like hope though, this future focus is more generalised and diffuse. According to Scheier and Carver (1985: 220), 'Optimists often appear to be optimistic "in general," in that their positive expectations are not limited to a particular behavioral domain or class of settings'. Optimism here is understood to be a relatively stable personality trait and one that provides for good health outcomes. Optimists as opposed to pessimists have higher levels of subjective well-being and have better recovery rates from mental health problems. As is the assumption with hope studies, psychologists have proposed that if the functional mechanisms of optimism can be better understood then it might be possible to teach them to others, thus providing significant benefits.

A number of characteristics of the optimistic person have been identified and these do seem to influence positive health outcomes. The first of these is their tendency to take direct action to solve their problems. Optimists also are more likely to plan how to confront difficult situations and are highly focused in their coping efforts. Optimists more so than pessimists tend to accept the reality of stressful situations and learn from them. Conversely, pessimists are less likely to confront stressful situations directly, tending either to deny their existence or avoid them.

Like Snyder's hope theory, Scheier and Carver's theory of optimism is predominantly a cognitive approach in which optimism is understood to be a cognitive process of broad goal appraisal. Individuals assess their capacity to achieve broadly defined goals or to move away from them. In a number of studies exploring the relationship between optimism and hope, there is a consistent finding that the two constructs are interrelated, but significantly different (Magaletta & Oliver 1999; Tennen, Affleck, & Tennen, 2002; Bryant & Cvengros, 2004). Each seems to be explaining a different facet of human processing.

Self-esteem

Self-esteem is a construct that has waxed and waned in popularity over most of the twentieth century. With the current dominant focus on cognitive processes in psychology, it is again acknowledged as an important aspect of human functioning. Self-esteem generally refers to the nature and content of an individual's self-appraisal. Coopersmith explained self-esteem by stating, 'By self-esteem we refer to the evaluation the individual makes and customarily maintains with regard to himself: it indicates an attitude of approval or disapproval, and indicates the extent to which the individual believes himself to be capable, significant and worthy' (1967: 4). More recent studies suggest that self-esteem is multidimensional rather than unidimensional and is therefore made up of several components. Harter (1999) identifies five dimensions of self-esteem: scholastic competence, social acceptance, behavioural conduct, athletic competence and physical appearance. Research suggests that an individual can vary in the concurrent degrees of self-esteem on each of these dimensions. In addition, self-esteem can also be understood to have a global quality. People have an overall sense of their own self-valuing usually determined via an integration of the various dimensions listed above.

According to Hewitt (1998), self-esteem, like hope, is largely built on goal-directed thinking. This means that self-appraisals are at least partly built on the relative success of goal attainment. According to Snyder, the difference in focus between self-esteem theory and hope theory is that hope theory examines the 'the goal pursuit process that elicits emotion and esteem' (2002: 258). He further argues that goal-pursuit thinking, particularly as explained in hope theory, effects esteem and not vice versa. Hence, while there is again some common ground between hope and self-esteem, there appears to be significant differences between the constructs.

Resilience

One final construct that sits comfortably within the field of positive psychology and that has resonance with hope theory is resilience. Research into the nature of resilience began when it was observed that in groups of children who had experienced very challenging experiences such as war, abuse, and deprivation, a proportion would emerge relatively unscathed and would mature into well-adjusted adults. Those who appeared to thrive psychologically were seen to possess resources that made them resilient. Masten (2001: 228) defines resilience as 'a class of phenomena characterized by good outcomes in spite of serious threats to adaptation or development'.

Resilience may also provide the individual with a capacity to weather overwhelming positive challenges such as early career success and overly social or work-based demands. In this respect, resilience allows for reactive recovery as well as proactive learning in situations of high demand and challenge. Luthans' definition of resilience captures these dual aspects. He states that resilience is 'the positive psychological capacity to rebound, to "bounce back" from adversity, uncertainty, conflict, failure or even positive change, progress and increased responsibility' (2002: 702).

After extensive studies in this area, it is now clear that resilience is a normal human capacity to adapt to the environment. Children draw on a range of internal and social resources to aid them in their developmental journey towards adulthood. While it is not fully clear why some children adapt more successfully than others, there is relative clarity on some of the important resources that resilient people draw on. Common characteristics of resilient people include an even temperament, proactive problem solving, high social skills, positive peer and adult interactions, intelligence, empathy, a sense of humour, high self-esteem and an internal locus of control (Garmezy, 1993; Harvey & Delfabbro, 2004). Benard (1991) categorised these traits and characteristics into five groups:

1 Social competencies or pro-social behaviour – traits that increase children's ability to maintain healthy relationships.
2 Well-developed problem-solving skills – the capacity to increase social influences in the environment and make choices about them.
3 Autonomy – a strong sense of identity and self-worth.
4 Religious/spiritual commitment – a concrete belief system.
5 Sense of purpose of future.

Resilience, like hope and optimism, orientates an individual to a positive future outlook. It varies from these other two constructs in several ways however. Even with the best of plans people experience overwhelming setbacks that may temporarily quash goal pursuit. One of the characteristics of resilience is its recognition of the need to respect the level of impact that such setbacks can have and allow the individual to set aside time, energy, and resources to recover and bounce back to a point of balance. A second distinguishing element of resilience is based in its capacity to deal with uncertainty. Hope, and to a lesser degree optimism, both rely on the pursuit of goals. Resilience goes beyond the certainties of goals and the current situation. Resilience provides a capacity to manage in circumstances that are uncertain and unpredictable. 'The resilience capacity uniquely searches for and finds meaning despite circumstances that do not lend themselves to planning, preparation, rationalization, or logical interpretation' (Coutu, 2002, in Youssef & Luthans, 2007: 780).

Hope has much in common with other positive psychology concepts and collectively they add value to a strengths-based view of human capacity. Hope from a psychology perspective incorporates both *will* (motivational) and *ways* (pathways) dimensions to the attainment of goals and a positive life outlook.

Neuroscience, imagination, and hope

One final area of academic exploration that contributes to our understanding of hope is neuroscience. Recent developments in neuroscience and its application to psychology and psychotherapy have added significantly to our understanding of human psychological functioning. As scientists have come to understand the workings of the brain better they have not only been awed by its complexity but amazed at its flexibility and integrative coherence. Influenced by mechanistic perspectives we previously understood the brain to be something like a machine, expecting to find in it fixed and separate mechanisms and components. Instead, research has provided us with quite a different picture of this organ as being highly malleable, adaptive, and integrated. One of the features of the human brain that distinguishes it from the brains of mammals and reptiles is the area known variously as the neo-cortex, pre-frontal cortex or executive brain. This is the area of the brain that provides us with the ability to be conscious of ourselves in the world, to regulate our emotions, and to plan and imagine our future.

The executive brain works with many other areas of neural functioning to regulate our instinctive and emotional responses (Cozolino, 2010). Unlike other species, humans have the capacity to think about their physical and emotional existence. Mammals have in varying degrees the capacity for emotion and to express care and concern for others, especially those in their kinship group. However, they have limited or no capacity to reflect cognitively on these emotions and to consider the future. The drive for survival is very strong in all species, but humans have the capacity to override their own survival instinct when they consider it necessary to do so. This ability comes from the powers of the executive brain. The executive brain provides us with many abilities, especially the ability to think logically, to access memory and bring it into conscious awareness, to pay attention to our emotions, and also to imagine a reality that is not necessarily evident. All of these abilities are important to the issue of hope in a number of ways.

As we discussed earlier, Snyder has highlighted the importance of identifying goals and pathways in the process of hoping. To do this requires a high degree of logical cognitive processing. It also involves the ability to access memories and to be aware of emotions. This is obvious because we select goals that are personally meaningful to us and that therefore have a connection to our past experiences. In this respect hope connects us with our past as much as it connects us with our future. We move towards our future in large part because of the experiences of our past and in this respect the past and future are connected.

Interestingly we know from studies in neuropsychology that there is a neural processing link between memory and imagination. Neuroimaging studies have demonstrated that similar areas of the brain are activated when we remember and imagine (Schacter & Addis, 2009). It appears that humans can use episodic memories to construct and simulate future scenarios in a highly flexible manner. As memory is dynamic it is also likely that imagining future scenarios may influence existing memory as many of the same brain processes are used in both. While we are yet to explore how this link may be applied to psychotherapy, it seems that our past and future are connected in more ways than we ever thought possible.

Another issue that relates to the executive brain's ability to link memory and imagination is that of defining reality. Our sense of reality is largely a function of our sense of perception and imagination. By perception we mean the human ability to use our senses to inform us of the world and our place in it. In the most basic form we use our senses to help us to orientate ourselves physically in the world. Perception though takes us beyond our senses by using the sense data we receive to interpret the world. Perception and imagination are both focused on defining reality, although in different ways. Perception focuses on present reality while imagination focuses on possible realities. O'Connor and Aardema (2005: 243) argue that our view of reality is mediated by imagination in three main ways:

(a) What I am doing exists alongside what I am intending to do – my projects in the world have a future, (b) Imagination creates the future and this creative aspect of seeing, fills up the space between what is and what is not, and (c) Living in reality is a matter of degree, and I exist in a gradient of awareness where different possibilities are associated with distinct senses of reality.

The idea here is that our sense of reality is never just an awareness of the immediate physical and social world around us but is also, in part, informed by our imagined or intentional world. Reality in this respect is never discretely in the present world or the future (imagined) world but somewhere in-between. To be human is to live somewhat between worlds.

If we consider our sense of reality to be a combination of perception and imagination, then hope becomes of even greater importance. Hope by its very nature involves a focus on future possibilities, of considering both the now and the not yet. To grasp reality we need to understand our past and future possibilities.

One final note about the link between the brain, imagination, and hope comes from studies in mentalization. Mentalization is the ability to focus on the metal state of oneself and others. Bateman and Fonagy state that 'Mentalization is mostly a preconscious, imaginative mental activity. It is imaginative because we have to imagine what other people might be thinking and feeling' (2006: 1). Mental health involves a realistic awareness and understanding of oneself and of others. When we fail to be able adequately to process our own thoughts, feelings, and behaviours and those of others, it affects our mental state. Recent neuropsychological studies have indicated that when systems of the brain that are associated with human attachment are activated (e.g., feelings of love), they can inhibit mentalization. The implication here is that positive attachment feelings enable a drawing together with primary others in part by limiting our evaluative processes (Bartels & Zeki, 2004). While this is, in general, a positive function it also provides an indication that the attachment system may also be involved in reducing mentalization when attachment experiences are highly negative (Bateman & Fonagy, 2006). In other words, when people, especially in childhood, experience primary relationships as being largely negative, it may impact on their ability to imagine. If our earlier premise is correct that reality is determined by a combination of perception and imagination, then those who have had poor attachment experiences may well be affected in their ability to perceive (imagine) both their own thoughts and intentions and those of others, leading to a confusion in their sense of reality. One of the tasks of psychotherapy is to help the client become more aware of themselves and of others – in other words, to imagine different possibilities, thus allowing for alternative meaning-making. When we more accurately understand our own thoughts and intentions and those of others, we are enabled to relate to ourselves and others in more grounded and realistic ways. This is where the capacity for imagination becomes vital. It may well be that hope is a key facility which enables a person to activate their ability to imagine and thus increase their mentalising capacity.

Neuroscience is now providing evidence that hope is not some optional extra aspect of human experience but an important part of living a healthy life. A salutogenic view of health and well-being suggests that optimal health comes about when we are able to organise our own inner resources well. There is growing evidence that the ability to imagine as an aspect of hope is one important dimension of the healthy self.

Summary

In this chapter we have explored hope from a number of disciplinary perspectives. Nursing research has greatly increased our knowledge of the place of hope, especially within terminal care. It has also provided a range of hope-based strategies that can be used in many other professional helping settings. The focus on hope-inspiration challenges professional helpers to consider their own capacity to hope and to convey hope. Psychology has also contributed significant research on hope, in particular highlighting its cognitive dimensions. The importance of goals, the ability to imagine different pathways to goal attainment, and the fundamental importance of motivation are well explained in Snyder's theory of hope. Psychology research has also clarified the distinction between hope and other related constructs such as optimism, self-efficacy, resilience, and so on. Finally, our advancing knowledge in neuroscience is shedding even more light on the functions and capacities of the brain and on how these relate to psychological health. It appears that memory and imagination form essential dimensions of the human capacity to be aware of self and others. Hope may well be more important in human functioning than we generally thought as it enables us to not only have a positive frame of mind but also to imagine new ways of being in the world.

QUESTIONS FOR REFLECTION AND DISCUSSION

1   Within the nursing literature referred to in this chapter, several metaphors of hope were mentioned. Which of these metaphors resonates best with your own experiences of hope? Why? Alternatively, can you think of your own metaphor of hope?
2   Cutcliffe found that hope could be implicitly projected on to patients and clients in therapeutic settings. What are the strengths and limitations of this perspective?
3   Snyder defines his theory of hope as a cognitive model. What are the strengths and limitations of approaching hope from a cognitive orientation?

4 Positive psychology has gained significant ground in the psychology literature and beyond. What do you like/dislike about positive psychology and its emphasis on positive human resources?

5 As hope has a future orientation, it is likely that our ability to imagine is directly linked to our capacity for hope. What practices might we employ to encourage healthy imagining?

4

How different theories of counselling and psychotherapy encourage hope

Hope and the common factors

One of the great research findings to emerge in counselling and psychotherapy over the past thirty years is that different models or approaches to therapy produce very similar outcomes. This has been affectionately dubbed the Dodo Bird Verdict after the dodo bird in *Alice in Wonderland*, who proclaimed 'Everybody has won and all must have prizes' (Luborsky, Singer, & Luborsky, 1975). This finding, while controversial, has spurred on further research efforts aimed at identifying why such different theoretical and practice perspectives produce similar therapeutic results. The search has led to another somewhat surprising finding, that there is a set of common elements across therapeutic models that are, in fact, the active ingredients in therapeutic change. As is now well known within the field, a set of 'common factors' has been quite consistently found to explain, at least in part, the Dodo Bird Verdict. The most well-known list of these common factors was identified by Lambert, Shapiro, and Bergin (1986) and Lambert (1992). In their review of outcome research across the range of approaches, it was found that about forty per cent of therapeutic change came from client variables or extra-therapeutic factors; thirty per cent came from the therapeutic alliance; fifteen per cent from the theory/technique; and another fifteen per cent from hope and expectancy.

Common factor 1: client variables or extra-therapeutic factors

It must be recognised that when clients come into therapy they bring with them not only a set of problems and conditions but also a set of potentials as well. Recognising this, it would be a highly limited view to place all or even most of the power for positive change in the hands of the therapist. As Bohart and Tallman (1999) argue, it is the client who holds the power for change. This view sits uncomfortably within the dominant medical paradigm, which sees the client as being much more passive, more akin to a receptacle for expert interventions. An emphasis on the importance of the client's resources should not obscure the expertise of the therapist, but neither should the therapist's abilities obscure the client's capacities to effect change themselves. The human potential for self-healing is well summed up in the following statement by Bohart (2000: 134):

> there is considerable evidence of a human capacity for self-healing. If so many individuals are capable of using naturally occurring self-healing processes on their own, it is no surprise that they are able to enter therapy and use widely different therapy approaches and procedures to self-heal, particularly since these approaches are themselves based on these same self-healing processes.

Different studies have found that while people can make enormous therapeutic gains without therapy, for those who do come to therapy, it is the active client who gains the most change. A number of factors appear to affect the likelihood of therapeutic change within the client:

- Commitment to the change process
- Expectation or hope of change
- Range and strength of support structures outside of therapy
- The quality of the therapeutic relationship.

All of these factors are about engagement by the client in the change process.

Common factor 2: the therapeutic alliance

Numerous studies confirm that a positive therapeutic alliance is one of the most important factors in predicting positive therapeutic outcomes (Bordin, 1979; Frank & Frank, 1991; Horvath & Symonds, 1991; Messer & Wampold, 2002). One of the main findings of research in this area is that the therapist plays a large role in determining the client's perception of the working alliance (Brossart et al., 1998). Apparently, clients take cues from therapists regarding the success of therapy. If the therapist connects well with the client and signifies that treatment is progressing positively the client is likely to feel good about the relationship and consequently begins to make improvements. In addition to these findings, it also has been observed that not only does the therapist's perception of the working alliance affect the client's initial and current perception, but such perceptions may have a lasting effect and carry over into future sessions.

While the importance of the client's initial perception of the working alliance cannot be understated, the maintenance of the working alliance cannot be presumed upon.

Horvath and Luborsky (1993) report that research into client cognitions during therapy suggests that clients' assessments of therapy are, in part, based on their own expectations of therapy. In this respect, the nature of the working alliance is interactive and thus relies on a reciprocal interplay between client and therapist factors. The ability of the therapist and the client to form an agreement about the nature of the goals and tasks of therapy seems to be an important component of the development of the working alliance. Therapists and clients often will have different expectations of the therapy process including the nature of short- and long-term goals. As Horvath and Luborsky assert, 'To establish a good alliance, it is important for the therapist to negotiate these immediate and medium-term expectations and link these to the client's wish to obtain lasting relief from suffering' (1993: 564).

The therapeutic alliance is probably the factor that best encapsulates the power of the common factors view of psychotherapeutic change. The alliance in this respect can be understood to be a pan-theoretical factor, one that is active across all forms and models of psychotherapy. Wolfe and Goldfried express this view well, stating, 'The therapeutic alliance is probably the quintessential integrative variable because its importance does not lie within the specification of one school of thought' (1988: 449).

Common factor 3: theories and techniques

The debate over which theory or technique is the most efficacious has stormed since the proliferation of approaches. Lambert's (1986, 1992) assertion that technique accounts for about fifteen per cent of the therapeutic outcome has certainly challenged researchers to explore the relative impact that technique has in the psychotherapy process. A wide range of studies using varied research designs targeting a diverse range of techniques and equally diverse range of mental health conditions has left us with inconclusive results. For example, a number of meta-analyses have found no substantial evidence to support the claim that specific treatment protocols are in themselves responsible for therapeutic change (Ahn & Wampold, 2001; Luborsky et al., 2002; Wampold et al., 2011). Conversely, there are other studies which have demonstrated that some specific techniques for certain presenting conditions produce better outcomes than standard psychotherapy (Task Force on Promotion and Dissemination of Psychological Procedures, 1995; Huppert, Fabbro, Barlow, Goodheart, Kazdin, & Sternberg, 2006; Siev & Chambless, 2007).

Current thinking in the field acknowledges that specific psychotherapy techniques and the underlying theories that support them are important to the change process. This is the case for several reasons. The first is the fact that therapists themselves need some guiding theory or system of thought to aid them in making sense of the client's presenting issues. Without some well-structured system of meaning-making the therapist would have little more to offer than a listening ear (not that that would not be beneficial). An additional benefit of the therapist having a guiding theory is that it provides confidence and belief in the effectiveness of therapy not only for the therapist but also for the client. This is a significant point as will be commented on later in this section, for expectancy of therapeutic success is itself part of the change process. A second reason why specific techniques are important is because there is some evidence, as mentioned above, that certain interventions are particularly efficacious for particular conditions in certain contexts.

Common factor 4: hope and expectancy

Hope and expectancy form the fourth common factor in Lambert's (1992) original set of pan-theoretical factors involved in therapeutic change. He estimated that this factor accounts for about the same amount of variance in client change as does technique, that is, fifteen per cent. It has generally been found that a client's expectations about therapy and its potential to aid them predicts both continuation in therapy and positive outcomes (Garfield, 1986, 1994). In a similar vein, it is well known that mental health treatments with a placebo also produce a significant degree of therapeutic change. It is argued here that hope is a form of expectancy, and like the therapeutic alliance, is one of the foundation stones of therapeutic change. Hope unites both therapist and client expectations about positive change. Hope theory as conceptualised by Snyder (1999), explains the therapeutic benefits of placebo and expectancy. In his view, both of these variables increase the client's agency thinking thus encouraging them to continue in therapy and to expect positive outcomes. Hope also motivates the therapist in the work of therapy.

It was Jerome Frank (1973) who argued strongly that hope was the unifying factor between a wide range of healing approaches including psychopharmacology, spiritual healing, and different forms of psychotherapy. Snyder (2000) agrees with Frank casting hope as a metatheory for psychotherapy. We would side with these authors and promote hope as a key integrating device within healing in general, and within psychotherapy more specifically.

Recent developments in what works in psychotherapy

The common factors perspective has advanced our understanding of psychotherapy by providing a powerful frame of reference for the change process. However, it has been unfortunate that therapeutic change has often been explained from two polarised positions; specific factors (techniques) and non-specific factors (common factors). These positions have arisen and are supported by different philosophies of knowledge, and as a result, proponents have found it difficult to come to agreement. Science, for example, prefers to see the world in terms of cause/effect relationships. Alternatively, the social sciences often see the world in more nuanced and multifaceted forms. While we are drawn to a view of psychotherapy as a science, we recognise the human and therefore multifaceted nature of human existence and its implications for psychotherapy. In reality psychotherapy is a merger of science and the humanities; both provide essential knowledge for the field. Counsellors and psychotherapists need a well-developed knowledge of theory and technique as much as they need a capacity to engage in the therapeutic relationship and hope.

In a review of the debate between the relative importance of technique and the therapeutic relationship, Goldfried and Davila (2005) argue that not only are both essential, they exist in a mutual interplay with each benefiting the other. Therapeutic change has many dimensions and there is a range of important principles of change. The common factors approach establishes overarching categories of change but these can also be identified in more specific terms. Bordin (1979), for example, explicated three specific aspects within the therapeutic alliance; bond, goals, and tasks. Duncan (2012) has more recently identified the benefits of feedback to both client and therapist in the change process. Beutler and colleagues (2011) demonstrate the benefits of client–therapist matching. Prochaska and DiClemente (2005) have observed the relevance of stages of the change process and of the importance of working with the client's readiness to change. Frank (1973) and Snyder (1999, 2000) have highlighted the importance of hope and expectancy in change. The complexity of change and especially the debate about technique verses relationship are well articulated by Goldfried and Davila in the following statement (2005: 427):

> As we hope is evident from reviewing these change principles, they do not lend themselves to an easy categorization as either technique-driven or relationship-driven. Indeed, that is the point. An understanding of therapeutic change cannot be reduced to simple comparisons of technique and relationship, but rather may be best understood in terms of the ways in which technique and relationship facilitate these more general principles.

Norcross and Wampold (2011a, b) recently reported the findings of the 'Interdivisional (APA Divisions 12 & 29) Task Force on Evidence-Based Therapy Relationships'. These findings again confirm the multifaceted dimensions of the therapeutic relationship. The report conveys the results of a number of meta-analyses of different aspects of the therapeutic relationship that have been found to be active in the change process. It is not surprising to find that the following features of the therapeutic relationship are highlighted as being therapeutically effective:

- Therapeutic alliance
- Cohesion in group therapy
- Empathy
- Collecting client feedback
- Goal consensus
- Collaboration
- Positive regard
- Congruence and genuineness
- Repairing alliance ruptures
- Managing countertransference
- Expectations
- Attachment style.

In addition to identifying aspects of the therapeutic relationship as being important in change, a number of methods of adapting counselling and psychotherapy to particular client characteristics were also found to be significant:

- Reactance/resistance level
- Preferences
- Culture
- Religion and spirituality
- Stages of change
- Coping style.

One of the conclusions of the task force is captured in the following statement:

> The therapy relationship acts in concert with treatment methods, patient characteristics, and practitioner qualities in determining effectiveness; a comprehensive understanding of effective (and ineffective) psychotherapy will consider all of these determinants and their optimal combinations. (Norcross & Wampold, 2011a: 98)

Our professional understanding of counselling and psychotherapy is beginning to mature as is evidenced in this more comprehensive and inclusive view of what is involved in therapeutic change. While there may well be some treatments that work particularly well for certain conditions, a whole view of the person necessitates the therapist embracing all the active features of the change process.

Expectancy and hope

One of the findings of the task force was that expectancy was highly likely to be an active ingredient in therapeutic change. A conservative approach to a meta-analysis of this construct by Constantino, Arnkoff, Glass, Ametrano, and Smith (2011) found a small but significant effect size for the impact of expectancy on change. This study differentiated expectancy from other similar constructs like *treatment motivation, therapy preferences,* and *credibility*, but did allow for hope as an aspect of expectancy. To clarify, a client may be highly motivated to engage in therapy but not highly expectant of positive outcomes. Equally a client might prefer a particular approach to therapy but not expect that it will effect any change. Credibility is similar to preference in that the client may come to understand the basic principles of an approach and affirm it, while still not expecting significant change.

Apart from finding support for the positive influence of expectancy on therapeutic outcomes in general, the study also noted the potential moderating effect of the therapeutic alliance on expectancy. This means that clients who establish a good therapeutic alliance with their therapist are a little more likely to experience positive expectancies about the outcomes of therapy. Again we see here an interplay, in this case between the therapeutic alliance, hope, and expectancy.

Contributions to the development of hope from established therapies

We have established that within the existing research, there is overwhelming support for the existence and benefit of a range of common factors across different approaches to counselling and psychotherapy. Apart from the importance of specific therapeutic techniques and the therapeutic relationship, it is clear that hope and expectancy are of fundamental importance in therapeutic change. In the following section we will explore, in brief, the particular contribution that several of the dominant theoretical approaches have in engendering hope.

Process-experiential therapies

Process-experiential therapies have in common a humanistic philosophical foundation and as such emphasise the inherent self-actualising capacities of the individual. A number of approaches contribute to what is known as process-experiential therapy, in particular, Carl Rogers' person-centred therapy and Fritz Perls' gestalt therapy. More recent theory development by Greenberg, Rice, and Elliott (1993) also fits within this tradition and is worthy of note. Perls drew attention to the importance of the client being an active processor within any change enterprise, often grounding therapy in a focus on the body and affective states. Rogers provided an enormous contribution to the field by emphasising the fundamental importance of the client experiencing in the here-and-now. He was one of the first to stress the centrality of the therapeutic relationship as the core element within therapeutic change. Impressively, Rogers was able to draw the field's attention to this fact at a time when more detached psychoanalytic interventions were in ascendency.

One of the outstanding contributions that Rogers made to the field of counselling and psychotherapy was his emphasis on the therapist and client making genuine relational contact. The formulation by Rogers of 'the necessary and sufficient conditions of therapeutic change' demonstrates his view that the therapeutic relationship is the central feature of therapeutic change.

For constructive personality change to occur, it is necessary that these conditions exist and continue over a period of time:

1 Two persons are in psychological contact.

2 The first, whom we shall term the client, is in a state of incongruence, being vulnerable or anxious.

3 The second person, whom we shall term the therapist, is congruent or integrated in the relationship.

4 The therapist experiences unconditional positive regard for the client.

5   The therapist experiences an empathic understanding of the client's internal frame of reference and endeavors to communicate this experience to the client.

6   The communication to the client of the therapist's empathic understanding and unconditional positive regard is to a minimal degree achieved. (Rogers, 1957: 96)

This formulation of therapeutic change is now well known as the 'core conditions' model. It has become common that particular attention is drawn to three of the conditions listed above, *acceptance*, *empathy*, and *genuineness*. Rogers took the view that people have a natural tendency or drive towards self-actualisation but that the lack of the core conditions in their life obscures or confuses people from a positive outworking of genuine personhood. When the core conditions are returned, a reorientation of life direction and health are facilitated within the individual. The centrality of the therapeutic relationship is a fundamental feature of this reorientation as it is through the relationship that the client experiences the core conditions for change. It is through a genuine encounter with another supportive person that individuals are able to be free to reconnect with themselves.

Jerome Frank agreed with Rogers that the therapeutic relationship is central to therapeutic change. He further expressed the view that it is through this relationship that the demoralised client is able to discover hope for change (Frank & Frank, 1991). While the early emphasis by Rogers on the therapeutic relationship has now essentially become a universal or pan-theoretical perspective taken on by all major therapies, it has always been a central premise of the humanistic therapies and of person-centred therapy in particular (Strupp, 1972; Castonguay, Constantino, & Grosse-Holtforth, 2006). It is therefore quite appropriate to assert that one of the primary ways in which the process-experiential therapies engender hope is through an emphasis on internal congruence and reorientation of the internal valuing process mediated through the therapeutic relationship.

One of the reasons that the person-centred approach has placed so much emphasis on the therapeutic relationship is because of its underlying belief in the self-actualising process. Rogers' most basic assumption (1957), along with other humanistic psychologists, was that given the right conditions, the individual would move towards self-healing and growth. This deep belief in an individual's desire and capacity for growth provided a respectful and sometimes awe-inspiring environment, highly facilitative for therapeutic change. The therapist's belief and expectation in the client's own capacity for change seems to inspire hope in the client. The very strong starting assumption in person-centred therapy is that change is possible.

While it could well be argued that other approaches to therapy hold equally positive expectations of clients' capacity for change, the basis for such a belief is often different. For example, in cognitive behavioural therapy change is possible on the basis of the client learning new ways of thinking and acting. In psychodynamic therapy change occurs when unconscious meanings and symbolised relationship patterns are brought into consciousness and resymbolised. In narrative therapy change occurs when negative personal and social discourses are deconstructed and then reconstructed on healthier grounds. All of these and other approaches to therapy capture highly powerful change mechanisms. What is different, however, in person-centred therapy is that it is the relationship that is the *summum bonum* of the therapeutic enterprise. It is the relationship that counts more than the technique or the clever interventions of the therapist. To put it another way, it is the relationship that provides the client with the rediscovery of his or her own hope for change.

Psychodynamic therapies

Psychodynamic therapies build on the foundations of Freud's psychoanalysis. There are many different approaches within psychodynamics but they all share in common a number of key principles:

1 The distinction between unconscious and conscious processes
2 The importance of early developmental experiences on adult life
3 The existence of defence mechanisms within the individual, especially transference
4 The centrality of the therapeutic relationship to the therapeutic process
5 The fundamental need to resymbolise unconscious meanings and relationship patterns.

One of the key differences between Freud's psychoanalytic approach and psychodynamic approaches is the different view of development. Freud argued that development was constructed around libidinal and aggressive drives or tendencies in the individual. Psychodynamic theorists emphasise the view that development is more about individuation, where individuation is best understood as the progressive formation of the self through relationships with primary others. The focus on the relationship between the therapist and the client has much in common with the humanistic schools of thought. The difference, however, lies in how the relationship is conceptualised. The psychodynamic therapist understands adult relationships as an outworking of internalised developmental patterns of relating. In this system of understanding, the individual is not simply relating to another consistently on the basis of a here-and-now interaction. Rather, he or she is relating, to a lesser or greater degree, on the basis of internal expectations about how the other 'is' in the world and how the other 'will' engage with them. Relationships are also highly influenced by individuals' unconscious views of themselves. Therapeutic relationships, in particular, highlight this complex interplay between the inner world images of *self* and *other* expressed by both client and therapist. The challenge of relationships within a psychodynamic perspective is to move to a more here-and-now experience of self and the other that is not determined by dysfunctional unconscious processes. This is achieved through the gradual growth in awareness of confused inner-world patterns or images of relationships and the transformation of them via the experience of healthy adult interactions (Scharff & Scharff, 2005). One of the key ways of encouraging this transformation of unhealthy unconscious structures is through the experience of a healthy and caring relationship with a therapist.

From a psychodynamic perspective, engaging in a healthy relationship is not as straightforward as it might appear in some other therapeutic approaches. This is because a genuine therapeutic relationship will inevitably involve the client playing out some unconscious processes with the therapist. This means that the client will, at times, transfer unconscious expectations about how others are in the world and therefore how they will relate to them. These uncomfortable (anxious or fearful) transferences will then be defended against by the client using defence mechanisms. It is in this context that the therapist has to try to provide a safe and genuine relationship with the client.

The therapist's task is a challenging one as he or she has to manage the experience of being the focus of the client's negative projections while at the same time not conforming to them. Part of the therapist's task is to hold safely the client's confused expectations and emotions for them while they are working through and reorganising their inner-world beliefs and images of self and other (Bion, 1962).

The idea of the therapist holding the client's unprocessed emotions is central to psychodynamic therapy and an important aspect in the development of hope within the client. The therapist holds the client's emotions by acting as a container for them until the client is able to hold them more adequately themselves. The central premise here is that unprocessed emotions and their related cognitions and symbolic meanings can become overwhelming for the individual, resulting in a shutting down of active processing usually via some form of defensive action. The therapist, by taking some of the burden of the emotional weight, provides the individual with space to more actively process the meaning underlying the dynamics of the situation. It is through the very act of the therapist 'sharing the load' of the emotional weight carried by the client that a rekindling of hope is possible. Without such therapeutic support, the individual is left floundering with the emotional turmoil brought about by unprocessed unconscious material.

From a psychodynamic perspective it could be argued that the therapist is not only holding some of the client's emotional burden but also holding hope for them until they can hold it for themselves. The notion of the therapist acting as a container has at least four key elements. The first is common to all therapeutic approaches and is referred to as the therapeutic (analytic) frame. This is the whole environment in which the therapy takes place and includes the physical setting, the organisational arrangements such as the number and frequency of appointments, the confidentiality of therapy, and so on. The second aspect of containment focuses on the therapist's task of holding the client's emotions by feeling their pain or, as some writers have expressed it, by 'suffering with' the client (Bion, 1962; Fleming, 2005). This requires a deep empathic connection with the client as would also be emphasised in person-centred therapy. When the therapist is able to *feel with* or *suffer with* the client, the client at some level, partly consciously and partly unconsciously, realises that another is deeply caring for them and holding out a positive expectancy for their movement towards greater wholeness and well-being. The third dimension of containment or holding is about *being with* the client. To be with the client in this sense is to be comfortable with the client experiencing psychological pain while not needing actively to intervene to relieve them of the pain. This form of holding involves the capacity to support the client by journeying with them as a fellow traveller. Such containment provides a place where it is safe and acceptable for the client to confront their emotional turmoil without unnecessary interference. The fourth aspect of containment is the therapist's own hope for the client's recovery or discovery of hope for themselves. One of the reasons people become therapists is because they have a deep belief in people's capacity for healing and a deep belief in the efficacy of the therapeutic process. It is the therapist's task to see strengths in the client that, for the moment, the client may not be able to see themselves. It is also the therapist's task to see potential pathways towards healing that the client cannot envisage. Interestingly, recent research has shown that the *therapist's* hope is a highly active ingredient in therapeutic change (Coppock, Owen, Zagarskas, & Schmidt, 2010). Psychodynamic therapies position the therapist as an important player in the change process and consider part of the therapist's role as holding hope for the client until the client is in a position to do so themselves.

Cognitive behavioural therapy

Cognitive behaviour therapists approach the task of therapy on quite a different premise than person-centred or psychodynamic therapists. Instead of a focus on realigning personal experience with an inner organismic compass through a genuine here-and-now encounter with the therapist as in person-centred therapy, or through a safe unearthing and playing out of unconscious processes through the supportive holding environment as in psychodynamic therapy, cognitive behaviour therapy (CBT) focuses on the relationship between cognition, behaviour, and emotion. As was highlighted in the first part of this chapter in the discussion on common factors, good therapists of any persuasion will pay keen attention to the therapeutic relationship. Apart from this focus though, therapists will tend to conceptualise therapy through their dominant theoretical frame of reference.

For the CBT therapist, the primary work of therapy is conceptualised within a more psycho-educational frame. The underlying premise is that the client is struggling with a problem due to faulty cognitions or mental schema associated with the problem topic. These maladaptive cognitions result in similarly maladaptive emotional and behavioural responses. While therapy can technically begin at any point by either focusing on behaviour, emotions or thought structures, the ultimate aim is to educate the client through a variety of means (e.g., information sharing, challenge, desensitisation, etc.), so that their assumptions are more adaptive than before, resulting in more appropriate beliefs and accompanying emotional and behavioural responses (McLeod, 2009).

While hope always resides within the support offered through the therapeutic relationship, it is also found within the potential benefits provided by the reorganisation of cognitive processes. In other words, learning to think and act differently provides its own hope for the troubled client. This more CBT-oriented view of hope is probably best expressed by Snyder. For Snyder one of the benefits of his theory is that it is premised on the capacity of the individual to break goals down into manageable sub-goals. While the existence of goals, pathways and agentic thinking is fundamental to his theory of hope, the application of the theory is dependent on an individual's ability and preparedness to examine the details of these components. Snyder suggests that one of the difficulties for many clients is that they are unable to break down their goals into manageable pieces. He says that the tendency is rather to pursue 'an ineffective search for a single-stroke solution to the presenting problem and an inability to break it down into manageable "bites"' (Snyder, 2000: 754). He adds that 'Consistent with hope theory tenets, cognitive-behavioral interventions train clients in the generalizable strategy of subgoal production' (2000: 754–5).

Another benefit of a cognitive behavioural approach to working with hope lies within the rational examination of pathways thinking. By definition, pathways thinking is about identifying multiple and alternative routes to desired goals. Often one of the problems clients face is that they have not been able to generate sufficient pathways options for their goals. The psycho-educational and cognitive focus of CBT is a very comfortable methodological fit for the examination of alternative pathways. CBT also capitalises on the iterative nature of pathways and agentic thinking. As new pathway options are discovered they tend to encourage motivation – the greater the motivation, the greater the energy that is directed towards finding further goals pathways. Snyder's views about the process of hope-oriented therapy are well captured in Box 4.1.

BOX 4.1   COGNITIVE BEHAVIOURAL THERAPY AND THE GENERATION OF HOPE

'To maintain the nascent sense of hopefulness very early in therapy, clients need credible answers to their fundamental shared question: How is this process going to help me get better? If during the early stages of treatment, the client is presented with a lucid rationale that outlines a plausible set of pathways for reaching the goal of symptomatic improvement (Frank & Frank, 1991), then hope should remain. Such a rationale serves two purposes: (1) it enhances pathways thinking by reassuring the client that the recently generated pathway (the thought of entering psychotherapy) will be efficacious, and (2) it stimulates agency thinking both indirectly via enhanced pathways thinking and directly by showing that the decision to seek expert help (an act of agency) was effective (i.e., "This therapist seems likely to be able to help me – I made a good decision!"). It is illuminating here to consider the very strong emphasis that cognitive-behavioral interventions place upon the therapist's ability to present a convincing, logical rationale for treatment, and to present this in the first therapy session (when it should, according to hope theory, have its maximal impact as a vehicle for catalyzing agency thoughts). In fact, many cognitive-behavioral manuals … provide therapists with a verbatim text for how to present treatments.' (Snyder, 2000: 757)

Mindfulness-based therapies

An approach to counselling and psychotherapy which has gained increasing attention in recent years is mindfulness-based psychotherapy. Mindfulness is not first and foremost a psychotherapy but rather a life practice of paying attention to each moment in a non-judgemental way. Kabat-Zinn, who is recognised as one of the most notable proponents of mindfulness in Western health literature, defines mindfulness as 'the awareness that emerges through paying attention on purpose, in the present moment, and nonjudgmentally to the unfolding of experience moment by moment' (2003: 145). It is usually associated with meditation, especially as it is practised within the Buddhist spiritual tradition. Mindfulness might simply be called a state of consciousness that enables an individual to have a connected but also detached awareness of him/herself, of others, and his/her surroundings. Meditation, as Kabat-Zinn (2005) explains, is not mindfulness itself but the scaffolding upon which it is built.

Mindfulness as a practice commonly found within human experience and across different spiritual traditions, is fundamentally about the practice of attention, and as such is a universal phenomenon (Kabat-Zinn, 2005). Most spiritual traditions explore the nature of attention and its benefits to spiritual enlightenment and wholeness. It is, however, through Buddhism that mindfulness has most effectively found its way into Western thought. One of the first formal ways it was introduced was in Kabat-Zinn's (1990) research on Mindfulness Based Stress Reduction (MBSR). Since this early work, much research demonstrating the effectiveness of mindfulness practices in clinical settings, has ensued. Before we demonstrate a link between mindfulness and hope, a more detailed explanation of mindfulness is necessary.

Shapiro and colleagues have developed a model of mindfulness that provides helpful insight into its working elements (Shapiro et al., 2006). They suggest that mindfulness is based on three axioms:

1 'On purpose' or intention
2 'Paying attention' or attention
3 'In a particular way' or attitude (mindfulness qualities).

In their view, each of these elements is necessary for mindfulness to be fully functional. As they express it, 'Intention, attention, and attitude are not separate processes or stages – they are interwoven aspects of a single cyclic *process* and occur simultaneously' (Shapiro et al., 2006: 375).

Mindfulness is most often associated with how one pays attention to one's moment-by-moment experience. While this is true, an element that is usually not addressed or recognised is the important place that intention plays in mindfulness. While non-judgemental awareness is one of the aims of mindfulness, this does not mean that it is without some direction or focus. As Kabat-Zinn explains, 'Your intentions set the stage for what is possible. They remind you from moment to moment of why you are practicing in the first place' (1990: 32). Intentions, however, are dynamic in nature and constantly evolving. Meditation practised initially for health reasons, for example, may later include a personal development intention. Intention therefore is an important component of mindfulness and essential for understanding it (Bishop et al., 2004; Shapiro et al., 2006).

Another way of defining attention is 'the process of becoming aware of one's own phenomenological experience in the moment'. Shapiro and colleagues note the importance of intention in phenomenology, commenting 'This is what Husserl refers to as a "return to things themselves," that is, suspending all the ways of interpreting experience and attending to experience itself, as it presents itself in the here and now' (Shapiro et al., 2006: 376). One important aspect of attention is its distinction between the experience of something and the presence of self as the observer of experience. In other words, the individual is not just someone having an experience as one who is singularly embedded within it, but is also someone who is aware of the experience, as it were, from the position of observer. This duality is an important feature of mindfulness as it is the capacity both to have an experience and also to be aware of having the experience that is at the heart of mindfulness.

The third axiom, *attitude*, is also important. One can have an intention and pay attention but from quite different attitudinal perspectives. The practice of meditation, for example, can be an application of fairly strict, clinical rules, which of themselves may lead one to a harsh or judgemental attitude to practice. Alternatively, meditation may include 'rules of thumb' which have embedded within them a non-judgemental stance. A key aim of mindfulness is to approach life in a non-judgemental manner without self-evaluation or interpretation. The primary attitudes promoted within mindfulness are patience, curiosity, non-striving, acceptance, and kindness towards the self, others, and the environment.

Mindfulness as an approach within counselling and psychotherapy can be regarded as a hopeful practice in two main ways. First, mindfulness prioritises personal self-awareness through a centredness of being. Such a practice of noticing oneself and one's environment provides a spacious and generous attitude of acceptance. Slowing down to pay attention to the present moment allows for a new level of awareness that is often missed due to distraction and busyness. Awareness can then bring with it a realisation that the present moment is 'good enough'. Such an awareness and acceptance of the ordinary provides an opportunity for hope to be present. This is not so much a specific hope for the future but a hope for the moment. Second, as we gain greater self-awareness we also gain greater awareness of others. To be self-aware is to be more insightful about our interconnectedness with all being. Mindfulness as a life attitude can provide a sense of peaceful equanimity that allows for hope in the everyday.

Postmodern therapies

Over the past twenty years there has been an enormous growth in what collectively are named postmodern therapies, including *feminist therapy, solution-focused therapy* and *narrative therapy*. These therapies, while different in various ways, have several key principles in common:

- There are no absolutes, only multiple realities
- There are multiple ways of knowing and these are equally valid
- Reality is personally and socially constructed

- There is no objective reality and therefore no certainty
- Therapy is a collaborative process of meaning-making
- Personal and social narratives are the dominant vehicles through which meaning is communicated and renegotiated.

Postmodernism, as the name suggests, is a philosophical shift away from the modernist assumptions about the nature of reality, how we know and how we construct personal and social values. Modernism, born from the Enlightenment search for knowledge and understanding of the universe, works on the assumption that reality is objective and fixed and that pathways of knowledge (epistemologies) are scientifically set and agreed upon. Knowing is not primarily personally constructed but objectively determined by scientific rules and principles. In modernism the knower and known are separate.

Postmodernism rejects the false dichotomy of knower and known, of subject and object, and argues that to know is an act of personal engagement with the object and hence knowledge is always personally constructed. Due to the perspective that knowing is an act of personal construction, the postmodernist also recognises that there are many wider influences on what shapes the individual's construction of reality. In this respect, knowing, and therefore our view of reality, is also influenced by many other contextual factors such a social milieu and physical environment. Hence, to know is not only a personal act but also a social or collective act of reality construction.

These assumptions about reality and epistemology orientate the postmodern therapist differently to those imbued with modernist assumptions. One of the first differences is a focus on narrative and language as the primary medium of understanding. While language is obviously essential in other therapeutic approaches, the emphasis is on verifiable and therefore objective conditions or understandings of the client's problems. Scientific evidence based on observation and measurement is primary in modernist approaches, whereas in postmodern approaches language and meaning construction is primary.

A central tenet in narrative therapy is that an individual's problematic beliefs about self and life arise from external oppressive stories that dominate the person's life. 'Human problems occur when the way in which people's [sic] lives are storied by themselves and others does not significantly fit with their lived experience' (Carr, 1998: 486). Within postmodern therapies psychological problems are understood to sit outside of the person as opposed to within the person. The problem is largely determined by the context in which an individual finds him or herself. As Carr further explains, 'Developing therapeutic solutions to problems, within the narrative frame, involves opening space for the authoring of alternative stories, the possibility of which have previously been marginalized by the dominant oppressive narrative which maintains the problem' (1998: 486). Narrative therapy as with other postmodern therapies holds that problems are not representative of identity or life but rather that problems *constitute* identity and life. In other words, reauthoring the narratives and imbuing them with different meanings changes lives because narratives constitute identity.

Postmodern therapists seek to collaborate with clients against the oppressive messages and practices that family and society have foisted upon them. Therapy is fundamentally a practice of identifying and deconstructing the negative dominant narratives from people's lives and of helping them to reconstruct preferred narratives. Carr argues that narrative therapists work from the premise that lives and identities are constituted and shaped by three main factors:

- The meaning people give to their experiences or the stories they tell themselves about themselves.

- The language practices that people are recruited into along with the type of words they use to story their lives.

- The situation people occupy in social structures in which they participate and the power relations entailed by these. (1998: 489)

Within a narrative framework of understanding problems are more appropriately defined by the individual than by science. The meaning the client gives to their story of struggle is more primary than some diagnostic label or even some externally recommended model of therapy. Epston, Stillman, and Erbes (2012: 77) explain the narrative position well, stating:

> Narrative therapy is about privileging the voice of those who consult with us, about working with their truth and their version of reality, instead of imposing an outside truth, even if that truth does come from 'empirical studies.' Put another way, science is about generalizing broad truths that apply to everyone, while narrative is about elucidating local truths that apply to those who construct them and live them.

One of the central contributions that the narrative and, more broadly, postmodern approaches to therapy make, is recognition that problems in living are not necessarily centred in the individual. While an individual's problems involve the individual, the problems arise because the individual is situated within a wider family, social and cultural context. In other words, the problems are more than the individuals. Emerging from this perspective are different ways of thinking about and working with problems in living. Externalisation, for example, is a strategy used particularly within solution-focused and narrative therapy, to separate the problem from the individual and to situate it outside within a wider context. For example, a client would be encouraged to externalise an experience of depression and see it as something that is outside oppressing them. This approach has many benefits, including allowing the person to see themselves as fundamentally OK and not defined by the problem, and highlighting the contribution of external voices from family and society in the problem construction.

The postmodern way of thinking inherently provides a different perspective on the issue of hope. If reality is fundamentally constructed and if no epistemology is privileged above another, then the individual is free to construct his or her own preferred version of reality which is alive and full of hope. The emphasis within postmodern therapies of constructing preferred identities focuses the client's attention on possibilities, on solutions, rather than on problems. Hope is possible because negative family and societal messages can be deconstructed and reconstructed to fit the individual's own preferences and interpretations. Shifting the site of the problem from within to outside the individual is a very powerful tool in the quest for a hoped-for future. New narratives of hope can transform lives in surprising and unexpected ways and are always possible.

Summary

In this chapter we have explored what factors within therapy are known to work and encourage positive therapeutic change. Primary among these is the therapeutic relationship. Without a strong therapeutic bond and a sense of direction forged through therapist–client collaboration, we know that therapy is likely to flounder. All good therapies and all good therapists value the place of relationship as central to the therapeutic enterprise. In addition to this, we know that the theory and technique of therapy plays a part in the change process. Good theories provide comprehensive and cohesive frameworks for understanding humanness, society, and problems in living. We have only reviewed, very briefly, some of these theories with the intention of highlighting their particular strengths and benefits in contributing to client hope. Our purpose here was not to recommend any one therapy as the therapy of hope, far from it. We value the contribution that each approach makes to ameliorating human struggle, pain, and suffering, and to providing an avenue for hope to emerge. In recognising these various contributions we recommend that therapists be open to working in integrative and pluralistic ways as we believe that doing so provides the greatest possibility for client hope to be found, ignited, or constructed (Cooper & McLeod, 2011).

QUESTIONS FOR REFLECTION AND DISCUSSION

1 The therapeutic relationship seems to be a key mediator of hope. Why do you think this the case? What is it about the relationship that provides an opportunity for hope to emerge?
2 Write down some key contributions that each of the approaches to therapy discussed in this chapter makes to engendering a hopeful life outlook.
3 Personal stories of hope are powerful mediums for encouraging hope. Tell someone (or describe in your personal journal) one of your stories in hope. Remember a story has a beginning, a middle, and an end.

5

Despair and anxiety as loss of hope

Despair and anxiety are key existential themes and also, one might say, the bread and butter of therapy. People come to counselling and psychotherapy for various reasons, some much more profound than others. At one end of the continuum problems are quizzical inquiries and issues about personal development and growth, and not overly disturbing or disconcerting. At the other end of the continuum, problems are catastrophic and debilitating. The majority of people though come to therapy because they are struggling with an issue of living that is perturbing and disconcerting. This is often characterised by experiences of despair and anxiety. It is our contention that despair and anxiety are often, but not always, manifestations of a loss of hope. In this chapter we will explore different perspectives on despair and anxiety and distinguish between when these states signal a loss of hope and when they do not.

Existential writers like Heidegger (1962), Spinelli (1997), van Deurzen-Smith (1997), and Yalom (1980) emphasise the importance of recognising the significant place of despair and anxiety in life. Heidegger understood the problem of living as a problem of *Being*. He was interested in the meaning of *Being* and argued that we had forgotten what *Being* was all about. He asserted that *Being* is best addressed not as an abstract concept, but through the experience of being itself. *Being* by its very nature is a relational encounter and not just a solo experience. One of the challenges of *Being* is to confront authentically the 'givens' of life. We have no control over our birth, the family circumstances into which we were born, our time in history, or the fact that we will die. Authenticity requires that we confront these facts and our responses to them. It requires that we be mindful to pay attention to our experiences, their impact on us, and our interpretations of them, because when we cease to pay attention we are living inauthentically.

The existential challenge of living authentic lives demands that we confront the issue of freedom and responsibility. Responsibility is best represented as choice, that is, the choice to pay attention. For the existentialist choice involves confronting guilt, despair, uncertainty, and anxiety. Guilt and despair arise when we realise that we have not always lived up to our potential, when we have chosen instead to forget *Being*. Anxiety results from the awareness of choice and the responsibility of making the best of our life because we know that life is short and that death is inescapable. While we may not be free to change the givens of our life, we are free to choose how we will live our lives within the constraints of human existence. The central issue in existentialism is how to live an authentic life.

In Chapter 2 we examined how different existentialist writers engaged with the issue of being authentic by exploring how they understood hope. In this chapter we extend these ideas and apply them to the issues of despair, depression, and anxiety. We explained earlier that Sartre and Camus saw no use for hope and regarded it as a hindrance to authenticity. Kierkegaard, Marcel, and Levinas conversely gave hope a central role in the task of authentic *Being*. For Kierkegaard (1844), existence requires us to manage the tension between the temporal and eternal. Our temporal nature demands constant attention to our relationships and the meanings we take from them. However, the effort and benefits of remaining authentic do not provide us with all the answers to life or assuage all our despairs and anxieties. While we gain hope through living a fully engaged life, this hope is not enough because we fall short of our own expectations and fall back into inauthentic ways of being. In this respect life is more than we can manage on our own. This is where we need hope for eternity, that is, a source of hope beyond ourselves. For Kierkegaard the authentic life is a paradox best represented in the tension between the necessity of self-effort and the recognition of our inability through self-effort to achieve authenticity. In one moment we are living successfully by the dint of our own efforts and in the next we lose focus and fall back into a forgetfulness of *Being*. One requires the patience of hope to hold this tension and press into the constant process of becoming truly oneself.

A seminal commentator on the question of existential existence is Ernest Becker. Among other issues, Becker was particularly interested in the human fear of death. He argued that the human capacity for reflectivity, while our greatest asset, is also the basis for anxiety as it enables us to be conscious of our own mortality. Becker asserted that if we were constantly aware of the fact that we will die, we would not be able to function normally. The awareness of our mortality is therefore largely repressed and usually only emerges into consciousness fleetingly. Becker argued that we as humans have a deep need to transcend our mortality and we try to do this in a variety of ways. Having children, creating works of art, desiring political power and influence, and seeking religious experiences are all examples of our attempts to transcend our temporal condition. Like other existential writers Becker sought to understand the dilemma of mortality and immortality. The central drive in this paradox was to derive meaning, to make sense of life. Munley and Johnson (2002) summarise Becker's thoughts about the fear of death in the box below.

BOX 5.1   FEAR OF DEATH

'In *Denial of Death* Becker (1973) wrote that of all the things that motivate humans, one of the most important is the terror of death; and that heroism is primarily a response to the terror of death. Drawing on the work of psychoanalyst Gregory Zilboorg, Becker shared the view that the fear or terror of death is universally present, primary and ever present behind humans' ordinary functioning as an aspect of self-preservation. However, the pure fear of death is not continuously present in one's mental awareness, since if it were, a person would be unable to function normally. Repression serves as a protector and allows humans to ignore the fear or transform the fear into part of life-expanding processes. Becker describes the existential paradox of humankind as the condition of "individuality within finitude". Humans are individuals; they have self-consciousness, a name, a personal history, and a symbolic identity, which stands out uniquely in nature. A person's mind has the capacity to create, speculate and to imaginatively project oneself to any place in the universe. Yet at the same time each person is an animal, destined for death and burial. Humans are conscious that this end is inevitable and that they will die. This is the terrible existential dilemma humans live with.

Becker (1975) wrote that humans desire eternal life and prosperity and create cultural symbols, which do not age or die, to alleviate their fear of death and to provide the promise of immortality.' (Munley & Johnson, 2002: 366)

The journey towards the authentic life subjects us to the tensions between possibilities and limitations, between an awareness of the enormity of existence and the demands of everyday life. True selfhood requires an awareness of these tensions and a deliberate choice to take responsibility for our growth and development. However, for Kierkegaard this responsibility is a relationship not just with self and others but also with the 'constituting power' or spirit that, as Hayes (2006: 85) expresses it, 'guides the dialectical development of the self and makes possible the synthesis of its various elements'. Thus for Kierkegaard, establishing a right relationship with oneself is dependent upon establishing a right relationship with God. When the individual is unable to engage with ultimate questions of *Being* he or she is likely to fall into despair. Patience is required to stay engaged in the process of becoming oneself. This patience is the hope that the trials of trying to live the authentic life will eventually pay off.

While Marcel holds much in common with Kierkegaard and the existential thesis of seeking to live an authentic life through paying attention to the experience of confronting the larger questions of existence, he identifies the action of hope differently. For Marcel, hope is tied to the issue of seeking to remain available (*disponibilité*) to relationships. This is because relationships form the central context in which the self emerges. The difficulty though, as mentioned in Chapter 2, is that we find it hard to remain available in relationships because relationships often leave us hurt or disappointed. To stay in a relationship requires an act of fidelity or commitment. However, fidelity is such a challenge that we require help from outside ourselves to maintain it. It is in this context that hope comes to our aid because hope provides us with the capacity to believe that we will be supported in finding the strength to maintain our fidelity.

Levinas (2001), like Marcel, understood openness to relationships as the primary pathway towards authenticity. He valued relationships because it is through them that we are most in touch with the immediate moment and it is our awareness of immediacy and all that it contains which is central to *Being*. Like all existentialists, Levinas sees *Being* as the fundamental existential issue, but his approach to *Being* emphasises, more than any other, the importance of the embodied state. According to Levinas, the needs and emotions of *Being* are aspects of embodiment. On the one hand we want to escape our earthly existence, and yet on the other hand our *Being* is largely defined by our temporality. Levinas' solution to the challenge of authenticity is to pay attention to our temporal embodied state via an engagement with our emotional and behavioural responses to others. He argues that when we stay open to the immediate moment of the relational encounter by 'welcoming the other' we are most in touch with *Being* and are most truly ourselves (Levinas, 1969).

The issue of hope comes into Levinas' argument through 'welcoming the other'. In his view, the other is always more than we expect. Otherness is a form of transcendence and will always surprise us. Hope resides not in some utopian vision of the future or in our own ability to achieve our own goals, but it is something that arises between people, a surprise of the unexpected. We are able to hope because relationships themselves provide the emergence of a new and surprising future. By paying attention to the ordinariness of our embodied state, that is, our needs and emotions especially as they arise in relationships, we maintain hope in becoming our authentic self.

Hope is important for Kierkegaard, Marcel, and Levinas, but in different ways. For Kierkegaard, hope as patience is necessary so that we do not ultimately despair of seeking authenticity or, as he would express it, of 'gaining one's soul'. Hope enables us to hold the tensions associated with the paradox of our temporal and eternal existence. For Marcel, hope also is an acknowledgement that we need strength from outside of ourselves to help us remain available to otherness. We need this hope because relationships are challenging and difficult but also because they are the ground in which our genuine self emerges. Levinas, like Marcel, agrees that a focus on otherness is the central issue and that it is through the relational encounter that hope arises.

Despair as loss of hope

These debates within existentialism provide a helpful framework for understanding despair and anxiety and ultimately their relationship with hope. Kierkegaard saw despair as representing stages along the journey towards authenticity. In a certain sense, despair is necessary if we are to discover our self, as it forces us to engage with the issue of *Being*. Despair arises at various points and in varying degrees in our life because we are unable to hold the tensions of existence. When we do not hold the inevitable tensions we fall into defensive mechanisms of inauthenticity. The first of these defences is the act of not paying attention. This is probably best seen in the busy but unthinking life. For Kierkegaard this is a stage where despair is present but unrecognised and he named this the *aesthetic* stage or 'sphere' of existence. He characterises this as a busy but mundane and largely fruitless form of existence. People at this stage of despair, as defined by Kierkegaard, are either not likely to come to counselling or, if they do, are not fully ready to engage with the central issues which trouble them. The movement forward beyond this stage of despair and readiness is to acknowledge the hidden existence of despair (the problem). In doing so, the individual then moves on to a different stage of despair known as the *ethical* sphere of existence.

In the ethical stage we are more able to acknowledge the existence of our struggles but we seek ways of resolving problems ourselves. The central dilemma in the ethical stage is maintaining a balance between *possibilities* and *limitations*. Typically we fall prey to the enticement of one end of the polarity or the other. We either overemphasise our limitations and play it safe by becoming one of the crowd, or overemphasise possibilities and fall into the romantic trap of ungrounded imagination. Referring to the individual who overbalances into possibilities, Hayes (2006: 87) insightfully explains 'he expresses an abstract sentimentality about the human predicament, without engaging with his own feelings and relationships; and he formulates grandiose plans without regard for the concrete conditions of his life'.

This loss of equilibrium is expressed defensively through one of two paths, the path of *weakness,* of not wanting to be oneself, or the path of *defiance,* of claiming oneself without reference to otherness. In the response of weakness we are aware, at some level, of our private pain and struggle but maintain a public reserve and non-engagement. In the response of defiance we stubbornly aim to become fully our self without the need of others or of the 'constituting power'. For Kierkegaard this aim is impossible to achieve without help from outside of the self. Not desirous of such help the person in defiance is ultimately left to maintain their despair and rage against the impossibility of change.

The only resolution to despair is finding the balance of *Being*, which is only gained by engaging with others and with the constituting power, God. As Kierkegaard (1989: 165) clarifies:

> the formula for that state in which there is no despair at all: in relating itself to itself and in wanting to be itself, the self is grounded transparently in the power which established it. Which formula, in turn, ... is the definition of faith.

This final stage or sphere of existence Kierkegaard names the *religious.*

Despair here is seen as a necessary aspect of the process of becoming an authentic self. Despair is not all bad as it spurs the individual on in the journey of becoming. Despair only becomes problematic when the individual becomes stuck in a stage or sphere of existence and ceases the struggle to become. In other words, the individual gives up hope either in his or her own capacity to effect change or gives up hope in there being any support from outside the self.

While Kierkegaard's existentialism has an avowedly theological underpinning, especially in its understanding of otherness, other expressions of this philosophy are less religious. However, central to much existential writing is the primacy of relatedness (otherness) in the individual's journey of becoming. In a less religious frame, otherness and transcendence is less about a personal God and more about people, nature, and universe. The importance of otherness though remains central.

Despair as guilt

As previously highlighted, the great challenge that existentialism sets before us is the task of maintaining a balance between possibilities and limitations, and remaining on the journey towards authentic selfhood. One of the outcomes of this struggle to maintain equilibrium is the recognition of the extent to which we fall into the extremes of the polarity and fail to reach our potential. This realisation often leads us to a place of guilt and ultimately despair.

It can be helpful to think of guilt as the result of a failure to live up to our own values. We have many personal values but some are more important to us than others and so subliminally we tend to arrange these into a hierarchy. When we reflect on our past as a failure to live up to our most prized values, we are tempted to feel guilty. As Thomas Oden explains, 'When I interpret the past as a negation of the very values that I hold most dear and that make my life meaningful, I experience guilt' (1992: 98). When we find no way of resolving guilt, the result is despair and depression. An interesting point to note here is that guilt is about the past and never about the future. We can only be guilty about what we have done or have failed to do, not what we might do in the future.

Therapy clients for whom guilt is a central concern are seeking a resolution to this negative experience. Sometimes guilt is a tangible awareness of specific acts we regret. At other times these are more esoteric regrets of having lived inadequately, or of failing to maintain equilibrium. Counselling and psychotherapy can offer much support to clients grappling with guilt as they seek to make new sense of their life story.

Psychoanalytic therapists have long held the view that some forms of depression are activated by internalised anger (Alexander & French, 1948). While there are many variables that contribute to depression in an individual, internalised anger in some depressive states has been validated as a contributing factor (Clay, Anderson & Dixon, 1993). Therapy can potentially assist clients struggling with anger by aiding them to normalise the experience of anger, by providing a site for catharsis, and by providing a space for clients to practise the expression of anger. However, if anger and depression are outcomes of an existential guilt, the client might well be served by being encouraged to explore the meaning of their perceived failure to live an authentic life. In such a situation, despair expressed as depression provides an opportunity for an increased self-awareness.

Despair as the dark night of the soul

According to the World Health Organization, depression currently stands as the fourth largest contributor to the global burden of disease. In many Western countries depression is ranked even higher as a leading illness. These statistics are alarming and worthy of serious reflection. Why is depression such an epidemic? While we know that many factors contribute to depression, some biological and others psychosocial, an existential understanding of it as a problem of living, as outlined above, provides a reasonable explanation for at least some depressive states. The term depression is a generic designation given to a range of psychosocial conditions. This range has meant that some forms of depression are better understood than others. In amongst the wide range of symptoms that collectively might be referred to as depression, we would like to suggest that sometimes what looks like depression is not depression, at least not as described in diagnostic manuals. Sometimes clients present with a number of depressive symptoms that, while typical of depression, do not collectively indicate depression. Of course this may be true for many presenting issues. Our concern though is not so much with a problem of a psychological nature but with what might be regarded as a spiritual or transpersonal problem.

A good example of an experience which has depression-like symptoms but which may well not be depression from a technical and diagnostic perspective is that which has been variously named the 'dark night of the soul' or spiritual emergence. The 'dark night of the soul' is a term first coined by the sixteenth-century Catholic priest, St John of the Cross, and is probably the best recognised name for a particular type of experience typified by deep personal turmoil and struggle. The dark night experience is one which usually lasts for an extended period of more than a year and which has at its centre a deep sense of spiritual questioning. While a number of the experiences inherent within the dark night are akin to depression, the critical difference between it and depression is the way the individual relates to the experience. Those who would identify as having a dark night experience are in some way or other conscious of their experience as a reorganisation of their meaning-making system from within a spiritual framework.

One qualification should be made here concerning the use of terms. The term 'spiritual' is being used in preference to 'religious', as many people who identify with a dark night experience may not be religious in the sense that they ascribe to a particular formal religious system of belief and practice. However, many people would describe themselves as spiritual. Wright, Watson, and Bell (1996: 31) define spirituality as 'A personal belief in and a personal experience of a supreme being or an ultimate human condition, along with an internal set of values and active investment in those values, a sense of connection, a sense of meaning, and a sense of inner wholeness within or outside formal religious structures'.

St John of the Cross used the metaphor of the progression from dusk to dawn as a description of an experience of deep angst and personal trial. The dark night of the soul is divided into two phases, the *night of the senses* and the *night of the spirit*. In the night-of-the-senses phase the individual finds that spiritual practices and ways of making sense of life no longer bring any feeling of joy or contentment. In this phase the individual continues to read, pray, meditate, and so on, but finds no spiritual comfort or connection with the transcendent. At these times it is also common that while some aspects of life continue on as usual and even may be particularly successful, other aspects of life – health, friendships, work, and so on – may be in turmoil or at least greatly unsatisfying. When the continued reliance on past meaning-making constructs and spiritual practices fail to deliver past rewards, the individual passes from the night of the senses into the night of the spirit. Metaphorically this is a transition to the darkness at midnight. At this point the strivings of previous ways of being are confronted as hollow artifacts of faith without substance. The night of the senses becomes a crisis of faith; a deep questioning of one's belief system that leaves the individual feeling abandoned and alone. Interestingly, throughout the two phases of the downward journey of the dark night, individuals usually are able to continue functioning in other aspects of their life. They may still go to work and run a family but the demands of maintaining normal functioning are great, usually resulting in exhaustion and varying degrees of low mood.

While much of the description of the dark night provided here is consistent with depression, a key point of difference is the meaning-making focus given to the experience by the sufferer. The person journeying through the dark night is aware that their struggle has primarily a spiritual base as opposed to a psychological one. May (1982: 91–2) describes the distinction between depression and the dark night well in the following statement:

> *Dark night experiences are not usually associated with* loss of effectiveness in life or work, as are primary depressions. Often, in fact, the individual is mystified at how well he or she is continuing to function.
>
> In the dark night one would not really have things otherwise. While there might be great superficial dissatisfaction and confusion, the most honest answer, the deepest response is that in spite of everything there is an underlying sense of rightness about it all. This is in stark contrast to primary depression in which one's deepest sense is of wrongness and, consciously at least, the desire for a radical, even miraculous, change is pervasive.

While there may be aspects of overlap between the dark-night-of-the-soul experience and forms of depression, the two experiences are largely different and are based in different aetiologies. One of these differences relates to the question of hope. While the depressed person can gain great psychological benefit from regaining hope, the person experiencing the dark night recognises hope as a central issue. Given that the dark night is founded on a spiritual belief system that inherently provides for a journey of transition designed to bring the individual closer to God or to some image of the transcendent, hope is not just a belief in the possibility of a brighter day, but a belief in benevolence. The focus of this benevolence will vary somewhat depending on the form of spirituality, whether sourced in a personal God, nature or universe. However, the challenge of hope is to believe in the character of the spiritual source. The question then becomes 'Will God, universe, spirit … be there for me and transition me to a new way of being?' This question is the test of faith. Hope in the context of spiritual challenge asks the believer to maintain belief without immediate evidence, to believe in the 'here but not yet'.

The likelihood that some clients may be experiencing a dark night of the soul, as opposed to depression, makes different demands on the therapist. To treat clients who are experiencing a dark night as though their problem is fundamentally depression, may not serve them well. The aware therapist is not only culturally aware but is also aware that different worldviews (which include spiritualities), require sensitivity and at times a different way of working.

Despair as anxiety

Like depression, anxiety presents in many guises and accounts for a high percentage of the global health burden. While everyone experiences anxiety in some form, between ten and eighteen per cent of the world population experiences clinical levels of anxiety. Clinical diagnoses include a range of disorders from Generalised Anxiety Disorder, which is based on protracted worry, to Obsessive Compulsive Disorder and Panic Disorder, which among other anxiety conditions can be profoundly disabling. Any condition that we experience as impinging on our quality of life, especially if it lasts for a protracted period, has the potential to lead us to despair. The various anxiety conditions, while varying in symptomatology, also have at their centre the common experience of prolonged anxiety. It seems that anxiety is a ubiquitous human experience, but with its clinical forms growing in incidence, we are left wondering again, 'Why is this so?'

The existential explanation of anxiety emerging out of the challenge of taking responsibility for one's life certainly has much to recommend it. The gift of freedom, while wonderful, seems to bring with it a host of problems. It is not surprising that existential thinkers have focused on despair and its offspring, guilt and anxiety, as primary life issues. Existential despair expressed as anxiety is usually understood to be about the loss of meaning and personal value. It also concerns an awareness of our own finiteness and the realisation that our current life will end. Paul Tillich (2000: 36) captures this view very simply by stating, 'Anxiety is finitude, experienced as one's own finitude'. It seems that to be alive is to be anxious. While the twin problems of finitude and loss of meaning are well argued causes of our anxiety, a more recent twist in the dilemma of *Being* suggests a significant new variation to this common view. In the postmodern world, anxiety may well be exacerbated by an *excess* of meaning. In this information technology age we cannot escape the plethora of IT gadgets and constantly streamed information. As well as issuing continual bursts of information, the postmodern age is also one of shifting and unstable worldviews. Historically worldviews were fairly stable and only shifted very gradually. Now the certainties of Enlightenment knowledge have been largely replaced by Quantum physics. In addition, the divide between Western and Eastern religions has substantially crumbled. Not only is knowledge increasing at an alarming rate, it is also being replaced just as quickly. The noted social constructionist Kenneth Gergen captures the impact of this boom of information well in the title of his book *The Saturated Self* and also in his comments that the postmodern individual is a 'populated self' full of 'downloaded' information.

On reflecting on this surfeit of information, Bingaman comments on the views of anthropologist Marc Augé, stating, 'Augé's assessment of the present postmodern or, to use his word, "supermodern" world is that it places considerable demands on our powers of observation and description, so much so that it leaves us with an acute feeling of disorientation' (2010: 666). One of the shifts that this new era has created is a movement away from a more stable 'truth' to a 'plurality of truths'. It seems that the plethora of knowledge and information demands that we become more comfortable with a multiplicity of ideas. While postmodernism and the new information age provide many benefits, with it comes a new anxiety. For the counsellor and psychotherapist seeking to support those troubled by anxiety, the challenge has increased. While we need to maintain the wisdom that anxiety is based in *finitude* and the *loss of meaning*, we also need to add to this base a view of anxiety as being grounded in an *excess* of meaning. The issue of finitude has not changed, but the challenge of aiding the client in their meaning-making has compounded exponentially. The certainties of the past, which were never as certain as they seemed, can no longer even provide an illusion of comfort. It is in this context that the benefits of hope may be even more necessary and longed for.

Anxiety has one feature in common with hope and that is they are both orientated to the future. In a certain sense anxiety and hope are opposites. The anxious person focuses on the future and anticipates their inability to perform or cope with life's demands. Anxiety also involves a belief that the future will present some uncontrollable threat. As Suárez, Bennett, Goldstein, and Barlow explain, anxiety requires a 'sense of uncontrollability focused on the possibility of future threat, danger, or other potentially negative events' (2009: 153). Conversely, hope looks to the future and expects that whether there is threat or not, the future will hold within it a positive outcome. Note here that hope is not an expectation of a rosy, carefree existence – rather, it is a positive expectancy grounded in reality.

Anxiety founded in an expectation of uncontrollability and threat is fundamentally about uncertainty. Given this, it has been postulated that negative reactions to uncertainty, known as *intolerance to uncertainty*, may be intrinsic to anxiety disorders. When intolerance to uncertainty is explored further, two key features are evident, the first being an intolerance of ambiguity. People with a high intolerance to uncertainty are more likely to interpret ambiguous situations as threatening. The result is that their physiological arousal is increased, which then exacerbates their cycle of fear. The second feature of intolerance to uncertainty is that sufferers overestimate future threat even if the probability of it occurring is very low (Carletona et al., 2012). Intolerance to uncertainty is such a powerful process that Carletona et al. believe that it is likely to be a transdiagnostic feature of anxiety conditions.

At its heart the intolerance to uncertainty is a drive towards control. The sufferer wants to be so in control of their life circumstances that anything outside of their control becomes intolerable. Of course this is the very thing that the existentialists have debated. In Kierkegaardian terms it is the tension between the temporal and the eternal, between a sensible self-control or agency and a trust (hope) in a certain positive or benevolent view of the future. Aiding clients in exploring and working with this tension becomes one of the central tasks of the therapist.

Summary

In this chapter we have explored the link between the loss of hope and despair and anxiety. Often, when hope fades despair expressed as depression results. Despair can be found in varying degrees and can take a number of different forms. While despair often challenges our mental health, it can also be the catalyst for positive change. Sometimes this change is found after an extended downward journey into turmoil and confusion.

This descent into struggle, however, can be the very doorway to new horizons. For some the loss of hope is more immediately experienced as the loss of certainty resulting in fear and anxiety. Whether our concerns lead us to states of despair or existential angst, hope remains at the centre of the recovery.

QUESTIONS FOR REFLECTION AND DISCUSSION

1 Despair can be thought of as a normal experience of life but one that is not lasting. It can also be a profound experience of giving up hope, of not wanting to continue the human struggle. How would you distinguish between these two degrees or levels of despair? What implication does this have for therapy?

2 Kierkegaard represented despair as having a three-stage progression, from the *aesthetic*, to the *ethical*, to the *religious*. At each point the individual gains a greater realisation of his or her struggle to maintain the balance of an authentic self. How might such a view of despair aid the counsellor and the client in exploring the experience of despair?

3 Intolerance of uncertainty has been postulated as being a central component of all anxiety conditions. What are your views on this assertion and how might such a view inform the therapist in their work of therapy?

SECTION 2

THE PRACTICE OF HOPE

6

The therapist's hope

Before exploring the range of hope-inspiring approaches and strategies used in counselling and psychotherapy, we first need to look at the person of the therapist. Who is this person that makes him or herself available to support, to care for, and heal others? What does the therapist bring to the therapeutic encounter that enables the development of hope? What about the therapist's own hope?

It is clear that counsellors and psychotherapists as a group have a deep belief in the possibility of therapeutic change – I suppose if they didn't then they are in the wrong job! Therapists tend to be hopeful people, and maybe it is this quality that encourages others to have hope? However, as we have seen in previous chapters, hope is not a static thing – it can ebb and flow. This means that therapists themselves are not always full of hope. They struggle like everyone else at times to make sense of life and to look positively towards the future. Snyder understood hope to have both trait-based and state-based dimensions and this means that it is both stable and unstable. The dispositional features of hope tend to be fairly stable, allowing hope to remain within firm parameters. Some people's base level is higher than others, enabling them to be high hopers. Other people's base level is much lower, making it more difficult for them to maintain a hopeful outlook. The state-based aspect of hope means that even though an individual might have a particular standard range of hope-oriented functioning, life circumstances can still impact them and either encourage or discourage hope.

It would seem that high-hope people not only have a dispositional advantage over low-hope people, but also an advantage in terms of intuitively knowing how to encourage hope even when their circumstances are not favourable. In other words, high-hope people have skills that enable them to bolster flagging hope. This ability to engender hope is encouraging because it means that there must be hope-oriented strategies and ways of thinking that can be learnt. The difficulty though is that these strategies and habits of mind are most often unconscious and tacit. The challenge is to try to unearth and identify how high-hope people maintain their buoyancy. Given that we typically expect counsellors and psychotherapists to be fairly hopeful people, researchers are now turning their attention to study the counsellor's hope.

Recent studies on therapist hope are already producing interesting findings. In one study which investigated the impact that both client and therapist hope had on therapeutic outcomes, it was found, somewhat surprisingly, that therapist hope in the client was a better predictor of positive therapeutic change than the client's own hope (Coppock et al., 2010). Whether this is the case in general or only in certain circumstances is as yet unknown. However, there appears to be some form of transfer of hope, expectancy, or belief from the therapist to the client, which impacts positively on therapeutic outcomes. Flesaker and Larsen (2010), in their study of reintegration counsellors working with women on parole and probation, also found that therapist hope was an important factor in recovery. Other studies confirm a link between hope-oriented qualities of the therapist and their influence on client hope. For example, Schachtel (1999) found that the therapist's capacity to maintain affective experience of hope impacted on the client's affective hope. In a similar vein, Snyder et al. (2000) found that high therapist agency correlated with high client agency. Given that agency (motivation) is a key feature of hope, it is not surprising that when it is modelled by the counsellor, the same energy is promoted in the client. These studies are encouraging in at least two ways: one, they show that an individual's *state-based hope* can be improved by interaction with another person, and, two, they mean that there are hope-engendering qualities of the therapist that are yet to be understood, which when better grasped may well improve the efficacy of therapy.

In an effort to understand therapist hope further we conducted two exploratory studies, the first examining therapist qualities which might be related to hope, and the second investigating ways therapists operationalised hope within therapy. This chapter largely draws on our findings and discusses the outcomes. In the first study we wanted see what therapist qualities might be positively linked with therapist hope (O'Hara et al., in press). There are, no doubt, many personal qualities of the therapist that are associated with hope. However, we planned to begin slowly and therefore proposed, based on previous research, that the constructs of the *differentiation of self* and *epistemic style* were likely to be positively correlated with hope. The differentiation of self is a concept which originated from family systems theory and was seen by Murray Bowen (1978), a psychiatrist and family therapist researcher, as being a defining dimension of the self which therefore was directly involved in human relationships. Skowron and Friedlander (1998: 237) define the differentiation of self as 'the capacity to maintain autonomous thinking and achieve a clear, coherent sense of self in the context of emotional relationships with important others'. Bowen thought that the differentiation of the self was made up of four key sub-components, *I-position, emotional reactivity, cutoff,* and *emotional fusion. I-position* is the capacity to hold onto one's own view of self and the world in a clear and logical manner, especially when under relational stress. *Emotional reactivity* is fairly self-explanatory and is the degree of emotional response that an individual usually expresses, again, particularly when under relational stress. Both *I-position* and *emotional reactivity* are considered to be intrapsychic qualities of the self. *Cutoff* and *emotional fusion* are more directly behavioural responses. Cutoff refers to an individual's behaviours that indicate emotional 'shutdown' and distancing from others. This can be expressed by an intentional lack of communication, snubbing, or physical distancing of oneself from others. *Emotional fusion* is the opposite of *cutoff* and refers to the need of an individual to be enmeshed with the other. This often expresses itself as an intolerance of conflict or a degree of acquiescence to the other's demands and expectations.

Epistemic style was the other construct we thought might be related to hope. This refers to how an individual prioritises and understands the nature and acquisition of knowledge. There are many different views about how epistemic style develops, but each has in common the perspective that as an individual develops cognitively and socially they move from a fairly literal view of knowledge as being something fixed and objective to something more fluid and subjectively constructed. The approach we took to identifying epistemology in our study was based on the work of DiGiuseppe and Linscott (1993) and Neimeyer and Morton (1997). This approach divides epistemology into two broad types, *rationalist* and *constructivist*. The rationalist sees knowledge as being largely objective, observable, and measurable, while the constructivist sees knowledge as predominantly indefinite and negotiable.

When we examined the correlation between the differentiation of self with dispositional hope and also compared their respective sub-components, we found some interesting results. First, the differentiation of self was strongly correlated with dispositional (trait) hope. This simply means that the higher a person's level of differentiation, the higher his or her level of hope is likely to be. Immediately this finding presents us with a challenge: 'How does one become more self-differentiated?' The concept of differentiation has been well defined in the research, but how is it facilitated? We don't believe there are easy answers to such questions but there is exciting scope here to pursue answers and new applications.

When the sub-components of self-differentiation were correlated with hope another piece of the puzzle began to emerge. While each of the sub-components of differentiation was positively correlated with hope overall, and with *pathways* and *agency* more specifically, the sub-component of *I-position* stood out as the most significant factor. This means that a person who has a well-developed sense of themselves and who can manage to stay cognitively focused and emotionally grounded is most likely to have a high level of hope. This finding demonstrates that while low, stable levels of *emotional reactivity, cutoff,* and *fusion* are found in highly differentiated people, it is those individuals with a well-developed *I-position* who are most likely to be high hopers.

A further task of the above analysis was the comparison of *I-position* with *pathways* and *agency*. It was found that *I-position* was most strongly correlated with *pathways* thinking. This was somewhat surprising because we had anticipated that *I-position* would correlate most strongly with *agency* thinking. In other words, a person with a strong sense of self would also have a strong sense of motivation. While this may well be true, the component that had the strongest link to *I-position* was *pathways* thinking. This is likely to mean that a person with a strong sense of self has a well-developed capacity to imagine and create new routes towards their goals.

In a final twist, when we compared the hope sub-components of *pathways* and *agency* with the differentiation of self, it was the agency component which demonstrated the strongest association with differentiation overall. This implies that the person who has a consistently high level of hope expressed as personal agency and motivation, is who is most likely to be highly differentiated.

It is clear from this study that the differentiation of self and hope are closely associated. *I-position* and *pathways* thinking align closely together and *agency* is clearly linked to overall levels of differentiation. Understanding the relationship between differentiation of self and hope may well help us support therapists in their work of fostering positive client change.

The second construct that we hypothesised was likely to be related to hope was epistemic style. However, we found that no clear relationship existed between epistemic style and hope. Epistemology is notoriously difficult to measure and so it is possible that the instrument may not have been sensitive enough to measure epistemology's link with hope. Alternatively, it may simply be that epistemology is not related to hope.

So in summary several key findings emerged from the study:

1 The differentiation of self is highly correlated with dispositional hope
2 The differentiation sub-component of *I-position* is most correlated with the hope sub-component of pathways thinking
3 The hope sub-component of agency is most highly related with the differentiation of self overall
4 Epistemology demonstrated no clear link with hope.

Recommendations

Based on this research we make the following recommendations:

1 That personal development of the counsellor is a high priority in training and in ongoing professional development.
2 In personal development, particular attention should be given to growth in the capacity to maintain rational functioning and emotional grounding while under relational stress or challenge.
3 The training of counsellors and psychotherapists should also incorporate education in the nature and function of hope and its applications personally and professionally.

How therapists facilitate hope in counselling

A number of studies have explored how therapists approach working with hope in therapy. Cutcliffe (2004, 2006a, b) investigated how bereavement counsellors inspire hope in their clients. He found three key actions of hope inspiration: forging the connection and the relationship; facilitating a cathartic release; and experiencing a good (healthy) ending. As seen in Chapter 3, Herth (1993) identified six categories of hope-fostering strategies: (a) sustaining relationships, (b) cognitive reframing, (c) time refocusing, (d) attainable expectations, (e) spiritual beliefs, and (f) uplifting energy. Larsen and Stege (2010a, b) distinguished between implicit and explicit hope-focused strategies. In the next chapter we outline, in some detail, different strategies that can foster hope in clients.

Table 6 Therapists' conceptualisations of hope and its operationalisation within therapy

Core category	Sub-category
A. Nature and source of hope	Nature • Positive expectancy • Positive feeling • Promise of positive change Source • Internal • External

B. Hope stance and orientation	Stance
	 • Hope in:
	   ○ different aspects of otherness
	   ○ impermanence
	   ○ intentionality
	   ○ transcendence
	 • Ambivalence
	
	 Orientation within therapy
	 • Hope:
	   ○ *in* the client
	   ○ *for* the client
	   ○ *in* the counselling process
	   ○ *in* life

C. Blockages to and difficulties in maintaining hope	Blockages
	 • Mental illness
	 • Traumatic experiences
	 • Grief
	 • Unconfronted aspects of the self
	 • Entrenched socio-economic circumstances
	
	 Therapist difficulties in maintaining hope
	 • Client not engaged
	   ○ in the process of therapy
	   ○ in *my* process of therapy
	 • Poorly developed therapeutic alliance
	 • Hopelessness as transference
	 • Poor client agency
	 • Entrenched socio-economic circumstances

D. The dialectic nature of hope and despair	• Two-sided coin • Acknowledgement of despair as the beginning of hope
E. Hope-focused strategies	• Relationship-focused strategies • Task-focused strategies • Transcendent and embodied strategies

Source: O'Hara & O'Hara, 2012.

Before moving on to identify such strategies we want to look at the ways therapists think about and conceptualise hope, as these understandings form the backdrop to how they then seek to work with hope in therapy.

To help us identify how therapists understand and orientate themselves to the issue of hope, we conducted a second study which asked therapists two main questions: (1) 'How do you understand and conceptualise hope?' and (2) 'How do you operationalise hope in therapy?' The study was a qualitative examination of these questions and the findings are summarised in Table 6 (O'Hara & O'Hara, 2012).

A. Nature and source of hope

Sixty-five therapists were recruited and were asked to complete a short-answer questionnaire focusing on the strategies they use to foster hope in therapy. An additional eleven therapists were interviewed regarding their views about the nature of hope and its operationalisation within therapy. The range of definitions provided by the participants was very consistent with existing research. The key definitional theme was that hope is an expectation of a positive future. It was also understood to have both cognitive and affective dimensions. In addition to the range of definitions of hope that were provided, the participants saw hope as having different sources. The sources identified are listed below.

- Internal source
  - Validation of self
- External source
  - Interpersonal support
  - Societal support and cultural wisdom (lore)
  - Spirituality

The internal source of hope was best summed up as a belief in oneself. This is particularly interesting in light of the findings of the first study reported above. These qualitative findings corroborate the quantitative results that identify the self-differentiation factor of *I-position* as being linked to a person's capacity to hope.

The external sources of hope were reported as being from three broad areas. The first of these is interpersonal support and refers to the importance of family and friends as the mainstay of one's support system. When people have strong relationships and a range of interpersonal connections, their general level of hope tends to be high. Hope was also perceived to be sourced through a wider set of societal relationships and cultural wisdom. Society can provide support for a hopeful outlook via a range of mechanisms, including membership of community, social and sporting groups. It might also include mental health networks and access to professionals likes doctors, nurses, social workers, psychologists, and counsellors. Inherent within these various social networks is a broader cultural set of understandings that can also support psychological well-being. Participants in the study referred to such knowledge as 'wisdom'. An example of this is the idea that in circumstances of pain and difficulty, it is of benefit to realise that 'This too shall pass'. Finally, spirituality was acknowledged as being an important source of hope. Spirituality is important because it provides a deep sense of meaning-making. Through our spirituality we make sense of the world. By trusting in a more transcendent dimension of our existence, we are often able to see past the transient troubles of the present moment and find a measure of calm and peace.

B. Hope stance and orientation

The participants in the study orientated themselves to the issue of hope in different ways and to different degrees. The first referred to the general stance taken towards hope. A helpful way of clarifying one's hope stance is to ask the question, 'What do you hope in?' The answers provided included hope in:

- Different aspects of otherness
- Impermanence
- Intentionality
- Transcendence.

The first hope stance position concerns *otherness*, that is, hope in relationship. Relationships consistently factor as the central source and foundation of hope. When we welcome and embrace relationships we welcome and embrace hope. It is through the encouragement of others that we are able to hope. The importance of relationships in the establishment and maintenance of hope is a central theme of this book. Without the support of others there would be little hope.

The second stance of hope is *impermanence*. This captures the very important belief in the possibility of change. Change can encompass many things, change in age and stage of life, change in the status of relationships from son or daughter to partner, parent, and friend. Impermanence also means that problems do not always stay static and remain. The fact that even our struggles have a limited life provides its own measure of hope.

Intentionality refers to the goal-focused dimension of hope. Snyder's work on hope highlights the centrality of goals, pathways, and agency and is a very good representation of this stance. To be hopeful from this perspective, one looks to the future with expectancy but with particular goals and intentions in mind. This stance presupposes a belief in the possible of the attainment of one's desires and goals. To hope is to take action to enable our intentions to be realised.

Finally, *transcendence* is a hope stance because it directs the individual's attention to support from outside the self. Those with a transcendent stance believe that the universe is predominantly benevolent and therefore oriented towards their personal good. For many with this stance, hope is also connected to the possibility of personal ongoing existence beyond the temporal world. Such a view provides hope because it establishes a system of belief that enables us to transcend the struggle of present-day difficulties.

Apart from the general stance taken towards hope by the therapist, the participants also commented on the more specific foci they applied to hope within therapy itself and particularly to individual clients. This is referred to as 'hope orientation within therapy' and four different types are listed below:

- Hope *in* the client
- Hope *for* the client
- Hope *in* the counselling process
- Hope *in* life.

Each of these four orientations is seen as being complementary but discrete. Hope *in* the client focuses on the therapist's belief in the client's capacity for change. Such a view is consistent with Rogers' (1957) assertion that if the necessary and sufficient conditions of change are met, especially the core conditions of unconditional positive regard, genuineness, and empathy, then the client's own resources for change will be enabled, transporting them towards health. This orientation implies a very positive view of human potential and therefore focuses hope in the client. The therapist pays attention to the client's own strengths and resources and seeks to nurture them until the client is able to fully activate these capacities themselves.

Hope *for* the client is about a desire for the client to do well, a deeply held concern for their well-being. Such an orientation highlights human kinship and connectedness. It is grounded in a deep empathy for the other. Hope for the client enables the therapist to *hold* the client's fears, pains, and despair, and to shoulder the burden for them for a time. Holding hope for the client occurs when the therapist is more focused on *being with, feeling with*, and some have suggested, *suffering with* the client (Bion, 1962; Borenstein, 2003; Fleming, 2005; Gravell, 2010). It is a form of burden-bearing that provides relief to the client long enough for them to move beyond the constraints of their present struggle.

Hope *in* the counselling process focuses the therapist's expectancy on the power and benefits of the whole therapeutic enterprise. It acknowledges the power of the human interchange and its potential to heal. It values both the skills of the therapist and the resources of the client. When hope seems at its lowest, the therapist holds onto the belief that the process of therapy itself will win the day.

The final hope within therapy orientation is founded on a belief in the generativity of life. The therapist is able to hold onto hope for the client because he or she can see beyond the present struggle and believes in the possibility of a brighter day. From this position the therapist is able to draw on a world and life view which is full of hope, and in so doing quietly inspire in the client a belief in the same. From this perspective life presents challenges to be overcome and offers opportunities for personal growth. Life is full of potential and new possibilities.

C. Blockages to and difficulties in maintaining hope

Even though hope is accepted as one of the four common factors of therapeutic change, it is not a factor that is always easy to establish. Therapists in the study recognised a number of difficulties that they saw had the potential to block the emergence of hope. In addition, there were a number of difficulties that the therapists themselves struggled with, which also limited hope's emergence. The identified client blockages were:

- Mental illness
- Traumatic experiences
- Grief
- Unconfronted aspects of the self
- Entrenched socio-economic circumstances.

The therapists acknowledged that substantial mental illness can act as a block to the establishment of hope or can be at least a significant limitation. This is not to say that those struggling with some form of mental illness cannot find hope. It does mean that in many cases the work of finding hope is made more difficult. The work of therapy is very much about finding hope for all those who seek it and therapists accept the challenge of helping those most in need. Another type of block that the participants in the study felt made the recovery of hope difficult was the client's experience of trauma. This was especially so if the trauma was experienced in childhood. Trauma was generally related to attachment-based problems or severe abuse of various kinds. Participant therapists saw trauma as setting up confusion in the individual's sense of self, and limiting the foundation stones from which hope can be built. The recovery of hope has very much to do with an individual's sense of self, as discussed earlier. Trauma by its very nature disrupts the self-construct, resulting in impairment of the individual's capacity for relationship. This disruption also impacts on the ability to trust, which is an essential feature of hope.

A third blockage to hope is the experience of grief. Grief can be seen to take two forms: normal grief, and pathological or complicated grief. Hope is difficult to find in either type but especially so in complicated grief (Drenth, Herbst, & Strydom, 2010). The normal grieving process challenges an individual's view of life and highlights human limitations and mortality. This process is not unhealthy and given enough time and support the grieving client will return to a balanced view of life. When this happens, hope returns. When grief becomes stuck and entrenched, hope is restrained. Complicated grief is not dissimilar to trauma and as with clients who have been traumatised, therapy offers significant opportunity for healing. Working through trauma and grief responses enables a more balanced form of meaning-making and thus a return to a hopeful outlook.

The next sub-category related to blockage of hope is unconfronted aspects of the self. This refers to those aspects of the self that we either do not know about or refuse to acknowledge, but that get in the way of healthy functioning. For example, if an individual holds a core belief that states, 'The world is against me and I will never get what I want in life', it will be very difficult to maintain a hopeful outlook. Another example of a hope-squelching core belief is, 'I am a bad person and therefore don't deserve good things to happen to me'. Sometimes people are consciously aware of holding such beliefs but quite often they are either unconscious or suppressed. When these aspects of self-belief are identified, challenged, and restructured, the result is an increased capacity to hope.

Apart from these blockages the participants in the study also acknowledged that hope was sometimes limited by external factors such as poverty, lack of education, racism, or some other socio-economic restrictions. Sometimes it is people's environmental circumstances that form the major blockage to hope. Some people, given the opportunity to change their socio-economic circumstances, might well find hope more easily.

In addition to the blockages just identified, a number of in-therapy factors were also recognised as impacting on therapists and their capacity to encourage hope in their clients. These were referred to as the 'therapist's difficulties in maintaining hope' and they are listed below.

- Client not engaged
    - In the process of therapy
    - In *my* process of therapy
- Poorly developed therapeutic alliance
- Hopelessness as transference
- Poor client agency
    - Entrenched socio-economic circumstances

The first two were variations of the same issue: the client not being fully engaged in the process of therapy. Of course any individual who participates in therapy is not fully focused all the time or even necessarily in agreement with the therapist all of the time. This is not problematic if generally there is a good connection between the therapist and client. Sometimes, however, clients struggle to fully engage in therapy even though they come along regularly. This may be the case for several reasons. One might be that they feel that they and the therapist do not really have common goals. Research confirms that when this happens therapy is less likely to be effective (Bordin, 1979). Another possible reason for a lack of engagement is that the client may not be ready or committed to change. Therapeutic change is very dependent upon the client's desire and motivation to change. If this is not present at the time of therapy there is little likelihood that therapeutic progress will be made. While general client engagement in the counselling process is essential, sometimes the problem is more nuanced. The client may have a level of willingness to participate in the therapy process but not be familiar or comfortable with the therapist's approach to therapy. Current research confirms that therapist–client matching is an important issue and is actually a factor in establishing and maintaining the therapeutic alliance (Beutler et al., 2011). A poor fit between the participants in therapy can make the experience uncomfortable for both the client and the therapist.

As is well known, the therapeutic alliance is a central factor in therapeutic change and therefore largely determines positive outcomes. Apart from mismatching and client readiness as just mentioned, the alliance can be limited by other factors. One of the important prerequisites for the establishment of a therapeutic alliance is a capacity in the client to form relational attachments. Some people, because of their developmental experiences, have a very limited capacity to form healthy attachments. Confused and chaotic attachment experiences in childhood tend to limit the possibility of forming secure adult relationships. While disruptive developmental experiences can make adult relationships more problematic, this does not mean that it is impossible over time to develop them. It does mean though that the task is more difficult and fraught, resulting in challenges to the establishment and maintenance of a hopeful outlook. Another limitation to the development of a healthy therapeutic relationship is the capacity in the client for psychological mindedness. This refers to the ability to think in psychological terms and to see the links between unconscious processes, cognitions, emotions, and behaviour. While some people find it relatively easy to see connections between past experiences or certain thought processes and feeling states and behaviours, others do not. A limitation in psychological mindedness means that the client may struggle to process what the therapist may be trying to do in therapy. Ultimately any factor which disrupts the therapeutic relationship between therapist and client limits the whole therapeutic enterprise and along with it hope.

A further difficulty that therapists encounter within therapy is transference. Transference is a defence mechanism first identified by Freud and it forms an essential part of the process of therapy, particularly within psychoanalytic and psychodynamic schools of psychotherapy. Transference is the process of projecting feelings and expectations that one has for one person onto another. Freud understood transference to be a defence mechanism because it provides some measure of protection from one's own feelings and thoughts that one unconsciously perceives to be too difficult to confront. There may well be good reasons why an individual is not ready to confront certain thoughts and feelings, especially if they are associated with unpleasant experiences from early childhood. Transference usually occurs when relating to another who unconsciously reminds us of the original offending other. The person with whom we are currently relating may not look like the person of the past, but some mannerisms or attitudes may appear to be similar enough to trigger unconscious defences. Transference is usually a process of projecting negative expectations onto another, but it can also include positive but unrealistic expectations of the other. For example, the other may represent an idealised person with whom one would like to share romantic feelings. The critical issue in transference is that it is fundamentally an unconscious process of projecting thoughts, feelings and expectations that one has for one person onto another.

Transference can form an important part of the therapeutic process because it provides the therapist with access to the client's intrapsychic processes and also allows the client to work through issues with a boundaried but aware other. When a client feels angry with a therapist it is either because they are angry within the context of the present therapist–client relationship or they are angry because the present relationship is representative of a past relationship. In the latter case the therapist receives the ire of the client but in reality is not the real object of the anger. The therapeutic relationship, however, becomes the site through which the client's anger can be processed and resolved.

The content of some projections sometimes demands that the therapist see the client in a negative light. For example, the client may expect that the therapist will see them as pathetic, troublesome, or hopeless. When this happens the client believes that the therapist will have a negative view of them and then relates to the therapist consistent with their own expectation. Hence, the client may unconsciously think, 'I believe you think I am pathetic, so I will act in a pathetic manner'. In such cases the therapist is caught in an interesting tangle of projective expectations, misapprehensions, and responses. Another example is when the client defines themselves as a victim and lives according to this persona. The projection then becomes 'I am a victim and I expect you to relate to me as a victim and not expect anything more of me'. There are many such scenarios, all of which can be very challenging to work with. To varying degrees these situations make the possibility of discovering hope for change much more difficult. The experienced therapist, however, maintains a belief in the possibility of positive change and holds onto hope.

A final difficulty that was identified by the therapists in the study was poor client agency. This refers to a limited ability to take action to improve one's situation. Agency is related to the concept of self-efficacy and of belief in one's own ability to engage with life and to effect change. Those with a high degree of self-efficacy see possibilities, look for alternatives, and take action. Some people are by personality much more incisive, creative, and action-oriented than others. Apart from personality differences though, an individual's level of agency might also be affected by upbringing and wider socio-economic circumstances. While poor socio-economic conditions are certainly external limitations, they can also impact the individual intrapsychically. This means that the experience of poverty, neglect, poor education, and so on might become internalised and therefore shape the individual's view of themselves. This then becomes its own blockage to hope. The issue of the self keeps recurring as a central feature of hope. Without a well-formed and grounded self it becomes difficult to hold hope.

D. The dialectic nature of hope and despair

Hope and despair are often co-occurring experiences. When one despairs, one needs hope. Despair is typically an experience which people want to be rid of. This is understandable as it is an unpleasant state. However, despair can also be an opportunity for growth. Despair demands our attention. It signals that all is not well. When we are in pain and struggle we are much more prepared to examine ourselves and to reflect on our life. Pain causes us to take stock and it increases our readiness to change.

Another interesting aspect of the despair/hope duplex is that we often think of them as non-compatible states. That is, we think that we cannot despair and hope at the same time. Flaskas (2007) argues that despair and hope are often at work simultaneously. Clients can, for example, express despair in one moment and soon after express hope in their future. It would be unwise for therapists to seek to rid clients too quickly of their despair, as the struggle is often an important part of the process of healing. When despair becomes debilitating and dangerous, then action must be taken to ensure the health and safety of the client. At other times, despair needs to be allowed its place in the healing process.

The therapists in our second study expressed similar ideas and saw despair and hope as a two-sided coin, one existing alongside the other. One of the functions of despair, it seems, is to draw our attention to the essentials of our struggles so that we can explore the possibility of change. In this respect, despair can become the beginning of hope.

E. Hope-focused strategies

The final set of findings from of our study was around how therapists operationalised hope within therapy. Participant therapists identified a range of different hope-focused strategies that they used in their own practice. Some of these were more implicit and others explicit, but each was aimed at encouraging clients towards a positive future outlook and ultimately towards positive change.

These various strategies were grouped into three main categories:

- Relationship-focused strategies
- Task-focused strategies
- Transcendent and embodied strategies.

The relationship-focused strategies highlighted the centrality of the therapeutic alliance in the establishment of hope. The capacity of the therapist to journey with the client in their struggles, questions, and reflections was seen as an essential aspect of engendering hope. Also mentioned was the benefit of therapist encouragement and recognition of client strengths. Often clients are unaware of their own strengths and abilities and this in itself is a hindrance to hope. The therapist is in a unique position of being a supportive observer of the client's strengths and so is able to offer insightful comment on their potential for strength-based action.

The therapists also identified an array of specific strategies or tasks that encourage the establishment of a hopeful outlook. These strategies included cognitive, goal-focused, blockage removal, and psycho-educational approaches to therapeutic change. Even though the relationship is central to the therapeutic enterprise, sometimes tasks and actions are required to facilitate change. The very decision to take action is often the point of change and signals the return of hope.

The final set of hope-focused strategies were categorised as transcendent and embodied. These approaches rely less on cognitive and behavioural interventions and prioritise acceptance of and engagement with present experience. The importance of one's feelings and physicality are highlighted and are seen as ways of grounding reality. When an individual is in touch with his or her own bodily and feeling states then a deeper awareness and acceptance of present difficulties is made possible. Transcendent approaches can also focus particular attention on awareness of otherness – other people, nature, and higher powers. From the perspective of the transcendent and embodied strategies, hope is founded in a grounded reality and in an awareness of otherness in all its possibilities.

Summary

The influence of the therapist's hope should not be underestimated. While there is no doubt that the client's own resources (hope being one of them) are fundamentally important in the therapeutic enterprise, the therapist also brings with him or her a wealth of knowledge and resources which help to shape the outcomes of therapy. As mentioned at the beginning of this chapter, there is now growing evidence that the therapist's hope is one of the variables responsible for encouraging client change. The therapist's hope can be thought of as being present first in the whole person of the therapist, and second in the actions and strategies employed by the therapist in therapy. The hope-inspiring strategies used by the therapist are drawn from their training and experience, but more fundamentally from who they are as people. As Buechler (2002: 277) aptly expresses it, 'It is who we are, as people, as company on the journey, that inspires hope'. It is important that the therapist remembers that they themselves are a source of hope for others.

QUESTIONS FOR REFLECTION AND DISCUSSION

1   What do you see as your primary source of hope?
2   The responsibility placed on the counsellor to hold hope is a substantial one. What are your thoughts about this aspect of your role as a counsellor?
3   The personal quality referred to as the *differentiation of self* was shown in the reported research to be positively correlated with an individual's dispositional (trait) hope. This implies that the greater one's level of self-development, the greater one's capacity to hope. What do you see as some of the implications of these findings for the counsellor and for counsellor training?
4   A number of blockages and difficulties in developing and maintaining hope were identified in this chapter. What do you see as the issues that most challenge you to maintain hope for clients? Why?
5   The dialectic nature of hope and despair can be puzzling. In what ways do you see despair as a catalyst for hope?

7

Hope in therapy: practical strategies

In this chapter we aim to identify and explore further a range of hope-focused strategies that can be used in counselling and psychotherapy. The majority of these strategies are not new to therapists' practices, as hope-based work within therapy is implicit. What may be new is the intentional use of strategies for the purpose of engendering hope in clients. As has been outlined in previous chapters, hope is made up of multiple spheres and dimensions. Hope can be both generalised and particular. In its more generalised form, hope is characterised by a deep belief in a good and positive future without the requirement of a specific goal or end in mind. Such a hope is more than optimism as it is based in a realistic and grounded awareness of future possibilities and limitations and in maintaining a positive expectancy. Particularised hope is more specific and directed in its focus. This type of hope is characterised as being goal-focused, strategic, and motivational. Those expressing a particularised hope aim to achieve a designated goal, and they move towards it expectantly. Both forms of hope are reflected in therapy in the client's expression of hope but also in how the therapist works with hope. Hence, at times the therapist is aware that the client's hope is less goal-focused but nonetheless central and important to their exploration of presenting issues. At other times, the therapist is aware that the client has a very clear goal but is struggling either with its attainment or its loss. One of the important tasks of the therapist is to assess the nature of the client's hope and to identify how best to work with them to achieve their goals, to regain meaning and hope where it is floundering or lost, and to move practically towards a positive future.

Implicit strategies

In exploring the range and types of strategies that therapists use in hope-focused therapy, Larsen and Stege (2010a, b) distinguished between *implicit* and *explicit* ways of working. They found that therapists often regarded their work as implicitly hope-focused and therefore not necessarily requiring direct reference to hope. When hope was referred to as an implicit aspect of the therapist's way of working, it was often understood to be fundamentally grounded in the dynamics of the therapeutic relationship. Two actions of the relationship that they noted as encouraging hope are: witnessing client hopelessness and pain, and highlighting client resources.

Relationship-focused strategies

Witnessing client hopelessness and pain

Therapists in Larsen and Stege's study asserted that witnessing client hopelessness was in itself a powerful means by which hope was supported. They state:

> On the surface it may seem implausible that listening carefully to hopelessness could open the door to hope; nevertheless, some therapists stated that compassionately attending to client pain is a vitally important aspect of implicitly supporting client hope. (2010a: 278)

In a study that explored how therapists operationalise hope O'Hara and O'Hara (2012) also found that empathic witness of the client's struggle engenders hope. The participant therapists in their study commented on the significance of acknowledging the client's pain as an aspect of recovering hope. Another type of witness was also found in this study in the form of the client hearing themselves tell their story of struggle to another. It seems the therapeutic relationship provided a medium through which clients became witness to their own story. The relaying of their own story to an empathic other appeared to provide a unique opportunity for self-reflection. Self-reflection itself is an avenue for recovering a sense of hope. It may well be that this is largely due to the establishment of a clearer sense of self. Researchers such as Meares (2005) and Bateman and Fonagy (2006) lend support to this possibility and argue that reflectivity plays a central role in self-organisation. Fonagy and Target explain that reflective function is 'the developmental acquisition that permits the child to respond not only to other people's behavior, but to his *conception* of their beliefs, feelings, hopes, pretense, plans, and so on' (1997: 679). They regard reflective function to be a central aspect of what Fonagy and others have called mentalization. Mentalization is defined by Levy et al. as 'the capacity to evoke and reflect on one's own experience to make inferences about behavior in oneself and others' (2006: 1029). Given this, it is not surprising that hearing oneself recount one's own stories of struggle enables a reorganisation of the self and through it a recovery of a sense of hope.

Highlighting client resources

The second aspect of the relationship that fosters hope occurs when the therapist notices and highlights the client's own resources. Sometimes this happens when the therapist points out initiatives the client has taken to foster positive change or highlights empowering responses the client has made to difficult circumstances. Collectively this aspect of therapy has been referred to as a strength-based approach and is particularly influenced by the works of White and Epston (1990) and De Shazer and Berg (1992). It is interesting how often clients are surprised when their strengths and abilities have been noticed and pointed out. It seems that people struggle to believe in their own capacities and when these strengths are noticed by a significant other, such as a therapist, they are encouraged to believe in themselves. A strength-based approach typically involves asking the client to remember a time when they used their strengths to good effect and then to apply these strengths to their current situation. For example, the client may be invited to think of a time when they didn't capitulate to others' demands (the exception) and to consider the benefits this produced. The therapist then may highlight this largely hidden strength and encourage the client to apply it in other situations.

Self-disclosure

Another opportunity for hope recovery that is mediated by the therapeutic relationship is therapist self-disclosure (Knox & Hill, 2003). The appropriate and judicious use of therapist self-disclosure has been demonstrated to enhance the therapeutic relationship and encourage client self-disclosure. In examining the research evidence Knox and Hill (2003: 538) concluded that:

> When used sparingly, when containing non-threatening and moderately intimate content, and when done in the service of the client, therapist self-disclosure can help establish and enhance a therapeutic relationship, model appropriate disclosure, reassure and support clients, and facilitate gains in insight and action.

Knox and Hill identified seven sub-types of self-disclosure. These include disclosure of:

- Facts
- Feelings
- Insight
- Strategy
- Reassurance/support
- Challenge
- Immediacy.

(For a full discussion see Knox & Hill, 2003).

These authors assert that self-disclosure used cautiously, and preferably not of an overly intimate nature, fosters a stronger therapeutic alliance that in turn enhances the possibility of a positive and hope-filled outlook.

Perspective change

Larsen and Stege (2010a) also identified a number of other implicit strategies for working with hope in therapy, collectively referred to as 'perspective change'. The various strategies involved in perspective change tend to be more cognitive than behavioural and are used to shift or expand the client's point of view. The strategies listed are *reframing, metaphor, externalisation,* and *humour.*

Reframing

Reframing involves reviewing the meaning the client attaches to a problem. This may be done in a number of ways, Socratic questioning and challenge being common approaches. Reframing is often used within cognitive therapy and when applied well, causes the client to re-evaluate their existing understanding of a problem and to propose possible ways of either resolving or managing it. A good example of this is seen in therapeutic discussions with those struggling with anxiety. Often people experiencing panic are overtaken with fear and imagine the worst. They expect that harm is likely to come to them in some way, and this fear leads to avoidant behaviour that only serves to exacerbate and reinforce the fear response. When such clients are asked what they imagine is the worst possibility, they often respond that they are likely to faint or embarrass themselves socially. When asked whether they could possibly manage such situations, that is, recover from fainting or survive the embarrassment, they usually are surprised to respond that they could. Confronting the existing meanings associated with a problem, in this case anxiety, provides the opportunity for a reframing of that meaning. In the case just mentioned, the client is encouraged not only to believe that they can manage panic situations, but they might also be encouraged to see such situations as opportunities for overcoming anxiety. Social encounters and feelings of panic, while still challenging, are reframed as opportunities for personal growth.

Metaphor

Metaphor can be a powerful tool in enabling perspective change as it provides associative links to alternative meanings. Metaphors often provide non-linear avenues through which new meanings can be forged (Kopp, 1995). The benefits of metaphor have long been recognised in psychotherapy. Long and Lepper (2008: 343–4) assert:

> Metaphor can be understood to help patients access memories and feelings ... to provide a shared entry for the therapeutic dyad into the patient's inner world, self-identity and ways of relating ... Metaphor is inextricably linked to the narratives we construct about ourselves to make coherent and meaningful sense of our lives ...

Lakoff (1993) has found that metaphor is a central organising principle in the way we think and therefore it is not surprising that its use facilitates a reorganisation of the self and through this the re-establishment of hope. Long and Lepper (2008) agree that the use of metaphor is an important part of the process of self-organisation. In this respect it forms an essential dimension of mentalization as conceptualised by Bateman and Fonagy (2006). In their study of the use of metaphor in psychoanalytic psychotherapy, Long and Lepper found that metaphor was used in eighty-nine per cent of mentalising exchanges between therapist and client. Meares (2005) likens metaphor to the external play space of the child. The adult no longer has a sandpit in which to play but does have the mental screen of the metaphor upon which to project thoughts and ideas. This being the case, metaphor allows the client the opportunity to reflect on and imagine new ways of being and in so doing to recapture hope.

Meares suggests that therapists should be mindful not to force metaphors upon clients as they need to emerge organically. He recommends that the therapist pay attention to the language of the client and to listen to metaphorical and analogous references and then to gently build upon them. In one example, he noted that a deeply depressed client who had been physically abused in relationships momentarily stepped out of her typical script of woe and commented that she really wished she could be a gypsy. The therapist, aware of this metaphorical shift, asked why being a gypsy would be so wonderful. The client replied that gypsies have the opportunity to travel, listen to music, dance, sing, and be free. This type of musing takes the individual away from the imperative of their dominant narrative or script and allows them an opportunity to see differently, even if only for a moment. When many more of these moments are experienced a platform is formed from which to launch challenges to old dominant narratives. When this occurs the reorganisation of self-expectations and beliefs is made possible.

Externalisation

Externalisation is a strategy that has been promoted by both solution-focused and narrative therapists and involves situating the problem outside of the individual. Typically the problem is personified and then represented by a common object present in the room like a vase or tissue box. The act of separating the problem from the client encourages a new sense of client agency in relationship to the problem issue. Similar to the identification of exceptions (as mentioned earlier), externalisation of problems often meets with surprise on the part of the client. When the problem is given voice via the licence of personification, the client is often able to gain a new perspective and to see the negative and often insidious power the problem has wielded in the client's life. Once the person recognises the heretofore manipulation of them by the problem, a new sense of agency emerges.

In reference to this strategy, I recall a case of a young woman who struggled with self-loathing. She constantly battled a highly critical inner voice that continuously told her how horrible she was. When externalised, the inner critic was given the name 'Revolting'. I asked the client to identify the daily onslaught of vitriolic comments shouted by Revolting. We briefly discussed these comments as they were identified, eventually collecting a long list. While this was a difficult task, it soon became obvious to the client that this diatribe of abuse was a ridiculous and unfounded assault. This was particularly evident when a second list containing the client's personal desires, goals, and qualities was itemised and compared with the list of negative qualities asserted by the inner critic. When an individual is able to gain some distance and perspective on a problem situation, hope can be more readily envisaged.

Humour

The use of humour was identified by Larsen and Stege (2010a) as another implicit hope-inspiring strategy. They suggested that humour provides an environment through which the client is more able, at times, to receive therapist challenge. The stress of different circumstances can sometimes be moderated through humour, allowing a review of the problem and potential perspective change. Humour has the capacity to ground the individual and to help to normalise the problem. It also provides an avenue for stress release and encourages one to step outside the struggle and take stock.

Summary of implicit hope-promoting strategies

Relationship-focused strategies

- Therapist witness of the client's hopelessness and pain
- The client listening to (witnessing) their own story in the context of an empathic other
- Therapist self-disclosure
- Noting and encouraging client's own strengths and resources

Perspective change

- Reframing
- Metaphor
- Externalisation
- Humour

Explicit strategies

In part two of their study Larsen and Stege (2010b) sought to identify explicit hope-focused strategies. They listed *cognitive/goals, behaviour, temporal aspects of hope, embodied emotion, relationships, psycho-education,* and *exploring threats to hope* as key strategies. O'Hara and O'Hara (2012) identified similar findings, adding *blockage removal, social engagement,* and *transpersonal strategies* to the list.

Cognitive/goal-focused strategies

A cognitive and goal-focused approach to hope is well developed in the work of Snyder (2000; 2002) and colleagues. As outlined in Chapter 4, Snyder's approach is based on the view that hope consists of *goals, pathways*, and *agency*. The aim is to encourage growth and clarity in each of these dimensions.

Goals

Goals themselves can be clarified by asking clients direct questions. The use of work-sheets can also facilitate goal clarification (see Appendix). In a study conducted in the University of Bern therapy outpatient clinic, Holtforth and Grawe (2002) identified the type and frequency of client goals of about 300 clients. From the range of problems presented, a list of five goal categories was identified. The percentages of clients presenting within each category is listed below.

Interpersonal goals – 74.5%
Coping with specific problems/symptoms – 60.3%
Personal growth – 45.9%
Well-being/functioning – 13.4%
Existential issues – 11.1%

When exploring the nature of goals, one of the emphases that Snyder sought to highlight was their positive nature. As evidenced in the research, the language of goals can be diverse. Goals can have a problem focus, a solution focus, or a more existential focus. The general tenor of goals though should contain a strong sense of forward movement towards positive change.

One of the potential difficulties of working with client goals is that clients are not always clear about them. Quite often people come to therapy because they feel frustrated with their life circumstances and know that there are problems, but at the same time are not clear themselves what the central issues are. One of the tasks of therapy is to help clients identify the key issues they wish to work on. Therapists need to be highly sensitive to the client's readiness to identify and articulate not just their problems but the resulting goals associated with alleviating them. The primary thing the therapist must remember is that therapy is a dialogue within the context of a therapeutic relationship. Therapy is not a task to perform but a relationship to develop, which has at its centre a purpose. In their book on *Pluralistic Counselling and Psychotherapy* Mick Cooper and John McLeod (2011) identify the importance of aiding clients to articulate their goals. They suggest a gentle introduction to the topic of goal identification and provide sample starter questions. These are listed below.

- 'Do you have a sense of what you want from our work together?'
- 'What do you hope to get out of therapy?'
- 'So I wonder what's brought you here?'
- 'What kind of things would you like to change in your life?'
- 'What do you see as the goals for this therapeutic work?'
- 'Where would you like to be by the end of therapy?'
- 'If you were to say just one word about what you wanted from this therapy, what would it be?'

- 'What would have to be minimally different in your life for you to consider our work together a success?'
- 'What will be the first sign for you that you have taken a solid step on the road to improvement even though you might not yet be out of the woods?' (Duncan, et al., 2004: 69) (Cooper & McLeod, 2011: 72)

If clients struggle to identify goals, the use of the 'miracle question', as promoted in solution-focused therapy, is worth considering. When using the miracle question, the therapist asks the client to imagine waking up the following morning to discover that a hoped-for miracle had occurred. The client is asked to identify what this miracle might be and to clarify specific details of the change in circumstances. The aim of the exercise is to aid the client in imagining new possibilities and to help them break free from a problem orientation and to move towards a solution orientation.

An additional issue that can cloud the identification of goals is the fact that goals exist in a hierarchy of values. Higher-order goals may look quite different to lower-order goals and even at times may seem to conflict. For instance, the goal of having a good work–life balance (or more appropriately, a work–leisure balance because work is life too) may conflict with reaching a certain level of seniority in one's job. The pressure to work longer hours to achieve recognition and promotion may vie for priority over the needs of family. The relative hierarchy of one's values largely determines the attention and energy we give to any life topic. If money is high on our list of values, and relationships is lower on our list (albeit still important), attention to money will be prioritised. What we value will be reflected in our goals and in the energy we give to them. The challenge for the therapist is to listen carefully to the client's values, usually evident in their use of language, and to help them identify not only the goals but the value emphasis inherent within them.

A final note about exploring goals in therapy concerns a clash of therapist and client priorities. When the client articulates goals that the therapist either doesn't value or thinks are not helpful for the client at this time, the therapist is left with a decision to make. Will the therapist follow the client in their pursuit of their stated goal or will he or she raise a discussion about the suitability of the goal? There is no easy answer to this question. A helpful principle to follow though is that we as therapists should value the client's own sense of direction and provide them the space to explore it, unless there is potential for harm to themselves or others. Therapists need to have the capacity to challenge the client when needed, but always within the context of valuing the client's autonomy.

Pathways

Snyder suggests that if client goals are not clear then it is difficult to move on to explore routes or pathway towards those goals. Goal pathways are basically strategies that can be employed to reach goals. High-hope people tend to have a developed facility in identifying a range of goal pathways. One of the hope-focused tasks of therapy is therapist–client collaboration aimed at identifying a range of possible goal pathways. One of the benefits of collaboration is that it encourages client agency and motivation. A number of suggestions for promoting pathways thinking are listed in Box 7.1.

BOX 7.1   A PATHWAYS CHECKLIST

To assist in the development of effective pathways, Snyder (1994: 189) offers the following checklist for pathways that could be shared with clients.

DO

- Break a long-range goal into steps or sub-goals.
- Begin your pursuit of a distant goal by concentrating on the first sub-goal.
- Practice making routes to your goals and select the best one.
- In your mind rehearse what you will need to do to attain your goal.
- Mentally rehearse scripts for what you would do should you encounter a blockage.
- Conclude that you didn't use a workable strategy when you didn't reach a goal, rather than harshly blaming yourself.
- If you need a new skill to reach your goal, learn it.
- Cultivate two-way friendships where you can give and get advice.
- Be willing to ask for help when you don't know how to get to a desired goal.

DON'T

- Think you can reach your big goals all at once.
- Be too hurried in producing routes to your goals.
- Be rushed to select the best or first route to your goal.
- Overthink with the idea of finding one perfect route to your goal.
- Stop thinking about alternative routes when one doesn't work.
- Conclude you are lacking in talent or are no good when an initial strategy fails.
- Be caught off guard when one approach doesn't work.
- Get into friendships where you are praised for not coming up with solutions to your problems.

Sometimes clients struggle to identify goals and this can be for two main reasons. The first is that the existing focus is too narrow and needs to be widened. For example, instead of focusing on one area of life, such as a problem at work, the field of reflection should also encompass relationships, leisure, family, personal growth, and so on. When a more holistic view of one's life and circumstances is incorporated into a discussion of goals, a clearer picture can emerge. The second reason that goals can be difficult to identify is because the problem is less about goal identification and more about issues of acceptance. The Western mind often thinks in terms of future attainment and success and less in terms of being present to the moment and of accepting what is. It is important that the therapist be mindful of this distinction and not press for goal attainment when attainment may not be the central issue.

Agency

Sometimes the client has a clear goal and a set of viable strategies to reach their goals but still struggles to engage with the task of goal attainment. Often when this occurs the problem is a lack of motivation. When motivation is limited, a perceived inability on the part of the individual to progress along the identified pathways towards goal attainment may be the cause. This ultimately comes down to self-belief. Dysfunctional thoughts like all-or-nothing thinking can scupper attempts at goal achievement from the outset. Clients can be greatly helped by having the opportunity to explore and challenge thoughts that limit their self-belief. A number of agency-promoting suggestions are listed in Box 7.2.

BOX 7.2   AN AGENCY CHECKLIST

Snyder (1994: 204) suggests the following agency checklist that could be shared with clients.

DO

- Tell yourself that you have chosen the goal, so it is your job to go after it.
- Learn to talk to yourself in positive voices.
- Anticipate roadblocks that may happen.
- Think of problems as challenges that arouse you.
- Recall your previous successful goal pursuits, particularly when you are in a jam.
- Be able to laugh at yourself, especially if you encounter some impediment to your goal pursuits.
- Find a substitute goal when the original goal is blocked solidly.
- Enjoy the process of getting to your goals and not focus only on the final attainment.
- Focus on physical health, including diet, sleep, physical exercise, and avoiding damaging substances (e.g., caffeine-laden products, cigarettes, alcohol).
- Closely observe your local world, including the little things happening all around you.

DON'T

- Allow yourself to be surprised repeatedly by roadblocks that appear in your life.
- Try to squelch totally any internal put-down thoughts because this may only make them stronger.
- Get impatient if your willful thinking doesn't increase quickly.
- Panic when you run into a roadblock.

- Conclude that things will never change, especially if you are down.
- Engage in self-pity when faced with adversity.
- Take yourself so seriously all the time.
- Stick to a clocked goal when it is truly clocked.
- Constantly ask yourself how you are going to evaluate your progress towards a goal.

Snyder developed two goal worksheets that can be used to aid clients in the identification of goals and in the development of pathways and agency thinking (see Appendix).

Hope as behaviour

Sometimes regaining hope is less about achieving goals than it is about re-engaging in life in ordinary, everyday ways. O'Hara and O'Hara (2012) suggest that hope-based action can take two main forms: (1) through *personal pursuits* such as hobbies and physical exercise, and (2) through *social engagement* such as joining a community group. The key feature of action as a strategy is that it takes the individual away from negative ruminative thoughts and inaction and reinvigorates them through activity. The very decision to take action is in itself an act of hope.

Temporal aspects of hope

While hope is usually focused on the future, past experiences can also be used to encourage hope. One example of this is the recounting of hope-filled experiences. Narratives of hope – both of one's own experiences and of those of others – can be a wonderful way of reinvigorating hope. Being aware of the temporal dimension provides the therapist with additional strategies. It provides the therapist with an awareness that hope can be drawn from the *past*, the *present*, and *future*. A present-oriented strategy like mindfulness focuses the client's awareness on the benefits existing in the present day. Examples might include the beauty of nature, the blessing of good relationships, the benefits of good physical health, and so on. Sometimes clients first need to focus on the present before they begin to look towards the future. Apart from the goal-based discussion listed above, one future-oriented strategy is the use of creative imagination. Clients can be encouraged to 'play around' with imaginative possibilities, to experiment in their minds with the way they would like their future to be. Such a strategy not only can provide new goals but also encourages agency thinking. It is often surprising what emerges when people stop long enough to allow themselves the opportunity to imagine.

Embodied emotion

Larsen and Stege (2010b) use the term *embodied emotion* to capture a sense of the client's emotional and physical states. For example, a client might be asked to reflect on how they are feeling physically or emotionally in reference to a problem topic. The aim here is to aid the person in associating with a deeper experiential sense of self and in so doing provide potential links between existing feeling states and pre-ferred feelings. This can be a very useful strategy when the therapist observes that the client may not be fully in touch with their own feelings. An increased awareness of feelings encourages an integration of the whole person, thus freeing up hope-filled possibilities.

Hope in relationships

As mentioned earlier, the therapeutic relationship is one of the primary avenues through which hope is encouraged. This is also the case for relationships in general. Human beings are primarily relational beings and so any growth and development in relationships, especially family relationships, encourages hope. Conversely, when rela-tionships struggle or fail there is often a corresponding diminishment of hope. One of the advantages of systems therapies is the priority they place on the individual's wider relationship system. Often when we work with individuals we can forget that the person lives within a wider context of relationships and these are central to his or her sense of meaning in life.

Psycho-education and hope

When considering hope, psycho-education can be applied in several ways. One of these is by informing the client of the multidimensionality of hope. While hope is often thought of in terms of goal pursuit, it can also be considered an attitude or life orienta-tion. Exploring hope via its many dimensions, as outlined in Chapter 1, may help the client find new and as yet undiscovered hope. According to Dufault and Martocchio (1985) hope consists of six dimensions: affective, cognitive, behavioural, affiliative, tem-poral, and contextual. These dimensions can be used as a reference point for clients to reflect on how hopeful they are in each of these areas.

Exploring threats and blockages to hope

Explicit questioning about potential threats to hope may help clients pre-empt problems and thus maintain a hopeful outlook. Quite often it is the 'What if?' question that creates problems for people. This is because the question is not answered. It is posed, but leaves the individual to ruminate on negative possibilities without actually fully engaging in problem solving. Exploring threats to hope enables the client to assess unconfronted issues that may impede the emergence of hope.

The development of hope is a process and as such needs time to grow. It is important that therapists respect client readiness for change and assess contextual aspects of the client's world. For example, it is quite appropriate for a client in a state of grief and loss to experience limited hope. Under normal circumstances hope will return over time. If hope does not return, especially when the client desires that it would, then there may well be unresolved issues blocking its re-emergence.

Social engagement

Social engagement can be a powerful stimulator of hope as it reconnects the individual with others and by doing so revitalises a person's own sense of self. Reconnecting with others can be a simple exercise of arranging a coffee with a friend or playing a game of scrabble with others or deciding to play a social game of sport. The very action of stepping beyond the confines of one's everyday routine provides the individual with the possibility of re-energising and recapturing an outward focus. When we are with others we are often encouraged by their stories of struggles and successes. Such engagements help to normalise our own life experience and places us on the path to a hopeful outlook.

Transpersonal strategies

Transpersonal strategies involve any approaches that aid the client to find meaning beyond everyday and standard psychological interventions. Examples of this include mindfulness-based meditation, acceptance-based strategies, spiritual practices, and breath work, to name a few. Mindfulness as an approach within psychotherapy has been recognised as a powerful medium through which new meaning can emerge. Such practices often are less cognitive in orientation and seek to aid the client to find meaning through a connection with a greater sense of otherness. Otherness may be conceived of as being based in nature, other people, or in some higher power. If deemed appropriate, clients can be encouraged to explore these avenues and through them to find new meaning in their circumstances.

At the heart of transpersonal psychotherapeutic perspectives is the view that not all of life can be explained by the rational scientific mind. While the advances in science wrought through the breakthroughs of the Enlightenment are appreciated, the transpersonal therapist also acknowledges that both personal subjective, cultural intersubjective and social interobjective dimensions of existence need to be acknowledged (Wilbur, 1996). In other words, not all knowledge is brought about through reason and observation. There are in fact multiple ways of coming to know something. Some of these are personal and subjective; others are social and cultural. Transpersonal approaches within therapy either use strategies that allow a broadening of standard cognitive ways of making meaning or employ more explicitly non-rational approaches such as meditation. Bibliotherapy and personal journal writing are examples of more cognitive avenues. Bibiliotherapy refers to the use of books and other forms of literature as sources of information for general reflection and for discussion within therapy. Journal writing has long been used as a method of externalising inner thoughts and feelings and can be a powerful tool for self-discovery.

Non-rational strategies include those that aim to quieten or place in abeyance the rational and problem-solving aspects of the mind. Meditation is an example of this and can take several forms, *concentrated* and *open meditation* being two examples. Concentrated meditation is the use of repeated words and phrases to block out unwanted thoughts. Open meditation, broadly, is an approach that encourages the mind to drift, with the aim of opening one's awareness. While meditation as a practice has its base in spiritual traditions, its more accepted use within counselling and psychotherapy has come through the introduction of mindfulness-based therapy.

Another example of an approach that has synergy with spiritual approaches to personal growth is acceptance and commitment therapy (ACT). This approach was developed by Hayes and colleagues (Hayes, Strosahl, & Wilson, 1999) and promotes:

1   Acceptance of one's emotions and experiences
2   Cognitive diffusion (flexible as opposed to rigid thinking)
3   Being present
4   Self-context as focusing on a transcendent sense of self
5   Values (discovering what is most important to one's true self)
6   Acting consistently with one's values.

One distinguishing feature of ACT is its focus on the acceptance of problem situations as opposed to the drive to change them. Proponents of ACT argue that the Western mind believes that there is some given sense of what is normal psychological functioning and that any deviation from this is problematic. The result of such thinking is an avoidance of experiences, behaviours or thoughts that we don't like. ACT practitioners encourage clients to stay present to their feelings and to be aware of their sense of self and then act in accordance with their own intrinsic values.

Traditional spiritual or religious practices such as prayer, ritual, and ceremonies can also be avenues through which people find hope. One of the great benefits of these practices is that they provide a framework for focusing personal awareness and the awareness of awe and otherness. When we begin to see ourselves and our life struggles within a greater context of the world, other people, nature, and the wider spiritual sphere, a reorientation of our perspective can occur and bring some sense of balance between the temporal and eternal, between possibility and limitation.

CASE STUDY

Bill came to counselling to discuss a problem with his in-laws. He and his partner had been together for ten years but he had never really felt comfortable with his wife's parents. There were several reasons for this. The first of these had its genesis in the early days of Bill and Susan's relationship when her parents expressed, quite clearly, their dislike of him. While they did not make many overt statements, their behaviour was unambiguous. Bill was taken aback at the time and Susan was quite good in acknowledging his concerns and hurt and in voicing her disappointment of her parents' behaviour. Once Susan's parents realised that their daughter's relationship with Bill was a long-term commitment they made some attempt at acknowledging him and accepting him into the family, at least in principle. In reality they remained displeased with Susan's choice and so were happy to have minimal contact with Bill. Susan still liked to see her parents on a reasonably regular basis and so Bill and her parents could not completely avoid each other. The ongoing cold approach to Bill by Susan's parents was the second key aspect of the problem for Bill. He couldn't understand how they could hold their position of dislike of him over such an extended period of time.

As time went on, Bill grew more and more angry about the situation as he became increasingly aware of the implicit disrespect in his in-laws' behaviour. This made it harder for him to feel comfortable with them, at times resulting in expressions of overt hostility towards them. Of course, this did not help his relationship with Susan. Bill was generally a well-meaning and amiable person who was reasonably self-aware. However, try as he might, he could not shift his sense of outrage at his in-laws' non-acceptance of him. He tried disciplining his thinking and saying to himself that it did not matter. He made jokes about them when he felt stressed by the situation. However, instead of getting better over time, the situation was only getting worse. Bill was losing hope of ever getting over this struggle with Susan's parents' rejection of him. Something had to be done.

Activity

Either by yourself or in groups of threes and fours reflect on this case and suggest two different explicit hope-focused strategies of working with Bill. Write down the key aspects of the respective approaches you have selected. In what ways do these explicit strategies primarily seek to encourage a new and hopeful outlook?

Summary

In this chapter we have outlined a range of different hope-focused strategies that can be applied in therapy. Therapists can work with hope both implicitly and explicitly. Even when hope is implicit it informs the nature and direction of the therapeutic encounter. While not necessarily mentioned directly, it helps to join the therapist and client together in a movement towards a new and acceptable future. When hope is explicit it allows for more direct dialogue about the nature of the client's hope. The range of strategies reviewed in this chapter is by no means exhaustive, however it does provide a useful set of ideas for therapists seeking to foster hope in others.

QUESTIONS FOR REFLECTION AND DISCUSSION

1 Some researchers have argued that working explicitly with hope is unwise and places expectations on clients to find hope. What are your views on this issue?

2 Two aspects of the therapeutic relationship that were identified as encouraging hope were *witnessing* the client's pain and struggle and *noticing* their strengths. Either in pairs or small groups, recount examples from your own experience (either as therapist or client) of the benefits of witnessing pain and noticing strengths.

3 One of the strategies identified as encouraging perspective change was metaphor. It was suggested that metaphor is a type of psychological space that encourages reflectivity. Why is metaphor and reflectivity so important in psychological recovery? How might you encourage clients' metaphorical, reflective thinking? When might metaphorical thinking not be encouraged within therapy?

4 Transpersonal strategies are numerous and often a little different from typical ways of working in therapy. What do you see as the benefits and limitations of transpersonal approaches in inspiring hope?

8

Hope for those with severe and enduring psychological challenges

So far in this book we have defined hope, explored different theoretical perspectives of hope, examined the therapist's hope, and identified a range of strategies that can be used to foster it. Implicitly our discussion has referred to the average, fairly healthy person who encounters problems in living. It is true that at times we all struggle with a loss of hope and so it is not surprising that the topic is familiar to us. For most of us though, given enough time and support we overcome our struggles and return to hopefulness. While this may be the case for the majority of people, whether participating in therapy or not, there are some for whom the return from the depths of pain and suffering is much more difficult.

Victor Frankl (1959), the famous existential therapist and holocaust survivor, said that suffering equals pain without meaning. By this he meant that as human beings we are all going to experience pain but that pain is bearable if we can associate meaning with it. When our pain has no clear meaning, when we can make no sense of our situation, then we experience suffering. Frankl's view captures a fundamental feature of some people's experience of life – ongoing pain and suffering without any meaningful resolution.

Many people who struggle with severe and enduring psychological challenges live relatively normal lives. This may seem a contradiction because we usually expect those with more complex psychological issues to be hospitalised or in some form of care. The reality is that enduring psychological problems are more 'normal' than we think. The imperfection of the human condition makes us all vulnerable to psychological challenges. The difference for those who struggle more than the average person is that something has disrupted their capacity to find new and facilitative meaning. They have been stymied in their efforts to integrate their experiences of life and to move past the stuckness of their problems. The significance of this issue to our interests in this book is that the experience of entrenched psychological problems presents a great challenge to an individual's capacity to hope.

In this chapter we aim to explore where hope fits in the context of severe and enduring psychological problems. It might seem that hope is a possibility for the 'normal', 'average'

person (whomever and whatever that is?), but what of the person with long-term problems? Is hope a possibility for them? To examine this question we first have to outline
what we mean by severe psychological problems and also provide some description of
their aetiology. As this is not a book specifically on advanced mental illness our discussion will necessarily be limited. However, it is possible to provide a considered summary
of our thoughts on the topic. Let us state at the outset that the discovery and maintenance
of hope for those with enduring psychological conditions is possible, but we acknowledge
that their road to hope is more difficult.

It would be unrealistic and academically inappropriate to lump a collection of diagnostic categories into one bundle as if they were all the same. Someone struggling with
schizophrenia endures different challenges to someone struggling with anorexia nervosa
or bipolar disorder. Each person's trials are unique and personal. However, it is important to note that all of our psychosocial struggles have in common a central confusion
around the nature of the self. Who we are, and how we process the nature of being, is
a universal human concern. Of course, the subject of self is more challenging for some
than for others, but no one escapes the need to process this central life topic. When an
individual's experience and understanding of themselves becomes more confused and
fraught than it is for the average person, it can be debilitating. The resulting psychological confusion varies in degree, making it difficult to place one diagnostic label on the
experience. However, in an attempt to find a common language for a range of enduring
conditions, which is also less tainted by pathological overtones, we have preferred the
term 'fragile process' (Warner, 1991).

Fragile process

Those with severe and enduring psychological problems all experience a certain degree
of intrapsychic and interpersonal fragility. Fragility refers to both internal and interpersonal experiences. It means that psychologically fragile people struggle to make sense of
others and to make sense of themselves. It also means that they have unstable emotional
states that can result in mood swings and unexpected behaviours. They often experience
their lives as being chaotic and empty. Margaret Warner refers to people with psychological fragility as being in a state of 'fragile process'. She explains (1991: 43):

> Clients who have a fragile style of processing tend to experience core issues at very high
> or low levels of intensity. They tend to have difficulty starting and stopping experiences
> that are personally significant or emotionally connected. And, they are likely to have dif-
> ficulty taking the point of view of another person while remaining in contact with such
> experiences.

People in a fragile process can appear disconnected and switched off or alternatively
highly focused and overly aroused emotionally. In therapy such a person may at times
seem to be passive, resistant, or of low mood for the majority of a session and then suddenly launch into energetic spurts of verbiage when aroused by a particular topic. Once

aroused the individual may struggle to find emotional balance again, not knowing how to switch off the overflow of emotion. In one moment the person is struggling to feel any emotion and in another they are struggling to contain their emotion.

Another feature of fragile process is the difficulty in understanding one's own thoughts and feelings as well as interpreting the words and intentions of others. This refers to a limitation in the process that Peter Fonagy and colleagues have named 'mentalization'. Bateman and Fonagy (2006: 1) state that, 'Mentalization simply implies a focus on mental states in oneself or in others, particularly in explanations of behaviour'. A client's limited ability to mentalise can play out in therapy when the therapist offers a supportive reflection to the client – for example, 'That must be frustrating' – only to be surprised that the client has taken umbrage at the comment, becoming suddenly angry. What is occurring here is a limitation in the ability to process the other's (in this case the therapist's) intentions. It is as if the normal cues that the other person offers are not noticed or understood. This limitation in mentalising ability means that the person lives in a fog of confusion even though to others, they may appear to live a relatively normal life.

Limitations in mentalization can leave people experiencing life as a fragile process. Try as they might to make sense of themselves, situations, and relationships, they are left confused, despondent, and angry. They appear to be caught in a cycle of misinformation, inflated or deflated emotional states, and relational turmoil. While a state of fragile process can come and go at a moment's notice, each individual does have a dominant style of experience. Some have what Warner refers to as a high-intensity fragile process and others have a low-intensity fragile process. Those with high-intensity experiences are more likely to react, explode in anger, and be entangled in relational conflict. Those with a low-intensity style tend to manage their confusion by being detached, withdrawn, and by living with a low degree of depression on a constant basis.

Aetiological considerations

A burgeoning field of psychological research is the area of attachment theory. This field is concerned with how human beings form and maintain relationships throughout the lifespan, even into old age. While we cannot do justice to the wealth of knowledge that exists in this area, a number of key features of attachment theory are worthy of consideration in helping us explore the issue of fragile process and eventually in understanding its relationship with hope.

One of the great tasks of early human development is to distinguish between the self and other. Object relations theorists like Mahler (1975) and Winnicott (1971) highlighted the importance of the child moving from an awareness of a part-object such as the mother's breast to a realisation that the supplier of milk and comfort was a separate whole person. The dependency of the infant is made easier when the child realises that the other is wholly committed to their care and nurture, as demonstrated by the provision of sustenance and other comforts. Beyond these initial needs the developing child now has the further task of discovering their own sense of self via the relationship with this benevolent other. This undertaking of discovering or forging a self is one of life's great tasks. This is particularly so when one considers that at birth there is no real sense of self. Russell Meares (2005: 18) points out this stark reality when he states:

> We are not born with a self. However, the I, or the ego, is neurobiologically given. At birth we have a rudimentary ego, which matures as the central nervous system matures. The self is merely a possibility, a potential that will arise through an appropriate engagement of the child as 'I' with mother and other care givers.

The child first gains an emerging sense of self through seeing their own reflection in the eyes of their mother. They begin to see that there is something different about themselves. However, this early differentiation will not be enough to establish a solid sense of self. The self grows in response to otherness, particularly an awareness of mother as other. Research has demonstrated that infants are genetically endowed by the age of two weeks with the ability to discriminate between their mother's voice and face and those of other people (Carpenter, 1974). Mothers too appear to respond to their babies in common ways, which suggests that there is a genetic predisposition to do so. They heighten their voice around the newborn and stroke the baby, being careful to speak in comforting tones. Both infant and mother are primed to interact and communicate in such a way that by two months of age the mother and baby are well meshed. They are so attuned to each other that there is clear evidence of each responding to each other's cues. Trevarthen (1974) has termed this interplay *primary inter-subjectivity*. This form of relating has also been called a proto-conversation for it has all the hallmarks of a real conversation – each person responding synergistically to the other. It is in this zone of personal social responsiveness that the self begins to really develop.

One of the key features of the interplay between the infant and the mother is the mother's tendency to adjust to the baby's state at any given moment. When the baby is happy the mother responds specifically to the child's mirth, even encouraging further smiles and giggles. When the baby is upset, the mother's response is again attuned to the needs of the child at that moment. This responsiveness has been referred to as *mirroring*. In fact, mirroring only describes aspects of this process of responsiveness, for the mother typically does much more than reflect the child's responses. She usually adjusts these responses by either intentionally heightening them or calming them down, thus providing a deep sense of connectedness and safety. The interplay between baby and mother is dynamic in nature. Referring to this dynamic matching process Meares (2005: 22) states:

> Matching responses of the social environment are an essential element of the development of self, not only in infancy but throughout development. Failure of these responses, particularly at critical points of development, such as adolescence, may lead to a disturbance in the sense of personal reality and diminished feelings of the rhythms and substance of the body.

At the heart of the proto-conversation is emotion. Emotion is not just conveyed by the baby through facial expressions and vocalisations but also via the body. Emotions are reflected in bodily responses in adults as well, although infants are uninhibited and reflect a greater congruence between emotions, behaviours, and bodily responses. Feeling states form an important part of responsiveness to the extent that when there is a mismatch in communication between people there is a corresponding feeling response in the communicants. The child who has been well mirrored and therefore who has had the opportunity to develop an early conversation, is one who has experienced emotional responsiveness. This responsiveness is also experienced by the child as a form of teaching or training in understanding emotional states. For example, when the child is upset the mother attempts to moderate the child's state by first matching the child in a form of responsiveness which acknowledges the child's distress but which then also provides examples of soothing responses. The child learns through these engagements how to work with their emotions. When they become more able to do this the developing sense of self is held more secure and is not normally overwhelmed by emotional turmoil. This process goes on through a range of critical moments in development right through to teenagehood. The result in the average person is a developed sense of self, an ability to manage emotions, and a knowledge of how to respond appropriately to others. Bateman and Fonagy affirm the place of this child–adult relationship and state 'The emotional tone of the adult in relation to a specific experience can offer the infant a clue about whether it is safe, and more generally the child expects to receive all types of knowledge about the world through the mind of a trusted other' (2006: 3).

Another feature of mentalization is empathy. For many, empathy largely equates to mentalization, although Bateman and Fonagy disagree. For them empathy forms an important part of the mentalising process but it also falls short of being the whole process. While empathy is generally defined as the identification with and understanding of another's feelings and motives, it is commonly used in a narrower sense to mean an awareness and appreciation of another's emotional state. Modern neuroscience has confirmed the existence in humans of mirror neurons, which can be activated when observing others' emotions. For example, when we see someone who is upset, the same neural response is triggered in us as is in the person experiencing the upset. While this process is no doubt involved in mentalization it is not the whole story as there is no reflective component in neural mirroring as there is in mentalization. In fact the ability to reflect and imagine forms an essential dimension of mentalization. It is the individual's ability to stand back from an emotional experience and to reflect upon it and imagine different possibilities that promotes growth in the self. Empathy offered by one to another is important in this process because it provides for matching and the development of attunement, and it is from this position of safety and connectedness that the individual has the opportunity to reflect and understand.

According to Meares (2005) our imaginative capacities are best evidenced in the form of metaphor. When we imagine we try to create images that portray meaning. When a therapist, for example, listens intently to their client's story he or she is not just listening to the words used but to body language and to unconscious communication, which is usually first felt before it is coalesced into thought. In order to track the volume of information present within the therapeutic encounter, the therapist creates images of the other and of their experiences. Meares explains this well by stating 'As the patient throws upon the screen glimpses of half-seen forms, faint outlines, the therapist tries to fill in the gaps and make out the shapes' (2005: 179). Meares believes that metaphor and empathy are linked because empathy seeks to grasp the somewhat intangible aspect of the other's inner life and this is done via imagining the inner landscape of the other. As Meares further clarifies, 'Metaphor is necessary to the empathic process since the intangible movements of inner life can only be conveyed by means of things that can be seen and touched. Emotions, at bottom, are always expressed in terms of metaphor' (2005: 179–80).

These aetiological considerations form an important foundation for understanding how to work with people experiencing fragile process. The therapist must understand that human beings need to experience relational attunement throughout the lifespan and that this need for attunement therefore is an essential aspect of therapy. Through empathic attunement the client is freed to get in touch with their own emotions and then to 'play' with them in the form of metaphor, which provides the opportunity to rearrange the meanings of events and experiences. Empathic representations open up a more expansive state of mind allowing an evolving narrative of the self.

Working with fragile process towards a recovery of hope

When the experience of empathy and attunement is disrupted or is inadequate in an individual's childhood development, the developing sense of self is confused and stagnated. This results in more limited mentalization and also in a reduced ability to self-sooth emotions. Under normal circumstances the child is aided in their incorporation of emotions not only through emotional matching with the mother and other caregivers but also through the provision of language to describe emotions. As the child grows, their cognitive capacity to identify and perceive nuances of meaning increases. Growth in cognitive ability though is not completely automatic. It also requires additional relational and language-based information to stimulate and feed the growth. Hence, when a parent provides a range of terms to describe the child's feelings, the child learns to discriminate between nuances of meaning that they then can apply to themselves and others.

The mentally healthy person therefore is one who has achieved a substantial capacity to be aware of their own inner states and the inner states of others, to reflect on these states and experiences through both cognitive and imaginative avenues, and to regulate their own emotions. The person who experiences fragile process is diminished in these essential skills. There are varying degrees of fragile process and so for some people their dip into a moment of fragile process may be occasional and may only occur when triggered by specific contexts and content. For others, the experience of fragile process is commonplace, even a daily occurrence. Someone troubled by fragile process, especially of the latter kind, finds life and relationships terribly confusing, anxiety-filled, and debilitating, commonly resulting in experiences of depression and despair. In this context, the discovery of hope is made particularly difficult because the mechanisms required to make meaning (a central component of hope) are dysfunctional. Each time the person tries to move towards health they are thwarted by the cycle of misinterpretation of their own inner states and of the inner states of others. They are also further ensnared by their own unfettered emotions. The only conclusions people caught in this cycle of confusion can reach, is that either there is something terribly wrong with them or there is something terribly wrong with others. This results in feelings of emptiness, badness, confusion, and anger.

What is missing for those in this situation is an experience of relational connectedness extended over a substantial period of time through which they are provided the opportunity to 'play' with their own inner states. Given the right conditions, psychotherapy provides such an opportunity. The process of forging a self was never meant to be done alone. We are social beings and while we may have reached physical and cognitive maturity as adults, there is no guarantee that we have completed the work of creating a self – this must be done with others. There are many insightful authors capable of outlining paths towards this self-maturity. We particularly appreciate the more psychodynamically informed works of Kohut (1977), Hobson (1971, 1985), Kernberg (2006) and more recently the works of Bateman and Fonagy (2004, 2006), and Meares (2000, 2005). The writings of humanistic authors like Rogers (1957), Gendlin (1964), Warner (1991), Greenberg, Rice, and Elliott (1993) are also recommended. To simplify our description of recovery from fragile process we are largely going to rely on the work of Russell Meares.

Meares proposes that recovery from disruptions to the self must follow the trajectory of normal development. This means that just as the child required an environment of intimate connection where mirroring and empathy were present, so too the adult caught in the mire of an undeveloped self needs these experiences. Intimacy, mirroring, and empathy provide the context within which the self can develop, but these processes are required not only to provide a safe and nurturing environment but also to enable the opportunity for inner exploration through play. To use Meares' terms, psychotherapy provides the opportunity for *coupling, amplification*, and *representation*.

Coupling

Growth in the self only really occurs in situations of safety. When an individual is anxious or fearful, access to their inner world is restricted. In the early stages of the psychotherapy process the client is naturally unsure of the situation as he or she has not yet built a solid relationship with the therapist and so experiences a degree of anxiety. This is a natural happenstance but it does mean that the nature of the conversation between therapist and client will, for a time, resemble something of the proto-conversation between the infant and parent. By this we mean that much of the time will be spent finding ways that the therapist can mesh and match with the client and establish a degree of intimacy. A very good demonstration of this process is Carl Rogers' conversation with Gloria in the classic film series (Scoop It, 2012). Rogers' demeanour here evidenced his ability to provide what he regarded as the core conditions for change – genuineness, empathy, and unconditional positive regard. We would affirm with Rogers that these core conditions are not just skills to perform but attitudes to hold towards the other.

One of the difficulties of reproducing, in a sense, the proto-conversation with an adult is that the spontaneity and responsiveness of the child no longer exist. The adult has learnt a complex web of defences and disguises that obscure his or her true feelings. This makes the task of coupling or joining with the other in an empathic encounter much more challenging. The mirroring relationship enjoyed by the infant and his or her mother is characterised by spontaneity and the matching of emotional states. When the child cries, for example, the mother responds appropriately by soothing and calming the child. When the child laughs the mother joins in the laughter. The client is not likely to provide such spontaneous expressions of emotion for fear of being misunderstood, of losing connection with the therapist or even of being devalued. Meares suggests that the therapist's response of reflecting the fragile client's words and feelings back to them may not be enough to engender a deepening connection. This is because such individuals have failed to develop a sufficient degree of mentalising ability and are thus prone to misread the intentions of the therapist. As Meares (2005: 169) very aptly explains:

> The subject is caught in a cage of mirrors. Sometimes the reflections are worse than ineffective. In responding merely to what is presented, the therapist may be perpetuating a system of compliance. Rather than a façade, what must be appreciated is often shown as if in disguise, since positive emotions or creative expressions had been met in the past with responses that seemed crushing. Because of this, the individual mentions something that is intensely charged with personal meaning, nonchalantly, matter of factly, or as if in passing.

Coupling only really occurs when the therapist is able to link with the most personal component of what the client has just offered. The aim of the therapist is to mesh with any genuine sense of *aliveness* present. While the client's emotions may not be spontaneous like the child's, any offering that has a sense of *specialness* brings the therapist and client together in a deeper way. As Meares further explains, 'By listening, in a particular way, to the exact words and the way that they are used, one may begin to be able to use words that are repeated, words that seem usually loaded, or words that have a particular ring in them, a means of entering into previously unexplored areas of psychic life' (2005: 174).

One example from my own experience highlights the power of such encounters. A man who had had a particularly traumatic childhood had been coming to therapy for some time and had by the session in question developed with me sufficient trust to begin to risk more emotional content. At a moment in one session there was a perceptible shift in his demeanour. He slowed right down and, looking at the floor exclaimed, 'It rattled me to the core'. As if to emphasise the solemnity of this moment, he followed this with a pause and silence, giving me the opportunity to catch up with him. Fortunately, I was able to stay with this silence for a moment and then commented, 'To the core?!' At my response he became teary and was eventually stifling heaving gasps. The sudden intensity of his emotion affected me, giving me a greater sense of how profoundly difficult his life had been. The fact that I could share some small portion of his pain was an important part of the healing process. When reflecting on this encounter, I was taken by the depth of feeling connection. I was also struck by the client's degree of comfort later in the session. It appeared that the few moments of deep emotional synergy had strengthened the relationship overall. We seemed now to be operating together on a different plane. While the rest of the session was not as poignant as those moments just described, there was a noticeable development in connectedness.

The therapist must have a developed ability to focus on the particulars of the client's words, bodily cues, and emotional tenor if he or she is to engage with potentially deeper moments in therapy. The difficulty is that the therapist also needs to pay attention to the wider context of therapy that includes his or her own inner states. The challenge increases with clients who struggle with fragile processes because they often offer little in the way of obvious moments of aliveness on which the therapist can focus. Not only that, the obscurity of what may well be of particular moment to them may be missed by the therapist, which only reinforces the client's view that nobody understands them, even the therapist. However, whenever the therapist is able to join with the client in a moment of 'fellow feeling' (the feeling state is the key) then the first critical stage of recovery, *coupling*, has occurred.

Amplification

The mother's coupling with the child through empathy and emotional mirroring is more than a mechanistic reflecting of the child's feeling state. Typically the mother joins in with the child but then adds to or subtracts from the child's affective experience. She reduces the child's negative feelings via soothing sounds and physical strokes and amplifies joyful states by joining in with the child's mirth.

> Amplification typically includes the enhancement of positive affect, which is very often muted. Amplification might also include the recognition of another affect which is less salient. For example, pleasure may be in the forefront of the expression but a sense of regret is also present. A third kind of amplification, extends the sense or meaning and so forth, of the words which are spoken. (Meares, 2005: 176)

It is important for therapists to recognise that they are not just reflecting their client's statements and emotions but also tentatively emphasising the very nature of their offerings within therapy. When a client says, 'I was really angry with him', the therapist can reflect back the statement as a feeling phrase but can do so in a number of different ways. The reflection can be conveyed simply as technical content, but it can also carry varying degrees of pathos, largely indicated by the tone of voice and by the intensity of the therapist's expression. Beyond this the reflection can also suggest via non-verbal cues, an emphasis, or even a question. Such responses are not only aimed at joining empathically with the client but also adding possibility. Possibility here is not so much about insight or cognitive information but rather it is a tentative opening of a door to client reflection, to a metaphorical play space in which the world of meaning can be manipulated. Just as the mother might place an emphasis on the child's immediate feelings state or add comment to a teenager's musings, so too the therapist can encourage the client to explore their own world of meaning.

Another key feature of amplification is that it gives value to the other. When the therapist suggests a particular emphasis, often non-verbally or with minimal verbal cues, the effect is to side with the client, to highlight the importance of their experience or point of view. Again the communication here has a feeling tone and is much more than rational argument. The client *experiences* (feels) valued. This is a particularly important dimension for those who struggle with fragile process because it counters one of their central developmental wounds. Those who have had disrupted or muted development are often left with underdeveloped mentalising abilities, but in addition they are also left with a negative view of themselves. Poor personal esteem is in part due to confusion experienced in relationships, but is also due to the lack of good 'fellow feeling'. When a parent or caregiver couples with the child a sense of relational synergy is produced, but along with this comes a mutually positive feeling. The child experiences good feelings in relationships and these feelings significantly inform them about the 'goodness' of their existence.

An example of this valuing dimension of amplification is found in a case of a young woman by the name of Clare. Clare was someone who did not come across as having any issues around personal worth. She was a bright, attractive, and generally vivacious individual with a healthy capacity to socialise. Once in therapy though she spent a good amount of her time crying and expressing depressed feelings. While she had developed many aspects of the self well, there were areas that remained shrivelled. One of the issues that had added complexity to her developmental trajectory was the presence of a congenital problem that could not be remedied. While the condition was not visible it did produce discomfort, resulting in anxiety and upset. Throughout her developing years her parents were generally supportive, however there was a degree of mismatch between their support and the child and teenager's need for empathic resonance. There was acknowledgment of her troubles but a lack of feeling tone.

Clare came to therapy to find a venue to process how to manage her health problem but also to confront her poor view of herself. Therapy with her was characterised by an interesting mixture of buoyancy and despair. In many ways Clare had a good understanding of her issues. Her understanding, however, did not provide her with the power to transform her feeling state, her self-criticism, and despair. It would require more than cognitive insight to resolve these issues. Clare needed to experience an empathic connection and a new self-valuing experience through the timely, subtle, valuing resonance with another. This slowly began to occur as Clare gained a sense that I not only appreciated her difficulties but also appreciated her. This did not come through a great deal of rational argument or Socratic reasoning, rather it came more through meaningful silence, and minimal therapist reflection, often involving only one word. Clare knew that she could be functional outside in her daily activities but collapse in the counselling room, and it would be understood. Clare knew at some deep level that healing came not so much through my affirmation but through our mutual sense of resonance.

Representation

Amplification provides a window into possibilities; it helps the individual to focus on their key issues with a different energy. However, the task of forging a more stable sense of self is not complete. For this to occur the ability to mentalise must be more firmly established. Through coupling and amplification the individual gains the building blocks to complete the process, but the building is yet to be built. The central requirement in the task of learning to mentalise is the opportunity to manipulate and play with one's own representations of reality. The clever explanations and interpretations of the therapist can hold back the process because it is not the client's process. The development of feeling tones is more critical than rational explanation because meaning is first attached to feeling. When the individual is in a feeling state of play and revelry they are, in fact, exploring new ways of being. The main task of the therapist is to help facilitate the client's entry into states of metaphorical musing. Imagination and metaphor are collectively a form of reflectivity and more than rational linear logic. Reflectivity can incorporate discursive logic but as a non-linear process it goes beyond it. The formation of the self requires a free space to move about in, a space in which to play with ideas, feelings and images. Those who have a diminished mentalising ability are characterised by a limitation in their creative imaginative functioning. To be able to be in touch with one's own inner states and also accurately (within reason) to perceive the inner states of others requires one to imagine.

Of course the difficulty is that those with fragile process do not easily move into this reflective, imaginative space. The fact that they struggle to perceive the actions and intentions of the therapist can block the very thing that would resolve their dilemma. The skilled therapist, however, is able, rather imperfectly, to facilitate this move towards inner exploration. Without the opportunity to join in empathic resonance with another, receive an affective sense of valuing, and have the opportunity to reflect in a playful imaginative manner while remaining connected to the other, the individual with fragile process will struggle to find hope. This is largely because their problem is a circular one. They need interaction with another to feel connected, but cannot connect because they have never really connected. As we have repeated throughout this book, hope is largely mediated through relationships. Those with fragile process exemplify the challenge we all have, except theirs is of a higher order of difficulty. We all need to feel valued and understood, to experience a deep resonance with another, and to have the ability to make sense of our life through reason and imagination – when we do, hope is not far away.

To illustrate the function of representation, we return to recounting a session with Clare. Clare was a high-functioning person with a challenging situation. She could do little to change her medical issues but she was in a position to rework her sense of self. Her highly critical inner voice was wreaking havoc in her life. However, she had established the building blocks of change through a deep resonance with me, the therapist, and now after a number of sessions there were the beginnings of a feeling change. This movement was particularly evident in one session when Clare expressed an imaginative desire to live on a tropical island free from the demands of the big city life. This statement came with a perceptible shift in her demeanour. She looked lighter and freer in herself as she made this statement. Noticing this, I was able to respond very simply with the words, 'Such freedom'. This response provided Clare with the opportunity to continue her revelry. She said, 'Yes, wouldn't it be wonderful to walk down the street, for people to know who you were and accept that you were living a carefree island existence?' In this moment, Clare was not thinking from within a rational linear mode of processing, she was rather playing freely with images and feelings and it was these images and feelings that were the heralds of change. After a few moments Clare said, 'So it's OK if I don't care what others think?' This was both an answer and a question to ponder. I interjected with, 'What are they thinking?' and she replied, 'They are thinking that there is something wrong with me' In this moment Clare exhaled and shifted in her seat looking surprised – a deep inner shift had occurred. Clare realised that her perceptions of others were inaccurate and that she really just wanted permission to relax and to accept that she was OK. It was from this moment that therapy moved into a new phase of consolidation.

Clare's story is a good illustration of the recovery of hope through empathic resonance and through a development in reflective functioning. Clare found the answers she needed when she felt secure that someone else grasped something of her struggle, allowing her to play with images, feelings, and ideas. One of the central requirements for people to discover and build hope is the capacity to imagine and reflect. Without this capacity there is no opportunity to see new possibilities. However, to be free to imagine we need the security of resonant relationships.

Summary

Hope might seem a possibility for the average person seeking help in therapy, but what of those with more severe and enduring problems? We have claimed in this chapter that while hope may be more difficult to find for those with more developed problems in living, it is still a possibility. One of the central foundations of hope is a healthy and well-formed self. When the self is confused hope is harder to find and maintain. In this chapter we have explored some key principles in the recovery of a healthy sense of self. A central aspect of such recovery is the ability to mentalise. Those who can mentalise are able to reflect upon their own thoughts and feelings well and are also able to assess the likely thoughts and feelings of others. The ability to mentalise is not a human given as it only develops in the context of secure and nurturing relationships. Therapy provides the possibility of experiencing nurturing relationships with informed professionals who are able to encourage the development of mentalization and through it the hope-filled self.

QUESTIONS FOR REFLECTION AND DISCUSSION

1 Victor Frankl said that suffering equals pain without meaning. What do you think about this?
2 Mentalization involves a number of abilities – what are these?
3 How might empathy be similar to but also different from mentalization?
4 With a partner or in a small group try to explain in your own words what is involved in the recovery steps of *coupling*, *amplification*, and *representation*.

SECTION 3

THE RESEARCH-INFORMED PRACTITIONER

9

Research, theory, and practice

In this chapter we want to highlight the importance of conducting research on key topics in counselling and psychotherapy, hope being one of these. Our aim in this chapter is twofold: one, to promote practitioner research in general, and, two, to promote research on hope in particular. We are strongly of the view that research is a vital part of building knowledge and skills that, in the end, will aid clients. Up until more recently counselling and psychotherapy practitioners have tended to have a certain aversion to research, claiming that it is too removed from practice. Therapists have questioned the relevance of university-based research, seeing it as overly theoretical and abstract. Thankfully, this view has changed substantially with therapists generally agreeing that research can, and often does, provide relevant knowledge that informs their practice. There are a number of reasons for this shift in view. In Britain counselling associations have been particularly good at promoting research through research conferences and journals. The majority of presenters at these conferences are either practitioners or university academics with a direct interest in practice. This has meant that much of the research reported at conferences and through association journals is about issues directly related to practice.

Another development in Britain that has drawn attention to the benefits of practitioner research is the development of the Clinical Outcomes in Routine Evaluation system (CORE). This clinical assessment system provides a range of client assessment and outcome measures that have had several advantages over many other similar systems. The first is that the measures are relatively short and easy to use. The second is that they provide a general assessment of client health structured in such a way that therapists can quickly gain an indication of client well-being in four different areas; *overall well-being*, *problem or symptom*, *general functioning*, and *risk*. Another benefit of this system is that it is a client self-report measure that can be used as feedback to clients themselves, thus incorporating assessment information as part of therapy. Finally, the data collected from clients using CORE can be stored in a personal, service, or national databank depending on user preferences, and therefore can provide statistical information on small through to very large cohorts. The flexibility of CORE means that it can be used by one therapist or a national register of therapists. Given these qualities, the CORE has been taken up as a routine measure within Britain by therapists in private practice, in community counselling settings, and in the National Health Service (NHS).

The CORE is representative of a new worldwide movement of client assessment in counselling and psychotherapy. Psychometric instruments developed by Michael Lambert and colleagues (1994), Scott Miller and Barry Duncan (2000), and Michael Barkham, John Mellor-Clark and colleagues (1998) have collectively drawn attention to the benefits of incorporating therapist–client feedback measures within the counselling process. As a result therapists have become more comfortable collecting data within their practice. These changes in practitioner perceptions of the relevance of research has greatly strengthened the profession and provided greater power for negotiations with governments and funding bodies. However, practitioner research is not the only kind of research, nor is it the research that attracts the most attention from governments and funders. The traditional view of research is that it is carried out by well-trained research experts who collect large bodies of data that can be generalised and organised into theories and practice guidelines. In Britain the National Institute for Clinical Excellence (NICE) consults with experts, examines findings predominantly from randomised controlled trials (RCTs), and makes recommendations based on these about preferred practice in counselling and psychotherapy and other health disciplines. Similar national health bodies serve the same function in the United States and in other countries. There are of course benefits to this level of scrutiny and dissemination of best-practice guidelines, however there are obvious limitations as well. Not all knowledge can be measured through RCTs. Although the data they provide is highly valuable, it should only be regarded as a portion of the knowledge that is relevant to the practitioner. RCTs form one important slice of the research-informed knowledge pie. The knowledge acquired through other methodologies and sources is also highly relevant.

Before taking this discussion any further it is important to provide a definition of research. McLeod offers a helpful definition by stating that research is 'a systematic process of critical inquiry leading to valid propositions and conclusions that are communicated to interested others' (2003: 4). He explicates the assumptions behind this definition by identifying a number of meaning components. These are outlined in Box 9.1 below.

BOX 9.1   ASPECTS OF RESEARCH

1   The concept of *critical inquiry*. Research grows out of the primary human tendency to need to learn, to know, to solve problems. These impulses are fundamentally critical; the need to know is the counterpoint to the sense that what is known is not quite right.

2   Research as a *process of inquiry*. Any research involves a series of steps or stages. Knowledge must be constructed. There is a cyclical process of observation, reflection and experimentation.

3   Research is *systematic*. There are two distinct sets of meanings associated with the notion that research should be systematic. The first is that any investigation takes place within a theoretical system of concepts or constructs. A piece of research is

---

embedded in a framework or way of seeing the world. Secondly, research involves the application of a set of methods or principles, the purpose of which is to achieve knowledge that is as valid and truthful as possible.

4   The products of research are *propositions* or *statements*. There is a distinction between research and learning. Experiential knowing, or 'knowing how', can be a valuable outcome of an inquiry process, but *research* always involves communication with others. Learning can occur at an individual, intuitive level, but research requires the symbolization and transmission of these understandings in the public domain.

5   Research findings are judged according to criteria of validity, truthfulness or authenticity. To make a claim that a statement is based on research is to imply that it is in some way more valid or accurate than a statement based on personal opinion. However, every culture has its own distinctive criterion or 'logic of justification' for accepting a theory or statement as valid. For example, within mainstream psychology truth value is equated with statements based on rational, objective experimentation. In psychoanalysis, truth value is judged on the basis of clinical experience.

6   Research is *communicated to interested others*; it takes place within a research community. No single research study has much meaning in isolation. Research studies provide the individual pieces that fit together to create the complex mosaic of the literature of a topic.

(McLeod, 2003: 43).

McLeod's definition does not qualify how to arrive at valid propositional knowledge and this is because there are many ways knowledge can be gained through research. Some of these require statistical expertise and others require human-inquiry-based methods. There is a wealth of methodologies for researchers of all persuasions to draw on. The main difficulty in counselling and psychotherapy research is the assumption that one approach to research with its attending methodologies is superior to others. For the majority of the twentieth century, 'scientific' research has claimed the mantle of superiority. This monopoly is now breaking down, largely due to the fact that it has not been able to answer all the questions raised. Other research approaches have demonstrated their capacity to provide answers to questions relevant to the field. The ascendance of scientific research in counselling and psychotherapy has also been restrained by a wider shift in worldview assumptions within academe. The emergence of the philosophy of science as a major field of study has enabled a challenge to old paradigms of thought. Rather than one philosophy of knowledge, *positivism,* asserting dominance, there is now a levelling process occurring where the relevance and importance of multiple approaches to knowledge are being equally valued. This is a particularly important development in counselling and psychotherapy because these fields are best thought of as being *interdisciplinary*. Therapists draw on knowledge and practices from many other disciplines including education, philosophy, the arts and humanities, theology, sociology, and psychology. Diversity adds strength to the field but also some confusion as these disciplines have different philosophical and methodological priorities.

Sanders and Wilkins (2010), in recognising the diversity of research, have identified a list of generic research approaches. Table 7 is an adaptation of the table they present.

Table 7 What research is

Approach to research	Definition
Informative	Describes a set of circumstances or domain of experience and offers an explanation of what is found.
Transformative	Concerns exploring practice within a particular setting with a view to changing the behaviour of the researchers or their attitudes. Transformative research is often the kind known as action research or action inquiry and may have 'political' aims or the aims of changing social situations.
Developmental	This occurs when the researcher's own self is changed and developed and arises from engagement in high level self-reflection. Developmental research occurs when the researchers are investigating aspects of their own experience.
Explanatory	This is about classifying, conceptualising, and building theories. Observation hypothesis formation, experimentation, and analysis are the main strategies for the implementation of explanatory research. The questions behind such research are 'what?', 'how?', and 'why?', and so explanatory research is close to the conventional view of research.
Expressive	This is to do with understanding the meaning of experience and allowing this meaning to become apparent. It requires the researcher to be a part of the research itself and to reflect deeply on what happens to them. It is essentially an exploratory approach in which synthesis is a principal strategy.

Source: Sanders & Wilkins, 2010: 3.

In principle, researchers can employ any one of these approaches. However, informative and explanatory research is predominantly carried out by full-time academics who are often expected to pursue quantitative research programmes that provide generalisable results. This type of research has served the profession well and has provided important insights into the processes and outcomes of therapy. One of the difficulties though is that 'scientific' research usually requires large sample sizes and very specific and, in many ways, restrictive conditions under which to conduct the research. For example, an RCT that explores the outcomes of cognitive behavioural therapy on veterans with depression will have very strict protocols. Some of these might include a participant cohort with no co-morbid conditions, a formal diagnosis of a particular type of depression, a certain age range, or a specified number of therapy sessions. If any of these conditions are not met, participant outcome data will not be included in the findings. These protocols can provide very beneficial information for therapists to integrate. The restrictions of this type of research however have created a dichotomy between the outcomes from trials (efficacy) and outcomes from actual therapy (effectiveness).

Efficacy research follows the strictest of protocols similar to those just outlined and tries to control for as many variables as possible. The benefit is a greater guarantee that results from studies can be associated with specific causal factors. In the example above, if veterans' depression begins to improve after participating in six sessions of CBT then it is likely that the cause of the improvement is CBT. Of course, there is no absolute guarantee that this is the case. Veterans may be getting better because they like the therapist and not because the specific interventions produced change. Having said this, the aim to control for influencing factors is a laudable one and worth pursuing. One of the interesting outcomes from this type of research however is that while participants gain improved clinical outcomes, application of the same therapeutic strategies in naturalistic settings may not result in the same level of benefit. This is because those in the average clinic are likely to have co-morbid conditions, have had their problem for a longer or shorter time than expected, and may not have been diagnosed. In other words, the therapy when applied in controlled conditions was *efficacious* (it got results) but was not as *effective* in general populations. This distinction has led some researchers to focus on what is known as *effectiveness research*, that is, research focused on improving outcomes in naturalistic settings.

Practitioner research

The distinction between efficacy and effectiveness has encouraged some practitioners to enter the world of research themselves. They usually do so out of a desire to pursue a personal/professional interest. For example, they may have had a number of clients with eating disorders and have an inkling (usually through their own professional experience) that a particular type of intervention produces positive change. There may be relatively little information in research journals on this type of intervention for such clients and so the practitioner researcher is inspired to find answers for themselves. This need to discover is the catalyst for most research, but especially for practitioner research. Academic researchers are also usually interested in their research projects, but sometimes their motivation is more external and comes from the lure of grants and promotion. Having said this, any good research is worth doing.

Practitioner research has a lot to offer the professions of counselling and psychotherapy for a number of reasons. Practitioner research:

1 Focuses on interests that arise from therapy
2 Deepens the therapist researcher's knowledge both of research principles and practices but also of their topic of inquiry
3 Increases the therapist's therapeutic skills
4 Usually incorporates reflexive self-awareness facilitating personal development
5 Is guided by a care and concern for clients and thus has a moral imperative
6 Is 'owned' by the researcher, making it personally meaningful
7 Can be disseminated to the profession in ways that are accessible to a wide audience, researchers, and practitioners alike.

As discussed above, at the heart of practitioner research is an internal motivation usually driven by curiosity aroused in the practice of therapy. Practitioners become curious because they have noticed something about a particular client group, an individual client, or something about their own functioning as a therapist that they want to find out more about. This curiosity highlights a difference between practitioner research and traditional research, which is that practitioner research is 'local' and pertains to their own site of practice. Traditional research is 'global' and seeks to makes generalisations that can apply to a multitude of settings. Practitioner research aims to make a difference to both practitioner and client at the site of practice.

Donald Schön (1987) argues that the distinction between traditional research and practitioner research is not just about the site of inquiry (i.e. global or local) but also about different epistemologies. Referring to traditional research as being based in a *technical rationality*, Schön argues that it relies on a positivist ontology (view of reality) and the valuable but limited epistemologies of *observation* and *reason*. One of the problems that Schön regards as inherent to technical rationality is an approach to knowledge that is overly objective and therefore removed from the real world of practice. The systems of inquiry that form the structure of traditional research function well in the context of well-formed problems. Statistical procedures, for example, work well when problems are defined and when the variables are identified. The challenge for the practitioner is that problems are not always so discrete and the variables are not always known. A number of quotes from Donald Schön in Box 9.2 below help capture his thoughts about the limitations of a technical rationality.

BOX 9.2   PROFESSIONAL PRACTICE AND THE LIMITATIONS OF A TECHNICAL RATIONALITY

Technical rationality is an epistemology of practice derived from positivist philosophy, built into the very foundations of the modern research university … Technical rationality holds that practitioners are instrumental problem solvers who select technical means best suited to particular purposes. Rigorous professional practitioners solve well-formed instrumental problems by applying theory and technique derived from systematic, preferably scientific knowledge …

But, as we have come to see with increasing clarity over the last twenty or so years, the problems of real-world practice do not present themselves to practitioners as well-formed structures. Indeed, they tend not to present themselves as problems at all but as messy, indeterminate situations. (Schön, 1987: 4)

These indeterminate zones of practice-uncertainty, uniqueness, and value conflict-escape the canons of technical rationality. When a problematic situation is uncertain, technical problem solving depends on the prior construction of a well-formed problem – which is not itself a technical task. When a practitioner recognizes a situation as unique, she cannot handle it soley by applying theories or techniques derived from her store of professional knowledge. And in situations of value conflict, there are no clear and self-consistent ends to guide the technical selection of means (Schön, 1987: 6).

Knowledge that is applied in professional settings like psychology, psychotherapy, nursing, teaching, and so on is often based on *practical knowledge* as much as it is on *technical knowledge.* The mathematics teacher knows the technical knowledge that he or she wants to teach students, but discovers that for some reason the students are blocked in their learning. The teacher then has to respond to the students' needs in the moment. There is no time to return to the textbooks to gain instruction about such situations. In a similar manner, the psychotherapist might be well steeped in various theories of psychotherapy but has to respond to the client's problem, right now, in the very moments of therapy. Polkinghorne identifies this situation by stating, 'Practical thinking is necessary to achieve a desired purpose in situations that are dynamic and fluid' (1999: 1431).

One of the challenges that emerges from situations of professional uncertainty is that the practitioner often feels obliged to find their answers in the library, in other words to return to technical knowledge. Of course this can be a very appropriate action and may well produce the desired results. However, the problems presented in practice-based settings are not always amenable to technical solutions (O'Hara, 2012). This is because such problems are not formed in ways that lend themselves to technical problem solving. What Schön, Polkinghorne, and others suggest is that practitioners have a type of knowledge that is well suited to solving more fluid, indeterminate problems. This practical knowledge comes from a merger of theoretical knowledge and experience. Through years of practice the practitioner builds up a wealth of knowledge that is often subtle and nuanced but nonetheless profound. Schön argues that this knowledge is often tacit because it is used in the everyday practice of one's discipline. He states, 'Perhaps there is an epistemology of practice that takes account of the competence that practitioners sometimes display in situations of uncertainty, complexity, uniqueness, and conflict' (1995: 29).

One of the unfortunate results of the ascendancy of one philosophy of science over others is the separation of knowledge forms. Instead of all forms of knowledge being equally appreciated and valued, technical knowledge claims that it speaks the greater truth. This claim has resulted in expectations of privilege bestowed by governments and the public. Historically, research which adheres to a technical rationality has gained funding and recognition over other forms of inquiry. In this context practitioners can be left wondering which way to turn. Will they prioritise technical knowledge over practical knowledge or the other way around? Unfortunately this is a false dichotomy. Both technical and practical knowledge is valuable in its own right and each has a contribution to make. Instead of a separation of knowledge there should be an integration that allows the professional to incorporate aspects of both into their field of practice.

Theory/practice gap

An example of the separation of knowledge forms is seen in what has been called the theory/practice gap. Argyris and Schön (1992) have demonstrated that theory and practice are not necessarily closely linked. They distinguish between espoused theory and theory-in-use. Espoused theory is the conscious view of what it is that informs our practice. The difficulty lies in the fact that what is espoused may not be what actually informs our practice. Theory-in-use, on the other hand, is the theory, assumption or belief that actually directs our practice. To illustrate the notion of theory-in-use it is helpful to think of a teacher in a classroom who is trying to decide what to do next. The teacher already has a lesson plan from which the lesson has been informed to the present moment, but now the teacher finds herself uncertain of the next step. To help decide which direction to take, the teacher looks at her watch. In this moment the teacher is actually not interested in the time, but in how much time is left before the end of the lesson. This is a vital piece of information for it is on the basis of the time remaining that the teacher will decide what to do. This decision is based on matching her knowledge of what the children are capable of managing within this timeframe, both in general and, more specifically, today. This type of knowledge is not taught at university, it comes from the experience of practice.

Argyris and Schön believe that the teacher, in this instance, is not actually operating on the basis of technical knowledge but a theory-in-use. In other words, the teacher's action is not a haphazard selection of last-minute strategies but rather an informed practice. Theory-in-use as a form of practical knowledge is really an organisational scheme of knowledge that comes from noticing, categorising, and organising knowledge gained from previous experience for the purpose of future use. Counsellors and psychotherapists employ practical knowledge throughout their practice. Therapy by definition is a sphere of practice full of unique, complex, and indeterminate situations in which the therapist is required to rely not only on their technical knowledge but on their theories-in-use.

Practitioner researchers have a great advantage in their research over traditional researchers because they are able to identify problems that emerge from their own practice. Their unique ability to combine technical and practical knowledge allows them insights into real-world dilemmas. Unlike the traditional researcher, they are not removed from the problems people encounter and they are not removed from their own practice of therapy. Being fully situated in the zone of practice enables the identification and application of interesting, personally motivating, and unique research.

Future research on hope and well-being

In light of the identified distinction between technical and practical knowledge outlined above, it is interesting to note a theory/practice gap in the area of hope studies. By gap here we do not mean a missing piece of information that needs to be researched, although there is much that we have yet to discover. The gap referred to here is the gap between the technical knowledge of hope and the practice of hope-focused strategies within therapy. As has been clearly identified in our discussion, hope is well known to be one of the common factors across therapies which contribute to therapeutic change. Most therapists would be able to list the notable four common factors without difficulty.

Some therapists would even be able to delineate these in more minute detail. However, if you were to ask therapists how they employ their knowledge of hope as a fundamental component of therapeutic change, many would struggle. This is not to suggest that therapists do not have some knowledge of how they might operationalise hope in therapy, but that this knowledge is more difficult to explicate because it is more tacit. The gap here lies between the assertion of technical knowledge and its practice, between what is espoused as the theory informing practice and the actual theory informing practice. We are often not aware that we are not practising what we preach. This is because our theories-in-use are embedded within our practice.

The topic of hope provides a good example of the gap between theory and practice. Of course this is one of the reasons for writing this book. We as health care practitioners agree that hope is important in therapeutic change and in general health and well-being, but have limited training in its application in practice. *Noticing gaps like this stimulates practitioner research.* There are endless opportunities for practitioners to research theory/practice gaps found in their own practice. One of the difficulties in discovering and working with such gaps, however, is their embeddedness. The fact that we are not easily aware of the inconsistencies in our own practice makes identifying them difficult. The key to identifying theory/practice gaps is practitioner reflectivity. Reflectivity requires us to step outside our everyday routine and to challenge our assumptions. We have to be prepared to confront our espoused theories, to be open to different points of view, and be prepared to use new tools of inquiry. Of course, this is where research can serve us well.

Qualitative research provides great opportunities for practitioners to become researchers because the various methodologies keep the researcher close to the subject and to the phenomenon of study. Some qualitative methods, in particular, recognise that there is little separation between researcher, subject, and phenomenon. This is because the researcher influences the outcomes of the research by both framing the research question and by being a part of the process of research as interviewer, data analyst, and reporter. While this can undoubtedly be problematic, it can also be an advantage because it means researchers must pay attention to their own subjectivity. It means they have to reflect on the research and on its impact on both the subject and themselves.

Disembedding practice

To discover our own tacit and embedded theories-in-use we need tools that help us to examine our practice and to identify our beliefs and assumptions. A number of specific methods can be employed for this purpose. Some methods that are highly useful in mental health research include *reflecting teams, interpersonal process recall,* and *personal/professional journals.* In some respects these approaches might better be called 'research techniques' and the term 'methods' left for research approaches such as grounded theory, narrative analysis, ethnography, and so on. Methods that are designed to provide the researcher with insight into their own practice or wider social and cultural practices is collectively called *transformative* or *participatory* research.

The *reflecting teams* technique emerged from the family therapy tradition and is also associated with solution-focused and narrative therapy approaches. A Norwegian family therapist, Andersen (1987), is credited with developing the technique and coining the term. Reflecting teams are structured around an observation of therapist and client(s) by observer therapists who are usually hidden behind one-way glass. At a particular point within the therapy process (this can vary) the observers join with the therapist and client and offer their supportive thoughts and observations. This method has not only proven to be a useful tool in providing client feedback, it has been particularly beneficial as a method in training therapists. One of the reasons the reflecting teams approach has been so successful in training is because it provides immediate feedback to the therapist on their practice. By definition, the observers are outside looking in and therefore are able to observe the process of therapy from a unique vantage point. The feedback provided to the therapist can therefore provide highly relevant insight into practice and facilitate therapist reflection on practice.

Interpersonal process recall (IPR) is another approach that encourages personal/professional reflection, making use of video recordings of therapy sessions as a form of review of practice. IPR in the form used by counsellors and therapists was developed by Kagan, Krathwohl, and Miller (1963). Baker, Daniels and Greeley (1990: 360) explain that:

> the recall process was derived to help students recall thoughts, feelings, goals, aspirations, bodily sensations, and many other covert processes in order to help them attend to these processes in the session and eventually to use the resultant awareness to foster self-and-client growth.

Elliott (1986: 504) lists a number of features of IPR that he believes make it a powerful tool for vivid recall:

> First, the recording acts as a cue to assist the participant in retrieving memory traces which would otherwise be lost in the welter of interfering information generated during any communication episode.

> Second, there is a recency effect for these memories: they can be much more readily activated and are noticeably more vivid when recall takes place ...

> Third, the IPR process slows down the interaction by allowing the informant to stop the tape in order to describe what he or she was experiencing at particular moments.

> Fourth, in instructing the informant [therapist], the researcher ... attempts to induce in the informant a *psychological set* in which attention is focused on specific experiences and perceptions which were occurring at that particular instant in time. Thus the informant is asked to do what he or she can in order to go back into the 'there-and-now' of the interaction, to avoid making inferences or generalizations, and to distinguish clearly between what is being recalled and what he or she is seeing now during recall.

> Fifth, IPR is carried out so as to make the informant feel safe.

One of the other beneficial features of IPR is that it 'allows therapists and researchers to gather information on the moment-to-moment perceptions, intentions, and reactions of clients and therapists during therapy sessions' (Elliott, 1986: 505). This is much more than can be gained from reviewing transcripts and recordings alone. IPR provides insight into the process of therapy and therefore is a medium through which practitioner researchers can identify topics of study that are of personal relevance.

A third example of a technique that can be used in practitioner research is the *personal/professional journal*. This type of journal holds the dual title of *personal* and *professional* as it is recognised that journaling even when focused on professional issues, especially in the field of therapy, also incorporates aspects of the personal. It is difficult to separate the person of the therapist from his or her practice of therapy. Personal/professional journals can be used in a variety of ways to enhance reflection. When employed to facilitate the disembedding of tacit theories-in-use the journal becomes a source of data itself. If the aim is to unearth tacit behaviours and assumptions, the reflexive researcher is benefitted by looking for patterns in their recorded thoughts and behaviours. This is best done by reading each journal entry and then recording a list of 'I tend to' statements. For example, a therapist may have outlined in his journal an interchange between himself and a client that he found to be curious, exciting, or troublesome. This outline would most likely include both personal and professional reflections on the event and also a description of what occurred. In reviewing the journal entry the therapist is in a position to step outside the moment of therapy and reflect upon it. He might then note patterns of thought and behaviour recorded in the journal. For example:

- I tend to focus on the content of the client's story and miss the emotional tenor present.
- I tend to like it when I can explain an idea or principle to the client as it makes me feel I am making a difference.
- I tend to be uncomfortable when the client doesn't know what to say or what to focus on.
- I tend to like it when we have developed together a client action plan for the coming week.
- I tend to enjoy the detective work of therapy, working out the causes and solutions to problems.

This list of 'I tend to' statements can be quite extensive and so will need to be organised into categories. From these categories several theories-in-use are likely to emerge. It is important to remember that a theory-in-use reflects very local, practice-based knowledge. Sometimes when we disembed our theories-in-use we are pleasantly surprised and sometimes we are not. It is not uncommon to find that what we espouse as our theory of practice is not consistent with our theory-in-use. We might say, for example, that we are comfortable working with emotions and seek to identify with clients the primary emotions at the base of their problems, but find that our practice does not demonstrate this. Returning to the sample of 'I tend to' statements above, we might tentatively suggest that the therapist's associated theory-in-use could be summed up in the statement:

I believe that therapy involves discovering the causes of problems, understanding their function in the client's life and finding practical action-based solutions, and doesn't require over-dwelling on emotions.

This theory-in-use, once identified, may not surprise the therapist and may only confirm his or her belief and practice. It may, on the other hand, be confronting and seem to be at odds with his espousals. This approach can also be used to explore other therapists' beliefs and practices, providing the opportunity to examine therapy processes with a larger sample.

Other practitioner research approaches

Research that seeks to disembed process dimensions of practice is one of many ways in which practitioners can explore topics of interests. As mentioned earlier, the availability of a variety of outcome measures, for example the CORE, OQ45, or ORS, has provided therapists with ample opportunity to collect data from their own practice. These measures can be used to:

- Explore overall effectiveness ratings of therapy
- Identify cohorts which score within a certain range on well-being and problem/symptoms
- Identify social role
- Identify client affective responses to therapy
- Monitor the therapeutic alliance.

There are many other well-recognised measures that can provide stimulus for practitioner research. Some of these will be discussed in the following chapter. Often practitioners believe that they are not in a position to use quantitative measures because they feel undertrained or because they think large sample sizes are always required. This is not the case. It is true that using client outcome measures within one's practice may not provide large-scale cohorts amenable to statistical generalisation. However, they are still highly valuable as variable indicators. Many researchers use quantitative measures on a small scale and combine this data with qualitative data, producing mixed-methods studies. As always in research, the central issue is whether the research design is fit for purpose – that is, will it provide useful information to answer the questions being asked.

The range of qualitative research methods is extensive, providing the practitioner researcher with an impressive array of possible approaches that can be used to explore their topics of interest. Some of these include:

- Phenomenology
- Ethnography
- Grounded theory
- Thematic analysis

- Interpretive phenomenological analysis
- Discourse analyse and conversation analysis
- Narrative analysis
- Heuristic research
- Autoethnography
- Action research.

This is not meant to be an exhaustive list of qualitative approaches and a detailed discussion is outside the scope of this book. There are many good texts on qualitative research, catering for both beginning researchers and experienced researchers. An example of a very good introductory text on qualitative research is John McLeod's *Qualitative Research in Counselling and Psychotherapy* (2011).

Summary

We have highlighted in this chapter the important place that research can occupy in informing the practitioner. Counselling and psychotherapy practitioners are more and more taking up the challenge to research their own work and to thereby add to the pool of knowledge we have about issues related to therapeutic change. The growing practice of using client assessment and feedback instruments has encouraged the growth in practitioners as researchers. Practitioner research can be conducted in a wide range of ways but it typically has a focus on 'local' research, that is, research related to the site of practice. A good example of local research is the notion of the theory/practice gap. This type of research centres attention on the differences or discrepancies between what therapists believe they are doing, and what they are actually doing in practice. While many topics and themes can be explored from the perspective of the theory/practice gap, hope is a topic that is highly relevant and amendable to investigation from within this framework. In the next chapter we provide information on a number of research instruments that can be used to explore hope and its relevance and application within therapy. Before looking at these instruments, it might be helpful to reflect on the following questions and even try the suggested activity.

QUESTIONS FOR REFLECTION AND DISCUSSION

1 Write a list of five research topics that you, given the opportunity, would like to explore. Share these with a partner explaining why they are of interest.
2 Have you noticed any potential theory/practice gaps in your own practice of therapy? What are they? What makes you curious about them?
3 Hope research can be applied in a wide range of areas. If you had the opportunity, what other area or topic would you combine research on hope with?

ACTIVITY

Either by observing a video of your practice of therapy or by reviewing a detailed personal professional journal focused on your practice, identify a list of 'I tend to' statements which capture aspects of your practice. Remember that these statements are *not* about preferred practice or tendencies but *actual* practice. Once you have a sufficient list of statements identify a theory-in-use statement.

I tend to:

_____

_____

_____

_____

_____

Theory-in-use statement:

_____

_____

_____

10

Hope measures and psychotherapy research

One of the advantages of hope as a topic of study is its versatility of application. Hope is really a metaconstruct and so has the potential to be linked with a wide range of other variables and concepts. A metaconstruct is defined as a theoretical level of organisation that has the capacity to provide coherence to a wide range of subordinate theories or ideas. A metatheory is a type of metaconstruct that operates at the level of worldview. Kuhn (1962), Pepper (1961) and others have identified a number of worldview paradigms that have informed the social sciences. Discipline-based theories function at a lower level of abstraction than metatheories and are necessary for the organisation of knowledge into functional units. It is possible that theories may diverge significantly at their own level of abstraction but converge at a higher level of abstraction. For example, person-centred theory and psychodynamic theory are quite divergent in many areas but both are representative of an organismic/developmentalist metatheory. This means that they share some fundamental worldview assumptions. In this case, they both hold a view of the person as a growing organism who develops through various life phases and stages. They both see the individual from a holistic perspective, acknowledging that the whole is greater than the sum of the parts. While our task in this chapter is not to develop a discussion about metatheory and worldview per se, we do wish to highlight the view that hope functions at a higher level of abstraction than does any single theory of counselling and psychotherapy. One of the qualities of hope is that it is a concept which is versatile enough to inform all approaches of counselling and psychotherapy.

Hope and well-being research

As a metaconstruct, hope provides a framework for the study of many other topics. Hope is just as much at home in studies of pathology as in studies of exceptional human performance. As a central ingredient in therapeutic change hope can act as a barometer or as a measure against which other constructs can be gauged. Hope also has the advantage of being well researched, as is evidenced by the existence of a number of established hope measures. These various measures can be applied to a wide range of potential investigations.

In the *Handbook of Hope: Theory, Measures and Applications* edited by Ric Snyder (2000), a list of topics and studies that have been linked to hope are reported:

- Children: raising future hopes
- Gray power: hope for the ages
- Hope and cultural diversity
- Hope and sport
- Hope and eating disorders
- Hope and trauma recovery
- Hope and anxiety disorders
- Hope and depression
- Hope and HIV/AIDS
- Hope and cancer
- Hope and acquired disability.

Some of the hope-based studies we are currently involved in include:

- Hope and bereavement by suicide
- Hope and empathy
- Hope and recovery from childhood sexual abuse
- Hope, the sense of self, and PTSD
- Hope education within schools
- Hope and the differentiation of self
- The therapist's hope.

Other possible topics of study which include a focus on hope are:

- Hope and resilience
- Hope and long-term conditions
- Hope and learning disability
- Hope and spirituality
- Hope and terminal illness
- Hope and therapist–client feedback measures
- Hope and well-being.

As can be seen from these lists, the scope for incorporating hope into research studies of well-being is extensive. In this chapter we outline a number of hope and well-being instruments that can be used in both traditional and practitioner research. Our aim here is to highlight the possibilities for research that involve hope. In particular, we wish to encourage the practitioner in his or her research efforts and to sow ideas for future research.

Hope instruments

This overview of research instruments begins with those directly related to hope and is then followed with other measures of well-being. For each instrument a brief description is provided. More detailed discussion of the psychometric properties can be found in the manuals related to each respective instrument.

Adult (Dispositional) Hope Scale (see Appendix)

Scale purpose

The Hope Scale was developed by Snyder et al. (1991) as a foundational measure of adult trait hope. It is a twelve-item self-report inventory and can be used with participants from aged fifteen upwards. This is a well-validated cognitive measure of hope and has been used extensively in research since its development. The scale takes only minutes to complete and is very easy to use. The Hope Scale has been utilised in a wide variety of research settings. It can be used in large-scale studies as an initial measure of hope or used in private practice as a feedback mechanism for both therapist and client. The scale can also be used to predict those people who have superior functioning.

Scoring

The scale provides two main sub-scale measures of Snyder's hope construct; *pathways* and *agency*. These two sub-scales when aggregated provide an overall measure for an individual's dispositional (trait) hope.

Adult Domain-Specific Hope Scale (see Appendix)

Scale purpose

The Domain-Specific Hope Scale developed by Sympson (1999), is similar to the Adult Hope Scale but focuses more particularly on dispositional hope within six specific domains – social, academic, family, romance/relationships, work/occupation, and leisure activities. A total score can be obtained, as can domain-specific scores. The measure provides an opportunity to identify an individual's hope as it functions in specific areas of life, thus providing a more targeted assessment that can be used in counselling or in life review.

Scoring

Participants are asked to rate the importance of and satisfaction in six life domains on a Likert scale (from 0–100). When scoring the six domains, participants are asked to rate the extent to which the items relate to them on an eight-point Likert scale. A total score can range from 48–384 and is obtained by aggregating the scores across the whole battery of items and the domain-specific score is obtained by aggregating the eight items within each domain.

Children's Hope Scale (see Appendix)

Scale purpose

The Children's Hope Scale was developed by Snyder and others (1997) and is similar in style to the Adult Hope Scale. The development of the measure is premised on the view that children are goal-directed and that their goal-directed thoughts can be evidenced in their pathways and agency thinking. The measure is well validated and is for use with children aged between seven and sixteen years.

Scoring

The scale has six questions that can either be read by children or read to them. The scale is hand scored and can be completed and scored within three to four minutes. Three of the items reflect agency thinking and three pathways thinking. The agency sub-scale assesses an active orientation about goals and the future, while the pathways sub-scale assesses a discovery perspective concerning finding ways of reaching one's goals. The two sub-scales can be combined to derive a total score.

Adult State Hope Scale (see Appendix)

Scale purpose

The Adult State Hope Scale was developed by Snyder and colleagues (1996) and is a six-item self-report measure (responses: 1 = definitely true to 8 = definitely false) that assesses goal-directed thinking within a given moment.

Scoring

The Adult State Hope Scale is designed to measure the present state of an individual's hope as opposed to their more enduring dispositional or trait hope. This can provide very beneficial clinical information when used regularly. Scores from the State Hope Scale can also be compared with the Adult Dispositional Hope Scale using the latter as a base measure of hope.

Herth Hope Index (HHI) (see Appendix)

Scale purpose

The Herth Hope Index is a twelve-item index adapted from the thirty-item Herth Hope Scale (HHS). It employs a four-point Likert scale and measures hope in terms of:

- Temporality and future
- Positive readiness and expectancy
- Interconnectedness.

The HHI is designed to capture the multidimensionality of hope with special attention to hope in clinical nursing populations. It is also designed to be sensitive to change in the hope scores of those in such populations.

Scoring

Scoring the HHI is a straightforward summation of the three separate domains. A total HHI score can range from 12 to 48 with higher scores indicating higher levels of hope.

Well-being measures

There is a wide range of measures of well-being, each capturing different aspects of health and human functioning. In this section we will briefly outline measures that can be used as stand-alone instruments in their own right or in conjunction with hope and other measures.

The Satisfaction with Life Scale (see Appendix)

Scale purpose

The Satisfaction with Life Scale was developed by Diener and colleagues (1985) to measure a global assessment of quality of life. The measure is designed so that the individual assesses their satisfaction on the basis of criteria that he or she has set for him/herself and therefore is not externally imposed. For example, a range of individual measures such as health or energy may be desirable but different individuals will place different values on them. This scale measures satisfaction across the whole of life to reach a score, rather than across individual domains.

Scoring

The scale has five questions and uses a seven-point scale. The answers are aggregated to reach a total score. The range and rating are indicated on the instrument.

The Perceived Stress Scale

Scale purpose

The Perceived Stress Scale was developed by Cohen et al. (1983) and measures the degree to which situations in one's life are appraised as stressful. Items were designed to assess how unpredictable, uncontrollable, and overloaded respondents find their lives. The scale also includes a number of direct queries about current levels of stress.

Scoring

The scale is a ten-item measure using a five-point Likert scale. While some items need to be reverse scored, the total score is derived from an aggregate of the all scores. This scale can be found at www.mindgarden.com/products/pss.htm

Depression Anxiety Stress Scale (DASS)

Scale purpose

The DASS is a set of three self-report scales designed to measure the negative emotional states of depression, anxiety, and stress. The Depression Scale assesses dysphoria, hopelessness, devaluation of life, self-deprecation, lack of interest/involvement, anhedonia, and inertia (Lovibond, & Lovibond, 1995). The Anxiety Scale assesses autonomic arousal, skeletal muscle effects, situational anxiety, and subjective experience of anxious affect. The Stress Scale is sensitive to levels of chronic non-specific arousal. It assesses difficulty relaxing, nervous arousal, how easily the participant becomes upset/agitated, and irritability/over-reactivity, and impatience. The scale is based in a dimensional rather than a categorical view of psychological disorder. The scale has been demonstrated to have good psychometric properties.

Scoring

Each of the three DASS scales contains fourteen items, divided into sub-scales of two to five items. As well as the forty-two-item questionnaire, a short version, the DASS21, is available with seven items per scale. Scores for each individual scale are aggregated to arrive at a score. A scoring template is available. This measure is available in the public domain at: www2.psy.unsw.edu.au/DASS/

Clinical Outcome Routine Evaluation (CORE)

Scale purpose

The CORE system provides a range of assessment instruments primarily designed to measure outcomes from therapy. It was developed in the United Kingdom 'as a set of measures that are applicable to all patients in psychotherapy regardless of the clinical settings, mode of therapy, or specific problems (clinical population) of the patients' (Barkham et al., 1998: 35). The most well-known of the instruments is the CORE-OM (Outcome Measure). It is a client self-report questionnaire designed to be administered before and after therapy.

Scoring

The instrument has thirty-four questions, uses a five-point scale, and identifies four dimensions:

- Subjective well-being
- Problems/symptoms
- Life functioning
- Risk/harm.

The responses are designed to be averaged by the practitioner to produce a mean score to indicate the level of current psychological global distress (from 'healthy' to 'severe'). Details of the CORE system can be found at www.coreims.co.uk/index.html

The Outcome Questionnaire 45 (OQ-45)

Scale purpose

The OQ-45 is a forty-five-item self-report outcome/tracking instrument designed for repeated measurement of client progress through the course of therapy and following termination. It is based on the work of Michael Lambert and colleagues (1994) and is a comprehensive and well-validated measure of client change. The instrument measures a range of risks and functioning across three domains: symptom distress (especially depression and anxiety), interpersonal functioning, and social role. It enables the clinician to assess functional level and change over time. Details of the OQ-45 can be found at: www.oqmeasures.com/page.asp?PageId=77

Outcome Rating Scale (ORS)

Scale purpose

The ORS is a therapy outcome measure initially developed by Scott Miller and Barry Duncan (2000) as a much shorter alternative to the OQ-45. It is based on the measurement of the same three functional domains: individual symptoms, interpersonal functioning, and social role. The main difference with the measure is that it uses a visual analog format to capture a measure of a client's current functioning across the three areas mentioned plus an additional overall rating of well-being. Details of the ORS can be found at: http://scottdmiller.com/?q=node/6

Therapeutic relationship measures

The Helping Alliance Questionnaire (HAq-II) (see Appendix)

Scale purpose

The Helping Alliance Questionnaire was developed by Luborsky and colleagues (1996) to measure the construct of the helping alliance as conceptualised by Borden and Luborsky.

Borden's notion of the alliance being made up of the bond, goals, and tasks influenced the development of the initial questionnaire and the subsequent second version of the questionnaire. The questionnaire is designed to be used in therapeutic settings and its use has reliably predicted therapy outcomes.

Scoring

The questionnaire has nineteen questions with responses arranged in a six-point Likert scale; three positive and three negative. To attain a global alliance score the positively scored items are simply aggregated and the negatively worded items are reverse scored, thus arriving at a total score.

Working Alliance Inventory – Short Form (WAI-S)

Scale purpose

The Working Alliance Inventory – Short Form is a revised version of the original Working Alliance Inventory developed by Horvath & Greenberg (1989). Like the HAq-II it is based on Borden's model of the working alliance. The short form version is a well-used measure of the working alliance and can be employed in a range of therapeutic settings.

Scoring

The measure consists of two sets of questionnaires, one being for the client and the other for the therapist to complete. It is well recognised that therapists do not necessarily rate the working alliance at similar levels to their clients. Hence the separate sheets are provided for therapist comparison. There are twelve questions on the questionnaires with a seven-point response scale for each. A copy of the Working Alliance Inventory – Short Form can be found at www.sfu.ca/~educwww/alliance/allianceA/

Conclusion

These different measures of hope, well-being, and therapeutic alliance represent only a small sample of instruments which could be incorporated in both small- and large-scale research endeavours. Many opportunities exist to develop research projects within private practice settings, university training, community-based settings, and in public health organisations. These measures can be used in purely quantitative designs or they can be combined with qualitative methodologies forming mixed-method designs. We hope that the range of ideas presented in this book have stimulated your own research appetite and set you on a path of discovery that not only increases your research capacity but develops your clinical skills as well.

11

Conclusion

Hope has long been recognised as an important factor in therapeutic change. Even before the common factors were recognised within the counselling and psychotherapy literature, hope was known to be a central component in healing. With the common factors established as key ingredients of therapeutic change hope has gained even greater recognition. While this is the case, there has been very little focus in research on how to operationalise hope within therapy. In large part, hope has remained an implicit aspect of the change process. The implicit nature of hope has also carried over into training programmes, resulting in it being acknowledged as a significant change variable but then largely ignored as a topic of study thereafter. When therapists are asked if hope is important in their practice of therapy most agree that it is. When then asked how they employ hope in therapy most therapists are less confident in their reply. It seems that hope is commonly acknowledged and then forgotten. This book has been written to help make hope more visible in the practice of therapy and to provide some recommendations about how therapists can operationalise it.

Acknowledging different theoretical influences

In the first part of this book we discussed a number of theoretical influences on how hope is understood. As hope is a metaconstruct it has been investigated from many disciplinary perspectives. The disciplines of philosophy and theology in particular have long recognised the significance of hope in human affairs. It is not surprising then that with the development of the professions in the twentieth century hope continued to exert its influence. This influence has been further advanced by nursing and psychology/psychotherapy researchers who have extended our understanding of the function of hope within many forms of healing and recovery. However, these advances have not resulted in unanimous agreement about the place of hope in health and recovery.

It is important to note that philosophers and theologians do not all hold hope in the same degree of esteem. Within existential philosophy, for example, hope has received mixed reviews. For some it is a central aspect of human functioning, for others it is at best a distraction and at worst a hindrance. Theologically hope varies in appeal as well. In monotheistic religions it is valued as a key virtue that enables us to live a balanced life. In Buddhism hope is acknowledged as contributing to daily functioning but is not viewed as a central component of spiritual transformation. These different philosophical and theological perspectives have demonstrated that we should not assume that hope is commonly understood. However, it is important to be aware of our own views of hope and of the influences that have helped shape them. While the various theoretical positions discussed here represent important perspectives on hope, there are many other positions which bear on the topic and which should be considered. In addition to this, we should note that the ideas that have shaped our thinking about hope have also shaped our professional practice. In fact, our practice reflects our understanding of hope whether we are consciously aware of hope or not. As evidenced in the participatory research literature, we always have local theories or theories-in-use. Being more aware of what influences our view of hope not only will inform us at a personal level but will also inform our professional practice.

Apart from the importance of being aware of our own views of hope in general, and of hope's place in therapy more specifically, as health care professionals we need to acknowledge that our clients also bring with them different perspectives. Given the often implicit nature of hope, client views may not be obvious and so it is important that we tread carefully and respectfully when approaching the topic. While much of our work with hope in therapy will be implicit there may well be times where it becomes an explicit focus. Whether working with hope implicitly or explicitly, we need both theoretical and practical knowledge of its nature and function and of how to foster it in others if we are to fully engage with it professionally.

The dialectics of hope and despair

One of the themes addressed in this book is the dialectic nature of hope and despair. It seems that the two conditions are intricately related. Many times people come to therapy because they are experiencing despair. Despair is best understood as a loss of hope, a loss of the ability to envisage a positive future. As we have seen, however, despair can also be the pathway that, in the end, leads us to hope. Despair can be a process of unmasking our illusions about self, about others, and about life. It can ground us in reality and send us looking for answers. When despair functions in this way it can open the door to hope. One of the ways in which despair can inadvertently help us is by requiring us to seek help. Without the experience of despair many would not come to counselling. Once linked with a therapist an individual has the possibility of accessing one of the greatest avenues of hope, the therapeutic relationship. Without doubt the therapeutic relationship is the *sine qua non* of therapeutic change. When we experience another as being deeply interested in our welfare, who has a capacity to appreciate our troubles and concerns, then we know that we are not alone in our struggles. To despair is a very human thing to do. Thankfully hope can be just around the corner. Of course despair can be a dangerous journey into confusion and mental illness and so it needs always to be carefully judged. As therapists we should be ever vigilant to consider our client's state of mind and to assess for risk. Having done so however, we should be ready to embrace the client's despair if and when it shows itself, as it may well be the turning point for change. When despair is present hope is close by.

The therapist's hope

We know that the client's own hope is central in the therapeutic change process, but what has not been as obvious is the importance of the therapist's hope. In several recent studies it was demonstrated that the therapist's hope was as much if not more predictive of positive therapeutic outcomes than was the client's own hope (Coppock et al., 2010; Flesaker & Larsen, 2010). These findings indicate that there is some transfer of hope from the therapist to the client. It is likely that the client draws on the therapist's hope in some way and in so doing bolsters their own hopes and expectations for change. It appears that the therapist's own hopeful life orientation is contagious, resulting in the client catching its benefits. This being the case, the therapist has a responsibility to examine his or her own orientation towards hope. How hopeful are we in our daily lives? Are there beliefs and experiences that limit our hope? How do we regain hope in ourselves when it has been challenged? Reflecting on such questions may not only benefit us personally but also benefit our clients as we progressively exemplify hope in our own lives.

Therapists' hope is also reflected in their use of theory and therapeutic strategies. Different counselling approaches encourage the client's hope in different ways. Our own theoretical preferences will in some ways shape how we work with hope. However, as a pan-theoretical construct hope also transcends the limitations of any one theory. This means that many hope-focused strategies can be incorporated comfortably into any theory of counselling. To do so however requires an awareness by the therapist of such strategies. In this book we have itemised and discussed a range of hope-focused strategies with the aim of equipping the therapist. These strategies come from therapists and so represent approaches that are already being used and recommended. No doubt there are many more ways of encouraging client hope, but we hope that the ideas and practices discussed here add significantly to therapists' capacities in working with hope.

Hope research

Research on hope has been growing over the past thirty years, greatly advancing our understanding of how it functions in peoples lives and also demonstrating how important it is for those in the caring professions to appreciate its place in care and recovery. Much of the research to date has focused on the patient's or client's hope and it is only recently that researchers have begun to turn their attention to therapist hope. Given that therapists' own hope influences therapy processes and outcomes, it is important to identify what contributes to them gaining and maintaining hope. What therapist qualities foster and support hope in their own lives and how do these personal/profession qualities influence therapeutic outcomes?

The growing practice of gathering regular client feedback provides opportunities to explore many different facets of therapeutic change, hope being one of them. Feedback mechanisms can provide information for both therapist and client, and when used collaboratively may well be an avenue through which hope is engendered. As the use of client feedback tools is still a relatively new phenomenon within the field, the opportunities for discovery are wide open.

The exciting thing about hope research is its breadth of application. As a metaconstruct hope can be linked to a wide array of other constructs. Researchers are only just beginning to tap the potential that such research may provide. In addition to the possibility of combining hope with other areas of interests, there is also extensive scope for innovation in research design. The multidimensionality of hope means that it is likely that its therapeutic benefits will only be fully realised through multi-method explorations. There is room for all types of research, ranging from traditional large-scale investigations to local practitioner research. Only time will reveal the full range of functions and benefits that hope provides.

Conclusion

This book has been written to draw attention to the benefits of hope and to the central place it holds in the therapeutic process. People have known through the centuries that hope is an important dimension of humanness and have sought to understand its function and influence. The knowledge gained in recent years has only served to increase the interest in hope, and especially how it can be fostered within therapeutic settings. It is our hope that this book serves to promote hope as a central component of therapeutic change and to help equip mental health professionals in inspiring hope in others.

APPENDIX

Settings goals

Set and make your goal

What is my goal? _____

What is my pathway to the goal?

_____

_____

How much do I believe I can make it?   a little   medium   very much

What makes me think I can attain my goal?

_____

_____

What probably will happen if I maintain this path to my goal?

_____

_____

_____

What might happen if I change my pathway?

_____

_____

_____

What is my back-up plan?

_____

_____

_____

What would I tell a friend if he or she came up with my goal and my pathway?

_____

_____

_____

What are the first three steps towards my goal?

   1 _____

   2 _____

   3 _____

How much do I believe I will accomplish my goal now?
   a little   medium   very much

Source: Snyder (2000). *Handbook of hope: theory, measures, and applications*. New York: Academic Press.

Goals worksheet

Domain	*Importance rating*	*Satisfaction rating*

Academic

Family

Leisure

Personal growth

Health/fitness

Romantic

Social relationships

Spiritual

Work

My selected domain is:_____

What would I have to do to increase my satisfaction in this domain?

_____

_____

My goal is: _____

To determine feasibility I asked three questions:

The answers I obtained were:

The main steps I will take to my goals are:

Here are the steps arranged in order from first to last:

Source: Snyder (2000). *Handbook of hope: theory, measures, and applications.* New York: Academic Press.

Hope Questionnaires

The Adult Hope Scale

Directions: Read each item carefully. Using the scale shown below, please select the number that best describes YOU and put that number in the blank provided.

1 = Definitely false
2 = Mostly false
3 = Somewhat false
4 = Slightly false
5 = Slightly true
6 = Somewhat true
7 = Mostly true
8 = Definitely true

____ 1. I can think of many ways to get out of a jam.
____ 2. I energetically pursue my goals.
____ 3. I feel tired most of the time.
____ 4. There are lots of ways around any problem.
____ 5. I am easily downed in an argument.
____ 6. I can think of many ways to get the things in life that are important to me.
____ 7. I worry about my health.
____ 8. Even when others get discouraged, I know I can find a way to solve the problem.
____ 9. My past experiences have prepared me well for my future.
____10. I've been pretty successful in life.
____11. I usually find myself worrying about something.
____12. I meet the goals that I set for myself.

Notes: When administering the scale, it is called The Future Scale. The *Agency* subscale score is derived by summing items # 2, 9, 10, and 12; the *Pathway* subscale score is derived by adding items # 1, 4, 6, and 8. The *total Hope Scale score* is derived by summing the four Agency and the four Pathway items.

Source: Snyder et al. (1991). The will and the ways: development and validation of an individual-differences measure of hope. *Journal of Personality and Social Psychology, 60*(4), 585.

The Domain-Specific Hope Scale

Please take a moment to contemplate each of the following life areas before you answer the questions in each section. If a particular question does not apply to you at this time, try to answer it as you would if they did fit your situation (e.g., you don't have a job right now so think of your last job). Using the scale below, select the number that best describes your response to each question.

1	2	3	4	5	6	7	8
Definitely false	Mostly false	Somewhat false	Slightly false	Slightly true	Somewhat true	Mostly true	Definitely true

Please take a moment to contemplate your social life. Think about your friendships and acquaintances and how you interact with others. Once you have this in mind, answer the following questions using the scale above.

Social relationships (friendships, casual acquaintances)

_____ 1. I can think of many ways to make friends.
_____ 2. I actively pursue friendships.
_____ 3. There are lots of ways to meet new people.
_____ 4. I can think of many ways to be included in the groups that are important to me.
_____ 5. I've been pretty successful where friendships are concerned.
_____ 6. Even when someone seems unapproachable, I know I can find a way to break the ice.
_____ 7. My past social experiences have prepared me to make friends in the future.
_____ 8. When I meet someone I want to be friends with, I usually succeed.

Academics (school, coursework)

1	2	3	4	5	6	7	8
Definitely false	Mostly false	Somewhat false	Slightly false	Slightly true	Somewhat true	Mostly true	Definitely true

Please take a moment to contemplate your academic life. Think about your classes and your coursework. Once you have this in mind, answer the following questions using the scale above.

_____ 1. I can think of lots of ways to make good grades.
_____ 2. I energetically pursue my school work.
_____ 3. There are lots of ways to meet the challenges of any class.
_____ 4. Even if the course is difficult, I know I can find a way to succeed.
_____ 5. I've been pretty successful in school.
_____ 6. I can think of lots of ways to do well in classes that are important to me.
_____ 7. My past academic experiences have prepared me well for future success.
_____ 8. I get the grades that I want in my classes.
_____ 9. If you read this question, place an X on the line.

Romantic relationships

1	2	3	4	5	6	7	8
Definitely false	Mostly false	Somewhat false	Slightly false	Slightly true	Somewhat true	Mostly true	Definitely true

Please take a moment to contemplate your love life. Think about your romantic relationships. Once you have this in mind, answer the following questions using the scale above.

_____ 1. I can think of many ways to get to know someone I am attracted to.
_____ 2. When I am interested in someone romantically, I actively pursue him or her.
_____ 3. There are lots of ways to convince someone to go out with me.
_____ 4. I can think of many ways to keep someone interested in me when they are important.
_____ 5. I've been pretty successful in my romantic relationships.
_____ 6. Even when someone doesn't seem interested, I know I can find a way to get their attention.
_____ 7. My past romantic relationships have prepared me well for future involvements.
_____ 8. I can usually get a date when I set my mind to it.

Family life

1	2	3	4	5	6	7	8
Definitely false	Mostly false	Somewhat false	Slightly false	Slightly true	Somewhat true	Mostly true	Definitely true

Please take a moment to contemplate your family life. Think about your family members. Once you have this in mind, answer the following questions using the scale above.

_____ 1. I can think of lots of things I enjoy doing with my family.
_____ 2. I energetically work on maintaining family relationships.
_____ 3. I can think of many ways to include my family in things that are important to me.
_____ 4. If you read this question, place an X on the line.
_____ 5. I have a pretty successful family life.
_____ 6. Even when we disagree, I know my family can find a way to solve our problems.
_____ 7. I have the kind of relationships that I want with family members.
_____ 8. There are lots of ways to communicate my feelings to family members.
_____ 9. My experiences with my family have prepared me for a family of my own.

Work

1	2	3	4	5	6	7	8
Definitely false	Mostly false	Somewhat false	Slightly false	Slightly true	Somewhat true	Mostly true	Definitely true

Please take a moment to contemplate your working life. Think about your job and job history. Once you have this in mind, answer the following questions using the scale above.

_____ 1. I can think of many ways to find a job.
_____ 2. I am energetic at work.
_____ 3. There are lots of ways to succeed at work.
_____ 4. Even if it's a lousy job, I can usually find something good about it.
_____ 5. I have a good work record.
_____ 6. My previous work experiences have helped prepare me for future success.
_____ 7. I can always find a job if I set my mind to it.
_____ 8. I can think of lots of ways to impress my boss if the job is important to me..

Leisure activities

1	2	3	4	5	6	7	8
Definitely false	Mostly false	Somewhat false	Slightly false	Slightly true	Somewhat true	Mostly true	Definitely true

Please take a moment to contemplate your leisure time. Think about the activities that you enjoy doing in your spare time. For some this may be sports or music or art. Once you have this in mind, answer the following questions using the scale above.

_____ 1. I can think of many satisfying things to do in my spare time.
_____ 2. I energetically pursue my leisure time activities.
_____ 3. If my planned leisure time activities fall through, I can find something else to do that I enjoy.
_____ 4. I can think of lots of ways to make time for the activities that are important to me.
_____ 5. Even if others don't think my activities are important, I still enjoy doing them.
_____ 6. My experiences with hobbies and other leisure time activities are important to my future.
_____ 7. I have satisfying activities that I do in my leisure time.
_____ 8. When I try to perform well in leisure time activities, I usually succeed.

Scoring information

Domain-specific hope scores are obtained by summing the eight items within each domain. Scores can range from 8 to 64, with higher scores indicating higher levels of hope within each domain.
Total domain-specific hope can be tallied by adding the scores from each of the six domains. Scores can range from 48 to 384, with higher scores indicating higher levels of total hope across domains.

Source: S. Sympson (1999). Validation of the domain specific hope scale: exploring hope in life domains. Unpublished Doctoral Dissertation: University of Kansas.

The Children's Hope Scale

Directions: The six sentences below describe how children think about themselves and how they do things in general. Read each sentence carefully. For each sentence, please think about how you are in most situations. Place a check inside the circle that describes YOU the best. For example, place a check (✓) in the circle (O) above 'None of the time', if this describes you. Or, if you are this way 'All of the time', check this circle. Please answer every question by putting a check in one of the circles. There are no right or wrong answers.

1. *I think I am doing pretty well.*

O	O	O	O	O	O
None of the time	A little of the time	Some of the time	A lot of the time	Most of the time	All of the time

2. *I can think of many ways to get the things in life that are most important to me.*

O	O	O	O	O	O
None of the time	A little of the time	Some of the time	A lot of the time	Most of the time	All of the time

3. *I am doing just as well as other kids my age.*

O	O	O	O	O	O
None of the time	A little of the time	Some of the time	A lot of the time	Most of the time	All of the time

4. *When I have a problem, I can come up with lots of ways to solve it.*

O	O	O	O	O	O
None of the time	A little of the time	Some of the time	A lot of the time	Most of the time	All of the time

5. *I think the things I have done in the past will help me in the future.*

O	O	O	O	O	O
None of the time	A little of the time	Some of the time	A lot of the time	Most of the time	All of the time

6. *Even when others want to quit, I know that I can find ways to solve the problem.*

O	O	O	O	O	O
None of the time	A little of the time	Some of the time	A lot of the time	Most of the time	All of the time

Notes: When administered to children, this scale is not labelled 'The Children's Hope Scale', but is called 'Questions About Your Goals'. The total Children's Hope Scale score is achieved by adding the responses to the six items, with 'None of the time' =1; 'A little of the time' = 2; 'Some of the time' = 3; 'A lot of the time' = 4; 'Most of the time' = 5; and, 'All of the time' = 6. The three odd-numbered items tap agency, and the three even-numbered items tap pathways.

Source: Snyder et al. (1997). The development and validation of the Children's Hope Scale. *Journal of Pediatric Psychology, 22*(3), 399–421.

State Hope Scale

Directions: Read each item carefully. Using the scale shown below, please select the number that best describes how you think about yourself right now and put that number in the blank before each sentence. Please take a few moments to focus on yourself and what is going on in your life at this moment. Once you have this 'here and now' set, go ahead and answer each item according to the following scale:

1 = Definitely false
2 = Mostly false
3 = Somewhat false
4 = Slightly false
5 = Slightly true
6 = Somewhat true
7 = Mostly true
8 = Definitely true

_____ 1. If I should find myself in a jam, I could think of many ways to get out of it.
_____ 2. At the present time, I am energetically pursuing my goals.
_____ 3. There are lots of ways around any problem that I am facing now.
_____ 4. Right now, I see myself as being pretty successful.
_____ 5. I can think of many ways to reach my current goals.
_____ 6. At this time, I am meeting the goals that I have set for myself.

Notes: The Agency subscale score is derived by summing the three even-numbered items; the Pathways subscale score is derived by adding the three odd-numbered items. The total State Hope Scale score is derived by summing the three Agency and the three Pathways items. Scores can range from a low of 6 to a high of 48. When administering the State Hope Scale, it is labelled as the 'Goals Scale For the Present'.

Source: Snyder et al. (1996). Development and validation of the State Hope Scale. *Journal of Personality and Social Psychology, 70*(2): 321–335.

Herth Hope Index

Listed below are a number of statements. Read each statement and place an [X] in the box that describes how much you agree with that statement right now.

	Strongly disagree	Disagree	Agree	Strongly agree
1. I have a positive outlook toward life.				
2. I have short- and/or long-range goals.				
3. I feel all alone.				
4. I can see possibilities in the midst of difficulties.				
5. I have a faith that gives me comfort.				
6. I feel scared about my future.				
7. I can recall happy/joyful times.				
8. I have deep inner strength.				
9. I am able to give and receive caring/love.				
10. I have a sense of direction.				
11. I believe that each day has potential.				
12. I feel my life has value and worth.				

Source: Herth (1992). Abbreviated instrument to measure hope: development and psychometric evaluation. *Journal of Advanced Nursing, 17*, 1251–1259. (1999 items 2 & 4 reworded.) Copyright held by Kaye A. Herth. No portion of the Herth Hope Index may be reproduced by any means without permission in writing from the copyright owner.

The Satisfaction with Life Scale

Directions: Below are five statements with which you may agree or disagree. Using the 1–7 scale below, indicate your agreement with each item by placing the appropriate number in the line preceding that item. Please be open and honest in your responding.

1 = Strongly disagree
2 = Disagree
3 = Slightly disagree
4 = Neither agree or disagree
5 = Slightly agree
6 = Agree
7 = Strongly agree

_____1. In most ways my life is close to my ideal.

_____2. The conditions of my life are excellent.

_____3. I am satisfied with life.

_____4. So far I have gotten the important things I want in life.

_____5. If I could live my life over, I would change almost nothing.

Source: Diener et al. (1985). The satisfaction with life scale. *Journal of Personality Assessment, 49*(1), 71–75.

The Helping Alliance Questionnaire (Patient Version)

Instructions: These are ways that a person may feel or behave in relation to another person – their therapist. Consider carefully your relationship with your therapist, and then mark each statement according to how strongly you agree or disagree. Please mark every one.

	Strongly disagree	Disagree	Slightly disagree	Slightly agree	Agree	Strongly agree
1. I feel I can depend upon the therapist.	1	2	3	4	5	6
2. I feel the therapist understands me.	1	2	3	4	5	6
3. I feel the therapist wants me to achieve my goals.	1	2	3	4	5	6
4. At times I distrust the therapist's judgement.	1	2	3	4	5	6
5. I feel I am working together with the therapist in a joint effort.	1	2	3	4	5	6
6. I believe we have similar ideas about the nature of my problems.	1	2	3	4	5	6
7. I generally respect the therapist's views about me.	1	2	3	4	5	6
8. The procedures used in my therapy are not well suited to my needs.	1	2	3	4	5	6
9. I like the therapist as a person.	1	2	3	4	5	6
10. In most sessions, the therapist and I find a way to work on my problems together.	1	2	3	4	5	6
11. The therapist relates to me in ways that slow up the progress of the therapy.	1	2	3	4	5	6
12. A good relationship has formed with my therapist.	1	2	3	4	5	6
13. The therapist appears to be experienced in helping people.	1	2	3	4	5	6
14. I want very much to work out my problems.	1	2	3	4	5	6
15. The therapist and I have meaningful exchanges.	1	2	3	4	5	6
16. The therapist and I sometimes have unprofitable exchanges.	1	2	3	4	5	6
17. From time to time, we both talk about the same important events in my past.	1	2	3	4	5	6
18. I believe the therapist likes me as a person.	1	2	3	4	5	6
19. At times the therapist seems distant.	1	2	3	4	5	6

The Helping Alliance Questionnaire (Therapist Version)

Instructions: These are ways that a person may feel or behave in relation to another person – their therapist. Consider carefully your relationship with your patient, and then mark each statement according to how strongly you agree or disagree. Please mark every one.

	Strongly disagree	Disagree	Slightly disagree	Slightly agree	Agree	Strongly agree
1. The patient feels he/she can depend upon me.	1	2	3	4	5	6
2. He/she feels I understand him/her.	1	2	3	4	5	6
3. The patient feels I want him/her to achieve the goals.	1	2	3	4	5	6
4. At times the patient distrusts my judgement.	1	2	3	4	5	6
5. The patient feels he/she is working together with me in a joint effort.	1	2	3	4	5	6
6. I believe we have similar ideas about the nature of his/her problems.	1	2	3	4	5	6
7. The patient generally respects my views about him/her.	1	2	3	4	5	6
8. The patient believes the procedures used in his/her therapy are not well suited to his/her needs.	1	2	3	4	5	6
9. The patient likes me as a person.	1	2	3	4	5	6
10. In most sessions, we find a way to work on his/her problems together.	1	2	3	4	5	6
11. The patient believes I relate to him/her in ways that slow up the progress of the therapy.	1	2	3	4	5	6
12. The patient believes a good relationship has formed between us.	1	2	3	4	5	6
13. The patient believes I am experienced in helping people.	1	2	3	4	5	6
14. I want very much for the patient to work out his/her problems.	1	2	3	4	5	6
15. The patient and I have meaningful exchanges.	1	2	3	4	5	6
16. The patient and I sometimes have unprofitable exchanges.	1	2	3	4	5	6
17. From time to time, we both talk about the same important events in his/her past.	1	2	3	4	5	6
18. The patient believes I like him/her as a person.	1	2	3	4	5	6
19. At times the patient sees me as distant.	1	2	3	4	5	6

Source: Luborsky et al. (1996). The revised Helping Alliance Questionnaire (HAq-II): psychometric properties. *Journal of Psychotherapy Practice and Research*, 6, 260–271.

References

Ahn H., & Wampold, B. (2001). Where oh where are the specific ingredients? A meta-analysis of component studies in counseling and psychotherapy. *Journal of Counseling Psychology, 38,* 251–257.

Alexander, F. G., & French, T. M. (1948). *Studies in psychosomatic medicine: an approach to the cause and treatment of vegetative disturbance.* New York: Roland.

Andersen, T. (1987). The reflecting team: dialogue and meta-dialogue in clinical work. *Family Process, 26,* 415–425.

Aquinas, T. (2006a). *Summa Theologiae: 2a2ae. 17–22 (v. 33).* Cambridge, England: Cambridge University Press.

Aquinas, T. (2006b). *Summa theologica, secunda secundæ partis* (Part II, Second Section) Question 17, Article 2.

Argyris, C., & Schön, D. A. (1992). *Theory in practice: increasing professional effectiveness.* San Francisco: Jossey-Bass.

Averill, J. R. (1994). Emotions are many splendored things. In P. Ekman & R.J. Davidson (Eds), *The nature of emotion.* New York: Oxford University Press.

Averill, J., Catlin, G., & Chon, K. (1990). *Rules of hope.* New York: Springer-Verlag.

Baker, S. B., Daniels, T. G., & Greeley, A. T. (1990). Systematic training of graduate-level counselors: narrative and meta-analytic reviews of three major programs. *The Counseling Psychologist, 18*(3), 355–421.

Bandura, A., (1982). Self-efficacy mechanism in human agency. *American Psychologist, 37*(2), 122–147.

Barkham M., Evans C., Margison F., McGrath G., Mellor-Clark J., Milne D., & Connell J. (1998). The rationale for developing and implementing core outcome batteries for routine use in service settings and psychotherapy outcome research. *Journal of Mental Health, 7*(1), 35–47.

Bartels, A., & Zeki, S. (2004). The neural correlates of maternal and romantic love. *NeuroImage, 21,* 1155–1166.

Bateman, A. W., & Fonagy, P. (2004). *Psychotherapy for borderline personality disorder.* Oxford: Oxford University Press.

Bateman, A. W., & Fonagy, P. (2006). *Mentalization-based treatment for borderline personality disorder: a practical guide.* New York: Oxford University Press.

Benard, B. (1991). *Fostering resiliency in kids: protective factors in the family, school and community.* San Francisco: Far West Laboratory for Educational Research and Development. ED 335 781.

Beutler, L. E., Harwood, T. M., Michelson, A., Xiaoxia, S., & Holman, J. (2011). Resistance/reactance level. *Journal of Clinical Psychology, 67*(2), 33–142.

Bingaman, K. A. (2010). A pastoral theological approach to the new anxiety. *Pastoral Psychology*, *59*, 659–670.

Bion, W. R. (1962). *Learning from experience*. London: Karnac Books.

Bishop, S. R., Lau, M., Shapiro, S., Carlson, L., Anderson, N. D., Carmody, J., Segal, Z. V., Abbey, S., Speca, M., Velting, D., & Devins, G. (2004). Mindfulness: a proposed operational definition. *Clinical Psychology: Science and Practice*, *11*(3), 230–241.

Bohart, A. C. (2000). The client is the most important common factor: clients' self-healing capacities and psychotherapy. *Journal of Psychotherapy Integration*, *10*(2), 127–149.

Bohart, M., & Tallman, K. (1999). *How clients make therapy work: the process of active self-healing*. Washington DC: American Psychological Association.

Bordin, E. S. (1979). The generalizability of the psychoanalytic concept of the working alliance. *Psychotherapy: Theory, Research & Practice*, *16*(3), 252–260.

Borenstein, L. (2003). The clinician as a dreamcatcher: holding the dream. *Journal of Clinical Social Work*, *31*, 249–262.

Bowen, M. (1978). *Family therapy in clinical practice*. New York: Harper & Row.

Brossart, D., Willson, V., Patton, M., Kivlighan, D., Jr., & Multon, K. (1998). A time series model of the working alliance: a key process in short-term psychoanalytic counseling. *Psychotherapy*, *35*, 197–205.

Bruininks, P., & Malle, B. F. (2005). Distinguishing hope from optimism and related affective states. *Motivation and Emotion*, *29*, 324–352.

Bryant, F. B., & Cvengros, J. A. (2004). Distinguishing hope and optimism: two sides of the a coin, or two separate coins? *Journal of Social and Clinical Psychology*, *23*(2), 273–302.

Buechler, S. (2002). Fromm's spirited values and analytic neutrality. *International Forum of Psychoanalysis*, *11*, 275–278.

Camus, A. (1955). *The myth of Sisyphus and other essays*. (J. O'Brien, Trans.). New York: Knopf.

Carletona, R. N., Mulvoguea, M. K., Thibodeaua, M. A., McCabeb, R. E., Antonyc, M. M., & Asmundson, G. J. (2012). Increasingly certain about uncertainty: intolerance of uncertainty across anxiety and depression. *Journal of Anxiety Disorders*, *26*, 468–479.

Carpenter, G. (1974). Mother's face and the newborn. *New Scientist*, *61*, 742.

Carr, A. (1998). Michael White's narrative therapy. *Contemporary Family Therapy*, *20*(4), 485–503.

Castonguay, L. G., Constantino, M. J., & Grosse-Holtforth, M. (2006). The working alliance: where are we and where should we go? *Psychotherapy: Theory, Research, Practice, Training*, *43*, 271–279.

Clay, D. L., Anderson, W. P., & Dixon, W. A. (1993). Relationship between anger expression and stress in predicting depression. *Journal of Counseling and Development*, *72*, 91–94.

Cohen, S., Kamarck, T., & Mermelstein, R. (1983). A global measure of perceived stress. *Journal of Health and Social Behavior*, *24*, 386–396.

Concise Oxford English Dictionary: main edition (12th ed.). (2011). Oxford: Oxford University Press.

Constantino, M. J., Arnkoff, D. B., Glass, C. R., Ametrano, R. M., & Smith, J. Z. (2011). Expectations. *Journal of Clinical Psychology: In Session 67*, 184–192.

Cooper, M., & McLeod, J. (2011) *Pluralistic counselling and psychotherapy*. London: Sage.

Coopersmith, S. (1967). *The antecedents of self-esteem*. San Francisco: Freeman.

Coppock, T. E., Owen, J. J., Zagarskas, E., & Schmidt, M. (2010). The relationship between therapist and client hope with therapy outcomes. *Psychotherapy Research*, *20*(6), 619–626.

Cozolino, L. (2010). *The neuroscience of psychotherapy*. New York: W. W. Norton & Company.

Cutcliffe J. R. (2004). The inspiration of hope in bereavement counselling. *Issues in Mental Health Nursing, 25*, 165–190.

Cutcliffe J. R. (2006a). The principles and processes of inspiring hope in bereavement counselling: a modified grounded theory study – part one. *Journal of Psychiatric and Mental Health Nursing, 13*, 598–603.

Cutcliffe J. R. (2006b). The principles and processes of inspiring hope in bereavement counselling: a modified grounded theory study – part two. *Journal of Psychiatric and Mental Health Nursing, 13*, 604–610.

De Shazer, S., & Berg, I. K. (1992). Doing therapy: a post-structural re-vision. *Journal of Marital and Family Therapy, 18*, 71–81.

Diener, E., Emmons, R. A., Larsen, R. J., & Griffin, S. (1985). The satisfaction with life scale. *Journal of Personality Assessment, 49*(1), 71–75.

DiGuiseppe, R., & Linscott, J. (1993). Philosophical differences among cognitive behavioral therapists: rationalism, constructivism, or both? *Journal of Cognitive Psychotherapy: An International Quarterly, 7*, 117–130.

Drenth, C. M., Herbst, A. G., & Strydom, H. (2010). A complicated grief intervention model. *Health SA Gesondheid, 15*(1), 415–423.

Dufault, K., & Martocchio, B. (1985) Hope: its spheres and dimensions. *Nursing Clinics of North America, 20*(2), 379–391.

Duncan, B. (2012). The partners for change outcome management system (PCOMS): the heart and soul of change project. *Canadian Psychology, 53*(2), 93–104.

Egéa-Kuehne, D. (2008). *Levinas and education: at the intersection of faith and reason*. New York: Routledge.

Eliott, J., & Olver, I. (2002). The discursive properties of 'hope': a qualitative analysis of cancer patients' speech. *Qualitative Health Research, 12*(2), 173–193.

Elliott, R. (1986). Interpersonal Process Recall (IPR) as a psychotherapy process research method. In L. S. Greenberg & W. M. Pinsof (Eds), *The psychotherapeutic process: a research handbook*. New York: Guilford Press

Epston, D., Stillman, J. R., & Erbes, C. R. (2012). Speaking two languages: a conversation between narrative therapy and scientific practices. *Journal of Systemic Therapies, 31*(1), 74–88.

Erikson, E. H. (1964). *Insight and Responsibility*. NewYork: Norton.

Flaskas, C. (2007). Holding hope and hopelessness: therapeutic engagements with the balance of hope. *Journal of Family Therapy, 29*, 186–202.

Fleming, M. (2005). The mental pain of the psychoanalysis: a personal view. *International Forum of Psychoanalysis, 14*(2), 69–75.

Flesaker, K., & Larsen, D. (2010). To offer hope you must have hope. *Qualitative Social Work, 11*(1), 61–79.

Fonagy, P., & Target, M. (1997). Attachment and reflective function: their role in self-organization. *Development and Psychopathology, 9*, 679–700.

Frank, J. (1973). *Persuasion and healing.* Baltimore: John Hopkins University Press.

Frank, J. (1995). Psychotherapy as rhetoric: some implications. *Clinical Psychology: Science and Practice, 1*(1), 90–93.

Frank, J. D., & Frank, J. B. (1991). *Persuasion and healing: a comparative study of psychotherapy* (3rd ed.). Baltimore, MD: Johns Hopkins University Press.

Frankl, V. (1959). *Man's search for meaning.* New York: Beacon Press.

Fromm, E. (1968). *Revolution of hope: toward a humanized technology.* New York: Harper.

Garfield, S. L. (1986). Research on client variables in psychotherapy. In S. L. Garfield & A. E. Bergin (Eds), *Handbook of psychotherapy and behavior change* (3rd ed.). New York: Wiley.

Garfield, S. L. (1994). Research on client variables in psychotherapy. In A. E. Bergin, & S. L. Garfield (Eds), *Handbook of psychotherapy and behavior change* (4th ed.). New York: Wiley.

Garmezy, N. (1993). Children in poverty: resilience despite risk. *Psychiatry, 56*, 127–136.

Gendlin, E. T. (1964). A theory of personality change. In P. Worchel, & D. Byrne (Eds), *Personality change.* New York: Wiley.

Gergen, K. (1991). *The saturated self: dilemmas of identity in contemporary life.* New York: Basic Books.

Goldfried, M. R., & Davila, J. (2005). The role of relationship and technique in therapeutic change. *Psychotherapy: Therapy, Research, Practice, Training, 42*, 421–430

Gombrich, R. (2011). Is hope a form of delusion? A Buddhist perspective. Unpublished paper presented at the conference of the European Network of Buddhist-Christian Studies entitled 'Hope: A Form of Delusion? Buddhist and Christian Perspectives', Liverpool Hope University, 1 July 2011.

Gravell, L. (2010). The counselling psychologist as therapeutic 'container', *Counselling Psychology Review, 25*(2), 28–33.

Greenberg, L. S., Rice, L. N., & Elliott, R. (1993). *Facilitating emotional change: the moment-by-moment process.* New York: Guilford Press.

Hammer, K., Morgensen, O., & Hall, E. O. C. (2009). The meaning of hope in nursing research: a meta-synthesis. *Scandinavian Journal of Caring Sciences, 23*(3), 549–557.

Harter, S. (1999). *The construction of the self. A developmental perspective.* New York: Guilford Press.

Harvey, J., & Delfabbro, P.H. (2004). Psychological resilience in disadvantaged youth: a critical overview. *Australian Psychologist, 39*(1), 3–13.

Hayes, H. (2006). To despair in the right way. *Existential Analysis, 17*, 84–101.

Hayes, S. C., Strosahl, K. D., & Wilson, K. G. (1999). *Acceptance and commitment therapy: an experiential approach to behavior change.* New York: Guilford Press.

Heidegger, M. (1962). *Being and time*. Oxford: Blackwell Publishing.

Herth, K. (1992). Abbreviated instrument to measure hope: development and psychometric evaluation. *Journal of Advanced Nursing, 17*, 1251–1259.

Herth, K. (1993). Hope in the family caregiver of terminally ill people. *Journal of Advanced Nursing, 18*, 538–548.

Hewitt, J. P. (1998). *The myth of self-esteem: finding happiness and solving problems in America*. New York: St. Martin's Press.

Hobson, R. F. (1971). Imagination and amplification in psychotherapy. *Journal of Analytical Psychotherapy, 16*, 79–105.

Hobson, R. F. (1985). *Forms of feeling: the heart of psychotherapy*. London: Tavistock.

Holtforth, M. G., & Grawe, K. (2002). Bern inventory of treatment goals: Part 1. Development and first application of a taxonomy of treatment goal themes. *Psychotherapy Research, 12*(1), 79–99.

Holy Bible, The (Jeremiah 29:11).

Horvath, A. O., & Greenberg, L. S. (1989). Development and validation of the Working Alliance Inventory. *Journal of Counseling Psychology, 36*(2), 223–233.

Horvath, A. O., & Luborsky, L. (1993). The role of the therapeutic alliance in psychotherapy. *Journal of Consulting and Clinical Psychology, 61*(4), 561–573.

Horvath, A. O., & Symonds, B. D. (1991). Relation between working alliance and outcome in psychotherapy: a meta-analysis. *Journal of Counseling Psychology, 38*, 139–149.

Huppert, J. D., Fabbro, A., Barlow, D. H., Goodheart, C. D., Kazdin, A. E., & Sternberg, R. J. (2006). *Evidence-based psychotherapy: where practice and research meet*. Washington, DC: American Psychological Association.

Kabat-Zinn, J. (1990). *Full catastrophe living: using the wisdom of your body and mind to face stress, pain, and illness*. New York: Dell.

Kabat-Zinn, J. (2003). Mindfulness-based interventions in context: past, present, and future. *Clinical Psychology: Science and Practice, 10*(2), 144–156.

Kabat-Zinn, J. (2005). *Coming to our senses*. New York: Hyperion.

Kagan, N., Krathwohl, D. R., & Miller, R. (1963). Stimulated recall in therapy using video-tape: a case study. *Journal of Counseling Psychology, 10*(3), 237–243.

Kant, I. (1788/2008). *Critique of pure reason*. Harmondsworth: Penguin.

Kelly, A. (2006). *Eschatology and hope*. Maryknoll, NY: Orbis Books.

Kernberg, O. F. (2006). Identity: recent findings and clinical implications. *Psychoanalytic Quarterly, 65*, 969–1004.

Kierkegaard, S. (1844). *Upbuilding discourses I-IV*. (D.F. Swenson and L. M. Swenson, Trans.). Minneapolis: Augsburg Publishing House.

Kierkegaard, S. (1989). *The sickness unto death*. London: Penguin.

Knox, S., & Hill, C. E. (2003). Therapist self-disclosure: research-based suggestions for practitioners. *Journal of Clinical Psychology, 59*(5), 529–539.

Kohut, H. (1977). *The restoration of the self*. New York: International University Press.

Kopp. R. R. (1995). *Metaphor therapy: using client generated metaphors in psychotherapy*. Bristol/PA: Bruner/Mazel.

Kuhn, T.S. (1962). *The structure of scientific revolutions*. Chicago: University of Chicago Press.

Lakoff, G. (1993). The contemporary theory of metaphor. In A. Ortony (Ed.), *Metaphor and thought*. Cambridge: Cambridge University Press.

Lambert, M. J. (1986). Implications of psychotherapy outcome research for eclectic psychotherapy research for eclectic psychotherapy. In J. C. Norcross (Ed.), *Handbook of eclectic psychotherapy* (pp. 436–462). New York: Bruner/Mazel.

Lambert, M. (1992). Psychotherapy outcome research. In J. C. Norcross, & M. R. Goldfried (Eds), *Handbook of psychotherapy integration*. New York: Basic Books.

Lambert, M. J., Lunnen, K., Umphress, V., Hansen, N., & Burlingame, G. M. (1994). *Administration and scoring manual for the Outcome Questionnaire (OQ-45.1)*. Salt Lake City: IHC Center for Behavioral Healthcare Efficacy.

Lambert, M. J., Shapiro, D. A., & Bergin, A. E. (1986). The effects of psychotherapy. In S. L. Garfield & A. E. Bergin (Eds), *Handbook of psychotherapy and behavior change* (3rd ed.). New York: Wiley.

Larsen, D., & Stege, R. (2010a). Hope-focused practices during early psychotherapy sessions: Part I. Implicit approaches. *Journal of Psychotherapy Integration, 20*, 271–292.

Larsen, D., & Stege, R. (2010b). Hope-focused practices during early psychotherapy sessions: Part II. Explicit approaches. *Journal of Psychotherapy Integration, 20*, 293–311.

Levinas, E. (1969). Totality and infinity: an essay on exteriority (A. Lingis, Trans.). Pittsburgh, PA: Duquesne University Press.

Levinas, E. (2001). *Alterity and transcendence*. New York: Columbia University Press.

Levy, K. N., Meehan, K. B., Kelly, K. M., Reynoso, J. S., Clarkin, J. F., & Kernberg, O. F. (2006). Change in attachment patterns and reflective function in a randomized control trial of transference-focused psychotherapy for borderline personality disorder. *Journal of Consulting and Clinical Psychology, 74*, 1027–1040.

Long, P. S., & Lepper, G. (2008). Metaphor in psychoanalytic psychotherapy: a comparative study of four cases by a practitioner-researcher. *British Journal of Psychotherapy, 24*(3), 343–364.

Lopez, S. J., Floyd, R. K., Ulven, J. C., & Snyder, C. R. (2000). Hope therapy: helping clients build a house of hope. In C. R. Snyder (Ed.), *Handbook of hope: theory, measures, and applications*. New York: Academic Press.

Lovibond, S. H., & Lovibond, P. F. (1995). *Manual for the Depression Anxiety Stress Scales* (2nd ed.). Sydney: Psychology Foundation.

Luborsky, L., Barber, J. P., Siqueland, L., Johnson, S., Najavits, L. M., Frank, A., & Daley, D. (1996). The revised Helping Alliance Questionnaire (HAQ-II): psychometric properties. *Journal of Psychotherapy Practice and Research, 6*, 260–271.

Luborsky, L., Singer, B., & Luborsky, L. (1975). Comparative studies of psychotherapies: is it true that 'everyone has won and all must have prizes'? *Archives of General Psychiatry, 32*, 995–1008.

Luborsky, L., Rosenthal, R., Diguer, L., Andrusyana, T. P., Berman, J. S., Levitt, J. T., Seligman, D. A., & Krause E. D. (2002). The dodo bird verdict is alive and well – mostly. *Clinical Psychology: Science and Practice, 9*(1), 2–12.

Luthans, F. (2002). The need for and meaning of positive organizational behavior. *Journal of Organizational Behavior, 6*, 695–706.

Magaletta, P. R., & Oliver, J. M. (1999). The hope construct, will, and ways: their relationship with self-efficacy, optimism, and general well-being. *Journal of Clinical Psychology, 55*, 539–551.

Mahler, M. S. (1975). *The psychological birth of the human infant.* New York: Basic Books.

Marcel, G. (1995). *The philosophy of existentialism.* (M. Harari, Trans.). New York: Carol.

Maslow, A. H. (1987). *Motivation and personality* (3rd ed.). New York: Addison-Wesley.

Masten, A. S. (2001). Ordinary magic: resilience processes in development. *American Psychologist, 56*(3), 227–238.

May, G. G. (1982). *Care of mind and care of spirit.* San Francisco: Harper Row.

McLeod, J. (2003). *Doing counselling research.* (2nd ed.). London: Sage.

McLeod, J. (2009). *An introduction to counselling.* London: Open University.

McLeod, J. (2011). *Qualitative research in counselling and psychotherapy.* London: Sage.

Meares, R. (2000). *Intimacy and alienation: memory trauma and personal being.* London: Routledge

Meares, R. (2005). *The metaphor of play: origin and breakdown of personal being.* Brunner-Routledge.

Menninger, K. (1959). The academy lecture: hope. *The American Journal of Psychiatry, 116*, 481–491. Retrieved 4 June 2008. Illiad.

Messer, S. B., & Wampold, B. E. (2002). Let's face facts: common factors are more potent than specific therapy ingredients. *Clinical Psychology: Science and Practice, 9*(1), 21–25.

Miller, J. F. (1983). *Coping with chronic illness: overcoming powerlessness.* Philadelphia: Davis.

Miller, S. D., & Duncan, B. L. (2000). *The outcome rating scale.* Chicago: Author.

Moltmann, J. (1993). *Theology of hope.* Minneapolis: Augsburg Fortress Press.

Morse J. M., & Doberneck B. (1995). Delineating the concept of hope. *Image, 27*(4), 277–285.

Munley, P. H., & Johnson, P. D. (2002). Ernest Becker: a vital resource for counselling psychology. *Counselling Psychology Quarterly, 6*(4), 363–372.

Neimeyer, G. J., & Morton, R. J. (1997). Personal epistemologies and preferences for rationalist versus constructivist psychotherapies. *Journal of Constructivist Psychology, 10*, 109–123.

Nietzsche, F. (1896). *Thus spoke Zarathustra.* (A. Tille, Trans.), London: Macmillan.

Norcross, J. C., & Wampold, B. E. (2011a). Evidence-based therapy relationships: research conclusions and clinical practices. *Psychotherapy, 48*(1), 98–102.

Norcross, J. C., & Wampold, B. E. (2011b). What works for whom: tailoring psychotherapy to the person. *Journal of Clinical Psychology, 67*(2), 127–132.

O'Connor, K. P., & Aardema, F. (2005). The imagination: cognitive, pre-cognitive, and meta-cognitive aspects. *Consciousness and Cognition, 14*, 233–256.

Oden, T. (1992). *Two worlds: notes on the death of modernity in America.* Downers Grove Ill: Intervarsity Press.

O'Hara, D. J. (2012). Reconciling technical and practical knowledge in psychotherapy through Polanyi's tacit knowing. *Counselling Psychology Review, 27*(1), 64–72.

O'Hara, D. J., & O'Hara, E. F. (2012). Towards a grounded theory of therapist hope. *Counselling Psychology Review, 27*(4), 42-55.

O'Hara, D. J., Meteyard, J., Andersen, K., & O'Hara E. F. (in press). The therapist's hope and its relationship with the differentiation of self and epistemic style. *Australian Journal of Counselling Psychology.*

Owen, D. C. (1989). Nurses' perspectives on the meaning of hope in patients with cancer: a qualitative study. *Oncology Nursing Forum, 16*(1), 75–79.

Pascal, B. (1958), *Pascal's pensees.* New York: E.P. Dutton and Co.

Pepper, S. C. (1961). *World hypotheses, prolegomena to systematic philosophy and a complete survey of metaphysics.* Berkeley: University of California Press.

Pieper, J. (1986). *On Hope* (Mary Frances McCarthy, Trans.) (originally Über die Hoffnung). San Francisco: Ignatius Press.

Polkinghorne, D. E. (1999). Traditional research and psychotherapy practice. *The Journal of Clinical Psychology, 55*(12), 1429–1440.

Prochaska, J. O., & DiClemente, C. C. (2005). The transtheoretical approach. In J. C. Norcross & M. R. Goldfried (Eds), *Handbook of psychotherapy integration* (2nd ed.). New York: Oxford.

Pruyser, P. W. (1963). Phenomenology and dynamics of hoping. *Journal for the Scientific Study of Religion, 3*(1), 86, 95.

Rogers, C. R. (1957). The necessary and sufficient conditions of therapeutic personality change. *Journal of Consulting Psychology, 21*(2), 95–103

Rogers, C. R. (1980). *A way of being.* Boston: Houghton Mifflin.

Rumi. *It is what it is: the discourses of Rumi – Chapter 16.* Retrieved from www.littleknownpubs.com/Rumi16.htm

Sanders, P., & Wilkins, P. (2010). *First steps in practitioner research.* Ross-on-Wye: PCCS Books.

Sartre, J. P. (1946/1989). Existentialism is a humanism. In Walter Kaufman (Ed.), *Existentialism from Dostoevsky to Sartre.* New York: Meridian Publishing Company.

Schachtel, E. G. (1959). *Metamorphosis: on the development of affect, perception, attention, and memory.* New York: Basic Books.

Schacter, D. L., & Addis, D. R. (2009). Remembering the past to imagine the future: a cognitive neuroscience perspective. *Military Psychology, 21*, S108–S112.

Scharff, J. S., & Scharff, D. E. (2005). *The primer of object relations* (2nd ed.). New York: Jason Aronson.

Scheier, M., & Carver, C. (1985). Optimism, coping, and health: assessment and implications of generalized outcome expectancies. *Health Psychology, 4*(3), 219–247.

Scheier, M., & Carver, C. (1993). On the power of positive thinking: the benefits of being optimistic. *Current Directions in Psychological Science, 2*, 26–30.

Schön, D. A. (1987). *Educating the reflective practitioner: toward a new design for teaching and learning in the professions.* San Francisco: Jossey-Bass.

Schön, D. A. (1995). The new scholarship requires a new epistemology. *Change, 27*(6), 26–34.

Scioli, E., Nyugen, T., & Scioli, A. (2011) Hope: its nature and measurement. *Psychology of Religion and Spirituality, 3*(2), 78–97.

Scoop It. (2012). www.scoop.it/t/the-gloria-videos

Seligman, M., & Csikszentmihalyi, M. (2000). Positive psychology: an introduction. *American Psychologist, 55*, 5–14.

Shapiro, S. L., Carlson, L. E., Astin, J. A., & Freedman, B. (2006). Mechanisms of mindfulness. *Journal of Clinical Psychology, 62*(3), 373–386.

Siev, J., & Chambless, D. L. (2007). Specificity of treatment effects: cognitive therapy and relaxation for generalized anxiety and panic disorders. *Journal of Consulting and Clinical Psychology, 75*, 513–522.

Skowron, E. A., & Friedlander, M. L. (1998). The differentiation of self inventory: development and initial validation. *Journal of Counseling Psychology, 45*, 235–246.

Snyder, C. R. (1994). *The psychology of hope: you can get there from here.* New York: Free Press.

Snyder, C. R. (1995). Conceptualizing, measuring, and nurturing hope. *Journal of Counseling and Development, 73*, 355–360.

Snyder, C. R. (1999). Hope, goal blocking thoughts, and test-related anxieties. *Psychological Reports, 84*, 206–208.

Snyder, C. R. (2000). *Handbook of hope: theory, measures, and applications.* New York: Academic Press.

Snyder, C. R. (2002). Hope theory: rainbows in the mind. *Psychological Inquiry, 13*(4), 249–275.

Snyder, C. R., Harris, C., Anderson, J. R., Holleran, S. A., Irving, L. M., Sigmon, S. T., Yoshinobu, L., Gibb, J., Langelle, C., & Harney, P. (1991). The will and the ways: development and validation of an individual-differences measure of hope. *Journal of Personality and Social Psychology, 60*(4), 570–585.

Snyder, C. R., Hoza, B., Pelham, W. E., Rapoff, M., Ware, L. Danovsky, M., Highberger, L., Ribinstein, H., & Stahl, K. J. (1997). The development and validation of the Children's Hope Scale. *Journal of Pediatric Psychology, 22*, 399–421.

Snyder C. R., Ilardi, S. S., Cheavens, J., Michael, S. T., Yamhure, L., & Sumpson, S. (2000). The role of hope in cognitive-behavior therapies. *Cognitive Therapy and Research, 24*(6), 747–762.

Snyder, C. R., Lapointe, A. B., Crowson, J. J., & Early, S. (1998). Preferences of high- and low-hope people for self-referential input. *Cognition & Emotion, 12*, 807–823.

Snyder, C. R., Sympson, S. C., Ybasco, F. C., Borders, T. F., Babyak, M. A., & Higgins, R. L. (1996). Development and validation of the State Hope Scale. *Journal of Personality and Social Psychology, 70*(2), 321–335.

Spinelli, E. (1997). *Tales of un-knowing: eight stories of existential therapy.* New York: New York University Press.

Stanford Encyclopedia of Philosophy (2010a). Existentialism. First published 23 August 2004; substantive revision 11 October 2010, page 6. Retrieved from http://plato.stanford.edu/entries/existentialism/.

Stanford Encyclopedia of Philosophy (2010b). Gabriel (Honoré) Marcel. Retrieved from http://plato.stanford.edu/entries/marcel/.

Stephenson, C. (1991). The concept of hope revisited for nursing. *Journal of Advanced Nursing, 16*, 1456–1461.

Stotland, E. (1969). *The psychology of hope.* San Francisco: Jossey-Bass.

Strupp, H. H. (1972). On the technology of psychotherapy. *Archives of General Psychiatry, 26*, 270–278.

Suárez, L., Bennett, S., Goldstein, C., & Barlow, D. H. (2009). Understanding anxiety disorders from a triple vulnerability framework. In M. M. Antony & M. B. Stein (Eds), *Oxford handbook of anxiety and related disorders*. New York: Oxford University Press.

Sympson, S. (1999). Validation of the domain specific hope scale: exploring hope in life domains. Unpublished doctoral dissertation, University of Kansas.

Task Force on Promotion and Dissemination of Psychological Procedures (1995). Training in and dissemination of empirically validated treatments: report and recommendations. *The Clinical Psychologist, 48*(1), 3–23.

Tennen, H., Affleck, G., & Tennen, R. (2002). Clipped feathers: the theory and measurement of hope. *Psychological Inquiry, 13*, 311–317.

Tillich, P. (2000). *The courage to be* (2nd ed.). New Haven: Yale University Press.

Trevarthen, C. (1974). Conversations with a two-year-old. *New Scientist, 62*, 230–235.

Vaillot, M. (1970). Hope: the restoration of being. *American Journal of Nursing, 70*, 268–273.

van Deurzen-Smith, E. (1997). *Everyday mysteries – existential dimensions of psychotherapy*. London: Routledge.

van Deurzen-Smith, E. (2010) *Everyday mysteries: a handbook of existential psychotherapy*. New York: Routledge.

Van Hooft, S. (2011). *Hope*. Durham: Acumen.

Wampold, B. E., Budgec, S. L., Laskaa, K. M., Del Rea, A.C., Baardsetha, T. P., Flückigera, C., Minamia, T., Kivlighana, M., & Gunna ,W. (2011). Evidence-based treatments for depression and anxiety versus treatment-as-usual: a meta-analysis of direct comparisons. *Clinical Psychology Review, 31*, 1304–1312.

Warner, M. S. (1991). Fragile process. In L. Fusek (Ed.), *New directions in client-centered therapy: practice with difficult client populations (Monograph Series 1)*. Chicago: Chicago Counseling and Psychotherapy Center.

Webster's Dictionary (2006) Webster's revised unabridged dictionary, WordNet 3.0, Princeton University. Retrieved from www.websters-dictionary-online.org

White, M., & Epston, D. (1990). *Narrative means to therapeutic ends*. New York: Norton.

Wikipedia. Retrieved from http://en.wikipedia.org/wiki/Buddhism.

Wilbur, K. (1996). *A brief history of everything*. Dublin: Gill & Macmillan.

Winnicott, D. W. (1971). *Playing and reality*. London: Routledge.

Wolfe, B. E., & Goldfried, M. R. (1988). Research on psychotherapy integration: Recommendations and conclusions from an NIMH workshop. *Journal of Consulting and Clinical Psychology, 56*, 448–451.

Woodbury, C. A. (1999). The relationship of anxiety, locus of control and hope to career indecision of African American students. *Dissertation Abstracts International, 59*(11-A), 4072.

World Health Organization. (2001). *Strengthening mental health promotion*. Geneva, World Health Organization (Fact sheet no. 220).

World Health Organization (2005). *Promoting mental health*. Melbourne: The University of Melbourne.

Wright, L, Watson, W. L., & Bell, J. M. (1996). *Beliefs: the heart of healing in families and illness*. New York: Basic Books.

Yalom, I. D. (1980). *Existential psychotherapy*. New York: Basic Books.

Youssef, C. M., & Luthans, F. (2007). Positive organizational behavior in the workplace: the impact of hope, optimism, and resilience. *Journal of Management, 33*, 774–800.

Index